Relics for the Present: Contemporary Reflections on the Talmud

Pardes | פרדס
Institute of Jewish Studies

מגיד
MAGGID

Levi Cooper

Relics for the Present

Contemporary Reflections on the Talmud

Maggid Books

Relics for the Present:
Contemporary Reflections on the Talmud

First Edition, 2012

Maggid Books
An imprint of Koren Publishers Jerusalem Ltd.

POB 8531, New Milford, CT 06776-8531, USA
& POB 4044, Jerusalem 91040, Israel
www.korenpub.com

ISBN 978 159 264 3608, *hardcover*

A CIP catalogue record for this title is
available from the British Library.

Printed and bound in the United States

We dedicate this book to our teacher and guide

Rabbi Zalman I. Posner

Rabbi emeritus of
Sherith Israel *Synagogue, Nashville, Tennessee,*
whose open heart and astute mind brought
the fullness of Judaism to so many.

Libby and Moshe Werthan

CONTENTS

BERAKHOT: CHAPTER TWO

BERAKHOT: CHAPTER THREE

BERAKHOT: CHAPTER FOUR

BERAKHOT: CHAPTER FIVE

PREFACE

A RELIC IS AN object surviving from an earlier time, carefully and conscientiously preserved, esteemed and venerated. It is a hallowed object of historical interest, of sentimental value, of unquestionable worth. The Talmud is such a relic.

This work explores the world of the sages, seeking relevance in the timeless texts of the Talmud. Each section analyses a passage from *Berakhot*, the first tractate of Talmud, chapters one to five, presenting the commentators' insights, searching for meaning and hoping to provide inspiration for our generation.

I began this project in 2005 at the beginning of the twelfth *Daf Yomi* cycle. *Daf Yomi* is a programme in which participants study a folio – two sides of a page – of Talmud each day. Those who maintain this pace complete the entire Talmud in seven and a half years.

The initial impetus for this project was provided by Amanda Borschel-Dan, then of *The Jerusalem Post*, who believed that there should be a weekly column on Talmud in Israel's oldest and largest English daily newspaper. Amanda had studied at the Pardes Institute of Jewish Studies in Jerusalem and had participated in my Talmud class.

Most of this work was written in the National Library of Israel, where readers like me are fortunate to be offered every assistance by the librarians. Joel Wolowelsky, a close family friend, has offered valued encouragement. I have benefited greatly from the editorial input of Yehudah Ber Zirkind, Yocheved Engelberg Cohen, Suzi Brozman and Nechama Unterman.

This work is jointly published by Pardes and by Maggid Books, a division of Koren Publishers Jerusalem. Since 1998, I have had the pleasure and the privilege to teach at Pardes. Matthew Miller and the whole Koren team have been professional and gracious.

Each passage in this book was first read and vetted by my wife, Sarah. Without her support – and the patience of our children Itai, Yedidya, Choni, Neta, Aviya and Adi – these reflections would never have seen light. Our parents and grandparents have also provided encouragement for all my endeavours.

I am happy to express my sincere gratitude to all those who have a portion in this work. I am humbled by the faith you have shown in me; I aspire to live up to it.

The release of the book coincides with the beginning of the thirteenth *Daf Yomi* cycle, and will offer a further opportunity for the English reader to connect to this global event.

The goal of the book is to make classic Jewish texts accessible, to contemplate the wisdom they impart and to consider the inspiration they provide for our times. My hope is that this work will provide a window into the wealth, depth and contemporary significance of the Talmud.

With gratitude to God,
Levi Cooper
Zur Hadassa

B. = *Talmud Bavli,* Babylonian Talmud
M. = *Mishna*
T. = *Tosefta,* addition to the *Mishna*
Y. = *Talmud Yerushalmi,* Jerusalem Talmud, Palestinian Talmud or Talmud of the Land of Israel

A full list of cited sources can be found at the back of the volume.

Berakhot
Chapter One

Why begin with *Shema*?

SHEMA, THE CENTREPIECE of the morning and evening prayers, is composed of a number of verses from the Torah. It consists of three paragraphs, opening with the famous verse: *Hear O Israel, the Lord our God, the Lord is one* (Deuteronomy 6:4). *Shema* focuses on our relationship with God, the tradition, the commandments and the Land of Israel.

Why does the record of the Oral Law begin with a discussion pertaining to *Shema*? *Shema* is not the first prayer recited in the morning, nor can it truly be classified as consisting of *berakhot* (blessings), the title of the first tractate. Furthermore, *Tractate Berakhot* begins the first order of Mishna – *Zera'im* (Seeds), which deals with agricultural laws; it is hardly obvious that *Shema* should be included in this section, much less form its opening discussion.

Rabbi Yeḥezkel Landau (1713–1793), better known by the title of his responsa, *Noda BiYehuda*, offers a number of explanations for the placement of the discussion of *Shema*. Originally from Poland and later serving in the rabbinate in Prague, Rabbi Landau answered questions from all over Europe. In addition to his responsa, he also authored an important supplement to the *Shulḥan Arukh* entitled *Dagul MeRevava*. He published his novellae on the Talmud under the title *Tziyun LeNefesh Ḥaya*, more commonly known by the acronym *Tzlaḥ*. It is at the beginning of this work that Rabbi Landau tackles our question.

He begins by quoting Maimonides (1138–1204), who suggests that since *Shema* is recited twice daily, this frequency justifies its place of pride. Rabbi Landau notes that if this were indeed the criterion, then the *Amida* prayer, which is recited thrice daily, would be a better candidate to open the Talmud.

A second possibility focuses on the order of the prayers. Perhaps *Shema* is discussed first since in both the morning and evening prayers it precedes the *Amida*. This approach falters, in light of the minority opinion that *Shema* precedes the *Amida* only in the morning prayer, while in the evening prayer the *Amida* precedes *Shema*. Granted, this opinion is not the halakhic norm and, in practice, *Shema* always precedes the *Amida*, yet Rabbi Landau is working with the understanding that an explanation that takes into account all opinions, even those that are not normative – that is, opinions that are not considered to be a required standard of behaviour – is to be preferred.

Indeed, the search for a universally acceptable explanation is a classic talmudic approach to problem solving.

Rabbi Landau further suggests that a parallel between the first Mishna and the first commandment at Sinai may be another reason for beginning with *Shema*. Before giving the Torah to the Jewish people, God presented His credentials – *I am the Lord your God Who took you out of Egypt* (Exodus 20:2). Therefore, at the outset of the human record of the Oral Torah, we begin by discussing *Shema*, thereby acknowledging that God is indeed the ruler.

A further explanation focuses on the legal status of the commandment to recite *Shema*. It is of Torah origin, and hence appropriately precedes the discussion of the *Amida*, which is an obligation of rabbinic origin. However, this explanation cannot be accepted by all, since according to one sage, the reading of *Shema* is of rabbinic origin as well.

The Torah origins of *Shema* lead Rabbi Landau to entertain an explanation that focuses on belief, since the bifurcation of the Written Law and the Oral Law may lead some to consider a dualistic God. To negate this perception, the Mishna opens with *Shema* – a statement of God's unity. *Shema* thus forms a bridge between the Oral and Written Laws, indicating that both corpora have one common origin.

Perhaps a slight variation on this theme could be suggested. Over the generations, the veracity of the Oral Law and the authority of its mediators have been questioned. Some have doubted the sages and the traditions they have imparted, while affirming the weight of the Written

Law. Accordingly, the Mishna opens by discussing *Shema,* a passage from the Written Law, thus highlighting the tight bond between the oral and written traditions.

Focusing on the content of *Shema* leads to other possible approaches. The first paragraph of *Shema* includes the injunction to propagate the tradition through education and learning: *And you will teach them to your children, and you will talk of them* (Deuteronomy 6:7). Rabbi Landau suggests that this passage elevates the relative importance of the Oral Law, a tradition passed down from generation to generation.

Perhaps the most satisfying approach suggested by Rabbi Landau considers the place of *Shema* in Jewish practice and collective memory. *Shema* is traditionally a statement of faith, to the extent that in many synagogues its first verse is proclaimed at the conclusion of the heartfelt Yom Kippur services. Over the generations, Jewish martyrs have followed the example set by Rabbi Akiva and recited *Shema* with their last breath.

In the first verse of *Shema* we proclaim the unity of God, and when reciting this verse we accept upon ourselves the kingdom of heaven. From a halakhic perspective, reciting this verse without meditating on its meaning renders the recitation invalid.

Asserting our relationship with God may be seen as a prerequisite for discussing the many issues raised in the corpus of the Oral Law. Before thanking God for granting us abundance, before humbly placing our requests before God, before plumbing the depths and details of our rituals and before exploring the Divine in our civil code, this special relationship between the Jewish people and God must be affirmed.

BERAKHOT 2A

Day or night: When do we start?

TRACTATE *BERAKHOT* OPENS with a discussion of the earliest and latest times for the recital of the evening *Shema* (*M. Berakhot* 1:1). The Talmud immediately questions the context of this statement, wondering why the sages did not begin with the time for the morning *Shema*, which is read earlier in the day (*B. Berakhot* 2a).

The Talmud explains the order by citing two biblical verses. The first passage of *Shema* speaks of an obligation to teach one's children and to speak of Torah *when you lie down and when you arise* (Deuteronomy 6:7). Thus the evening *Shema* recited before retiring should precede the morning *Shema* which is read upon waking.

The Talmud goes on to cite a verse which supports the general approach of Jewish law that night precedes day. At the end of each day in the biblical description of creation, the phrase *and it was evening and it was morning* is used to signal the end of the day's work. Here too, evening precedes morning, thus validating the discussion of the evening *Shema* first.

The night-before-day rule applies in a different context as well. The Torah tells us that it is forbidden to slaughter an animal and its offspring on the same day (Leviticus 22:28). The same term – *yom eḥad*, one day – is used in this context as well as in the creation story. Thus our sages conclude that the day follows the night for calculating the twenty-four-hour period during which an animal and its offspring cannot be slaughtered together (*M. Ḥullin* 5:5).

In Jewish tradition, each twenty-four-hour period begins at sunset; hence the morning is really the middle of the day. Shabbat begins in the evening, as do all the festivals. This curious order can be considered a defining feature of the Jewish calendar, and one that sets it apart from non-Jewish calendars.

However, it is not so clear-cut that the night precedes the day in

Jewish tradition. The very same biblical verse quoted by the Talmud – *and it was evening and it was morning* – is read very differently by one of the medieval biblical commentators. The Frenchman Rabbi Shmuel ben Meir (c. 1085–1158), known as Rashbam, followed in the footsteps of his illustrious grandfather, Rashi (1040–1105), authoring biblical and talmudic commentaries. Rashbam's commentary on the Pentateuch is exceptional for its succinct style and its bold devotion to the literal meaning of the text. As such, Rashbam makes no attempt to align his comments with normative law. On a few occasions, his words blatantly contradict halakha, though he viewed Jewish law as authoritative.

Noticing that the biblical verse avoids using the term *laila* (night), Rashbam suggests that the passage should be read *and the day set and it was dawn.* Thus dawn concludes the day, and the new day begins at sunrise.

Rashbam never suggests that this interpretation should affect Jewish law. Nevertheless, in an unrelated halakhic realm – the Temple service – the day preceded the night. Sacrificial leftovers from the day's service were burned on the altar in the evening and no new sacrifices were offered. When sacrifices were to be eaten on the day they were offered, they could be consumed through the entire night, but not the following morning (see Leviticus 7:15).

Thus when the sages are faced with someone who forgot to pray *Minḥa* (the afternoon prayer), they question whether the supplicant could make up this lost prayer by reciting the evening prayer twice (*B. Berakhot* 26a–b). Given that the prayers are modelled on the Temple service, then, perhaps, once evening has arrived and the previous day has passed, the prayer can no longer be offered, just as sacrifices in the Temple were not offered at night. Alternatively, perhaps the afternoon prayer may be recited in the evening, since the remainders of offerings were allowed to be burned on the altar even at night.

The Talmud also offers an alternative model for the three daily prayers. It records an opinion that the three daily services date back to our forefathers: Abraham established *Shaḥarit,* Isaac introduced *Minḥa,* and *Ma'ariv* was the innovation of Jacob. Significantly, it was Abraham, our first forefather, who established the first prayer – that is, the morning *Shaḥarit* – and not the evening prayer.

Indeed, other biblical verses also support the position that the day precedes the night. When Moses sat in judgment, he received people *from the morning until the evening* (Exodus 18:13–14). In the curses delineated at the end of the Torah, we are told that the situation will be so dire that *in the morning you will say "when will evening come?" and in the evening you will say "when will morning come?"* (Deuteronomy 28:67). In both these passages the day precedes the night.

Thus we see that Jewish tradition offers two paradigms for the order of the day. The normative approach is that the night precedes the day, and this view permeates Jewish life. Another approach exists which maintains that each calendar day begins in the morning. This view was reserved for the Temple.

Why did our tradition not adopt the Temple model as the normative practice? This system would certainly fit our lifestyle – each morning we wake up to a new day. Why was the night-precedes-day paradigm preferred? We can suggest that our forebears sought to establish when we begin our day. Does the day begin with our gulping down a quick breakfast and racing off to earn a livelihood? When there is a holiday, does the day start with oversleeping? Or perhaps the day should begin with coming home to the family and sitting around the Shabbat table?

By adopting the night-before-day system, our sages convey a message about priorities. True, we must work to support ourselves and our families, but employment is merely a means, not an end. Our day really begins when we arrive home from work, when we sit down and enjoy a festive atmosphere with loved ones. Thus the day starts in the evening, in the home, together with the family.

BERAKHOT 3A

Greeting with peace

IN JEWISH LIFE, there is a time for all things: *A season is set for everything, a time for every experience under heaven* (Ecclesiastes 3:1). Thus, the discussion of *Shema* opens by delineating the appropriate time for its recitation. Tangentially, the Talmud includes the story of Rabbi Yose, who was travelling on the road when the appointed time for prayers arrived (*B. Berakhot* 3a).

Intending to pray, Rabbi Yose entered a ruined building in the Jerusalem area. While he was praying, Elijah the prophet came and waited by the doorway, perhaps even guarding the entrance. When Rabbi Yose concluded his prayers, Elijah approached him and said: "*Shalom alekha rabbi* – peace unto you, my teacher." Rabbi Yose responded: "*Shalom alekha rabbi umori* – peace unto you, my teacher and my master."

After the initial greetings, Elijah berated Rabbi Yose: "My son, why did you enter this ruin, thus endangering yourself?"

Rabbi Yose responded, perhaps with an innocent look on his face: "To pray."

Indeed, it is considered preferable to pray indoors rather than outdoors. Yet Elijah was not placated, since Rabbi Yose endangered himself by entering such a ruin. Elijah asked: "Why did you not pray on the road?" Or, perhaps, in a more accusatory tone: "You should have prayed on the road!"

"I feared that I would be interrupted by passersby," responded Rabbi Yose, justifying himself not on the grounds of a preference for the indoors, but rather on the grounds of finding a quiet place for solitude.

Still not mollified, Elijah continued: "You should have prayed an abridged prayer," thus minimising the chances of interruption from passersby.

At this point, Rabbi Yose interrupted the tale of his discussion with Elijah, and declared that from this short exchange he learned three things: "I learned that one should not enter a ruin, I learned that one may pray on the road and I learned that one who prays on the road should pray an abridged prayer."

Indeed, chance encounters at times can leave lasting impressions. It may be only a short conversation, a few words exchanged; yet much can be learned from such interactions. Rabbi Yose certainly felt that his encounter with Elijah the prophet left him with three important halakhic lessons.

Rabbi Yaakov Reischer (1661–1733), author of the three-volume *Responsa Shevut Yaakov,* points out that a fourth lesson can also be derived from this conversation. Rabbi Reischer, born and raised in Prague, served in the rabbinate in a number of communities in Europe – Rzeszów, Anspach, Worms and Metz. He also authored a commentary entitled *Iyun Yaakov* on the aggada, the non-normative sections of the Talmud. On this passage, Rabbi Reischer notes that Elijah did not interrupt Rabbi Yose's prayers even though he believed that Rabbi Yose should not have been praying in such a manner. Rabbi Reischer points out that this shows the importance of not interrupting another's prayers. Rabbi Reischer concludes that the reason Rabbi Yose did not say that he learned four lessons from this discussion is that undoubtedly, he was already aware of this law. Therefore he did not list it as a lesson learned from his brief interaction with Elijah.

I would like to suggest a further lesson that can be gleaned from this exchange.

Rabbi Yose was one of the important contributors to the Mishna. He was a student of his father Ḥalafta and of the great Rabbi Akiva, and was known for his mildness of manner and moderation in halakha. A tanner by trade, Rabbi Yose lived in Tzippori in the Galilee. Normative practice often follows Rabbi Yose's opinion because of the logic with which he approached halakhic questions. Among his students was the famed Rabbi Yehuda the Prince, compiler of the Mishna.

Despite Rabbi Yose's illustrious biography, surely Elijah the prophet would be considered his superior. It is somewhat surprising, therefore, that Elijah opened the discussion by addressing Rabbi Yose with a title of respect: "Peace unto you, my teacher." This is especially interesting since Elijah did not approve of Rabbi Yose's actions and was about to scold him.

To be sure, Rabbi Yose returned the greeting appropriately: "Peace unto you, my teacher and my master." And indeed, further on in the story, Elijah called Rabbi Yose "my son." These titles, though, do not mitigate the oddity of the great Elijah the prophet approaching Rabbi Yose and calling him "my teacher."

We might suggest that herein lies a fifth lesson that can be derived from the story. Despite Elijah's greatness and mythic status, he did not deem it beneath him to approach Rabbi Yose and address him respectfully. Different achievements in society or different roles in the community should not lead us to the mistaken belief that any party is undeserving of respect.

This is reminiscent of a passage later on in this tractate (*B. Berakhot* 17a). The Talmud records favourite teachings of various sages. One of the teachings that Abbaye was known for was: "One should increase peace with his siblings, with his relatives, with every person and even with a gentile in the market." Supplementing Abbaye's instruction, the Talmud relates a tradition about Rabban Yoḥanan ben Zakkai: "No one ever greeted him first, not even a gentile in the marketplace."

Elsewhere in rabbinic literature, *shalom* (peace) is listed as one of the names of God. For the Almighty loves peace, pursues peace and greets all with peace (*Derekh Eretz Zuta, Perek HaShalom*, 5). Furthermore, God greets those who are more distant from Him before He greets those who are closer to Him (*Bemidbar Rabba* 8:4; *Midrash Shmuel* 28:6).

What is the significance of being *makdim shalom*, being the first to greet the other with peace? A greeting is an invitation. Though it requires little investment, it is also too easily ignored. It is a starting point for a relationship, or at the very least, indicates a respect for the other.

Delusions of grandeur or inflated self-perception should not cloud our vision. Every person should be treated with the respect that is due to him or her as a human being.

BERAKHOT 3A

Roar and coo

THE MISHNA RECORDS different opinions regarding the latest appropriate time for the recitation of *Shema* in the evening. According to Rabbi Eliezer, it is *sof ha'ashmora harishona,* the end of the first watch. The sages, however, propose midnight as the latest time, and this is accepted as the halakhic ideal. The opinion of Rabban Gamliel, who permits the recitation of *Shema* throughout the night until the light of dawn, is accepted for those who missed the earlier time (*M. Berakhot* 1:1).

Despite this normative ruling, the ensuing discussion in the Talmud (*B. Berakhot* 3a) attempts to clarify the opinion of Rabbi Eliezer and to determine when the first watch ends. The Talmud concludes that there are three watches; thus the end of the first watch is a third of the way through the night.

Rabbi Eliezer cites the biblical verse: *The Lord will roar from on high, from His holy abode He will make His voice heard, He will roar a mighty roar over His habitation* (Jeremiah 25:30). Noting that the term "roar" is used three times, Rabbi Eliezer adds that at each watch God roars like a lion.

Later in the Talmud, we are told that God roars like a lion, crying out at each of the three watches: "Woe to My children whose sins have caused Me to destroy My House, burn My Sanctuary and exile them among the nations of the world."

Immediately following this passage, Rabbi Yose recounts his meeting with Elijah the prophet in a dilapidated building in Jerusalem. After scolding Rabbi Yose for choosing to pray in a dangerous place, Elijah asked: "My son, what sound did you hear in this ruin?" We may be inclined to explain Rabbi Yose's entry into the ruin as an attempt to find a place for praying which would be free from the distractions and interruptions of passersby. Elijah, however, understood that a *ḥurva,* a ruin, is an auspicious place for prayer. Rabbi Yose's sincere, heartfelt prayer in the *ḥurva* may have merited him a glimpse of some hidden realm.

Indeed, Rabbi Yose answered: "I heard a heavenly voice cooing like a dove and saying: 'Woe to My children whose sins have caused Me to destroy My House, burn My Sanctuary and exile them among the nations.'"

Rabbi Kalonymus Kalmish Shapira of Piaseczno (1889–1943), writing during the Holocaust, referred to this passage. On January 20, 1940 the Piaseczno Rebbe told his followers of the value of prayer that comes from a place of ruin. Drawing on the reality of life in the Warsaw Ghetto, and connecting this harsh existence to Rabbi Yose's experience in the *ḥurva*, the Piaseczno Rebbe implored his adherents to redouble their efforts in prayer, prayer that would come from a place of destruction.

Let us return to our talmudic passage. Elijah responded to Rabbi Yose's report by revealing more details of God's grieving. Elijah gave his solemn word that the heavenly voice resounds in this fashion three times daily. Furthermore, even when the Jews enter synagogues and study houses and respond to the *Kaddish* prayer exalting the great name of God, God responds: "Fortunate is the King Who is praised this way in His House." Bemoaning the fact that such praise is not being said in the Temple but only in exilic places of worship, God continues: "Woe to a Father who has exiled His sons, and woe to the sons who have been exiled from their Father's table."

Perhaps the story of Rabbi Yose in the *ḥurva* is cited because, as in the previous discussion of God's nightly roar, we find God grieving over our yet-to-be redeemed state of existence. However, a striking difference between the two passages jumps out at the reader. In the first description, we find God roaring like a lion; in the second account, we find God cooing like a dove. What can we learn from these vastly different portrayals of lament?

We might suggest that we are offered two paradigms for anguish over the exilic reality in which we live. We may roar like lions with fearful voices that resound in the streets and alleyways, heard by all and sundry. All who hear the roar may be shaken, but as the echo of the roar grows fainter, the impression fades until it is only a memory. Alternatively, we may coo like doves, barely audible and easily ignored, yet always there in the background.

In many areas of life, we have a choice as to how we express ourselves. People unhappy with the social injustices of our time can shout from the rooftops, post signs on every street corner and organise mass demonstrations. Alternatively, they may express their feelings in the privacy of their own homes, educating their family and community about the importance of social justice and making their small contribution to better the world.

What is the difference between these two avenues? Each one provides something which the other lacks. The roar of the lion may keep the issue in the public eye, but it does not necessarily ensure that the individual will internalise the values expressed. On the other hand, actions that may appear to be relatively insignificant and limited to the home may leave an indelible impression on the family, even though there is no guarantee that the message will permeate beyond the confines of the individual's home.

Which paradigm can better help us maintain our awareness of our unredeemed state of existence and transmit to the next generation a desire for better times?

I would like to suggest that herein lies the key to understanding the juxtaposition of these talmudic passages. The sages present us with two Divinely sanctioned paradigms. Both public and private articulations of a desire for change and improvement are legitimate, and crucial for society. Neither expression alone can achieve the dual goals of internalising values and sending a strong message to the outside world. Improving our society can be achieved only by a combination of the roaring of the lion and the cooing of the dove – by public proclamation and by private inculcation.

BERAKHOT 3B–4A

War as a solution, diversion or catalyst

BEFORE GOING TO bed we may set an alarm, but in the morning hours we often turn over and hit the snooze button, wishing for a few more minutes of sleep.

King David had a unique alarm clock. Before retiring, he would hang his harp above his bed. When a northern wind blew at midnight, it played the harp, waking him from his royal slumber. The Talmud relates how King David would get up at that point and study Torah until dawn (*B. Berakhot* 3b–4a; *B. Sanhedrin* 16a–b).

One day, the sages entered at dawn with the tidings that the people of Israel were in need. King David responded: "Let them go and support each other." He was either addressing the wealthy who could support the poor, or encouraging commerce and trade so that the entire nation would be self-sufficient.

One of the commentators points out that King David was punished for this response. His coffers were full; yet rather than feed the needy, he kept this money to build the Temple. As punishment, King David did not merit building the Temple, and the task fell to his son, King Solomon (*Anaf Yosef*).

The sages petitioning King David were not satisfied with his solution, and retorted: "A mere grasshopper or handful of food cannot satiate a lion, nor can a pit be filled with earth by digging more earth out of it." Resources were insufficient to satisfy all, even if they were redistributed more equitably.

Perhaps looking up from the tome he was studying, King David delivered a distant response: "Go and stretch forth your hands against the legions." King David's solution was to plunder neighbouring countries in order to increase supply.

This response, cold as it may seem, turns even more chilling, for the Talmud goes on to describe how the ensuing battles were Divinely sanctioned. The notion that God would authorise war as a means to solve socio-economic problems is certainly a troubling one.

This disconcerting conclusion may have been what led one commentator to offer a different interpretation. King David was suggesting that they battle the Amalekite legions who were raiding the cities of the Land of Israel and disrupting commerce. By routing these bands, King David aimed to restore supply lines and economic growth (*Margaliyot HaYam*).

Following this approach, it would be inappropriate to describe King David's response as detached. King David offered a solution that struck at the heart of the problem – the marauding gangs who were looting food supplies and having a negative impact on the economy.

To be sure, the Talmud itself makes no reference to David's attack on the Amalekites. However, the language used by King David in his response is similar to the biblical text describing the event (see I Samuel 30).

Though we may have soothed our disquiet over this talmudic passage, the troubling image of Divinely sanctioned war as a solution to socio-economic problems rears its worrisome head again in another aggadic passage (*B. Temura* 16a).

In the last moments of his life, Moses turned to his trusted deputy and ordained successor, Joshua, offering him a final opportunity: "Ask me about any uncertainties that you have."

Joshua was shocked and offended: "Did I ever leave you, even for a moment, to go to another place!?" The thought that Moses would suspect him, his star student, of not having a clear grasp of the knowledge with which he was entrusted, hurt Joshua.

With poetic justice, the passage describes how on the first day of his leadership Joshua forgot some 300 laws and was uncertain about 700 others. Moses was no longer alive to restore the lost Torah; it appeared that Joshua failed as bearer of the tradition.

The people of Israel were incensed and demanded Joshua's head. With the bloodthirsty mob calling for his death, Joshua turned to God for help. God, however, refused, saying that the Torah has left the heavenly sphere and has been given to humans. As such, we humans – with all our frailties, including forgetfulness and violence – must operate without Divine intervention.

Not wanting to leave Joshua to the unruly masses, God offered an alternative solution: "Go and occupy them with war." Here too, God endorsed war as a solution to an internal problem confronting the Jewish people.

Once again we find a commentator who tries to mollify readers of this text. "War" is not referring to a physical battle against an enemy; rather it is referring to *milḥamta shel Torah,* the war of Torah – engaging our heritage and battling to discover new understandings and points of connection. God refused to restore the forgotten laws, and instead advised study as a means to placate the people. Perhaps this was even a means to reveal the missing Torah (*Afikei Yam*).

Though this explanation puts an entirely different and much more positive spin on the passage, it is difficult to defend as the straightforward meaning of the text. The Talmud buttresses God's instruction by referring to the beginning of the book of Joshua, which opens: *And it was after the death of Moses...* (Joshua 1:1), and then continues with the story of the conquest of the Land of Israel. The Talmud is offering a creative reading of the first verse of the book of Joshua: And it was *consequent* to (meaning a consequence of) the death of Moses that Joshua called the people to war.

We are left with two talmudic texts in which we are confronted with the disturbing prospect of God suggesting a war to solve internal challenges.

Troubling though this thought may be, perhaps we could suggest that war in these cases is not being offered as a solution, but rather as a diversion. Both texts describe internal strife among the Jewish people: resources allocated inefficiently and unfairly, and the loss of part of a national treasure. They were faced with these adversities, and lacked the means to resolve them. So God advocated diverting the attention of the people with an outside stimulus – war.

Indeed, this is hardly comforting for a peace-loving and peace-desiring nation, for a country that calls its army a defence force, for a people who pray daily for tranquillity and serenity. The talmudic passages remain chilling – upsetting, to my mind – but they may push us to focus intensely on internal issues of disunity and inequity. War should not be a solution or a diversion; rather the frightening prospect of war should be a catalyst for re-evaluating our priorities.

BERAKHOT 4A

Admitting that we don't know

ON THE EVE of the Exodus from Egypt, Moses warned of the looming tenth plague. *And Moses said: Thus said the Lord – Around midnight I will go out amongst Egypt, and every first-born in the land of Egypt will die* (Exodus 11:4–5). The Talmud wonders why the time given for this fateful event is inexact: around midnight (*kaḥatzot*). The sages reject out of hand the possibility that this could have been the Almighty's word, for our all-knowing God would surely have said: "At precisely midnight (*baḥatzot*)." Accordingly, the ambiguity is attributed to Moses. The Talmud offers three explanations for Moses' opting for an imprecise description (*B. Berakhot* 3b, 4a).

The first one is that God told Moses that the slaying of the first-borns would occur *baḥatzot*, exactly at midnight; however, when relating the Divine plan of action, Moses, not knowing the precise moment of midnight, changed *baḥatzot* ever so slightly and said *kaḥatzot* instead. This minor alteration removed the precision from God's original statement. Moses did not wish to quote a time whose correctness he would be unable to prove, should he ever be challenged about it (*Tosafot*).

As we said, the Talmud does not entertain the possibility that it was God who did not designate a specific time for smiting the first-borns. Rather, God stated a precise time, but Moses sought to blur the Divine statement. It seems that the Talmud is shying away from any imprecision associated with God (*Maharsha*). Such a suggestion suits the continuation of the talmudic passage, where even the previous assumption that Moses was unaware of the clear-cut moment of midnight is rejected. Thus the following two explanations assume that Moses also knew the exact instant of midnight.

The second explanation maintains that precisely twenty-four hours before the designated time, Moses related God's warning: *Like this midnight* (kaḥatzot) *I will go out amongst Egypt.* According to this reading, the Hebrew letter *kaf* is not used to express approximation (around midnight), but to convey similarity (like midnight; see also Genesis 18:10, 14; II Kings 4:16–17). Although Moses may not have quoted God verbatim, he did not change the meaning of the original message. In fact, Moses reinforced God's words by relaying them at a precise moment – exactly twenty-four hours before the event.

A third possibility – and one from which the sages derive a practical lesson – is that although Moses knew the instant of midnight and heard God specify that moment, Moses adjusted God's warning. The Talmud explains that this change was driven by Moses' concern lest Pharaoh's astrologers err in their reckoning of the midpoint of the night. Such a mistake would lead them to think that midnight had come and gone with no plague inflicted, and they would then accuse Moses of being a charlatan. By not quoting precise times, Moses ensured that such a claim could never be brought against him, thus dodging the risk of losing his credibility.

With Moses' course in mind, the Talmud recalls a rule mentioned elsewhere (*Derekh Eretz Zuta* 3): "Teach your tongue to say, 'I don't know,' lest you get caught in a falsehood." The task of saying "I don't know" may sound easy. If someone were to ask us to build a rocket that could reach the moon, the majority of us would have no hesitation in saying that we don't have the expertise required for such an undertaking. Is it really so difficult to teach our tongues to say, "I don't know"? Moreover, why does such a practice require training?

Perhaps the following Hasidic tale, as retold by Rabbi Ḥayim Elazar Shapira of Munkács (1871–1937), will help shed light on our sages' words. Rabbi Zev Wolf of Zbaraẓ (d. 1822) once came to spend Shabbat in Lublin at the Hasidic court of his master, Rabbi Yaakov Yitzḥak

Horowitz (1745–1815), better known as the *Ḥozeh* (Seer) of Lublin for his exceptional perceptive powers to see far, wide and deep.

On Friday night, the Seer turned to his disciple and, wishing to honour him, asked him to share some Torah insights. Rabbi Wolf responded: "Not now."

The next morning, the Seer of Lublin once again offered his student the opportunity to present a Torah thought to all those present. Rabbi Wolf replied as he had the previous evening: "Not now."

The Seer understood that Rabbi Wolf was waiting for the third meal of Shabbat to offer his Torah thoughts and therefore refused to speak until then. Thus, as Shabbat waned and all were gathered for the final meal of the day, the master once again turned to his disciple expectantly.

Rabbi Wolf's response this time was different: "I don't know what to say."

The Seer of Lublin was taken aback: "If you don't have any Torah to share with us, why didn't you say so when I first asked you on Friday night, or at least earlier today?"

Rabbi Wolf respectfully replied: "I am surprised at my master's question. I was merely following the talmudic directive to teach your tongue to say, 'I don't know.' All Shabbat I have been teaching myself to say this; all Shabbat I have been trying to confess that I did not have an insight to share. Only now do I have the courage to admit that I don't have anything to say."

This tale casts a different light on the talmudic passage. We often find ourselves in situations where we are expected by our peers, teachers, parents, congregants or community to have answers. Our sages are urging us to have the courage to admit when we don't know.

Undoubtedly, the Jewish slaves in Egypt as well as their Egyptian overlords expected Moses, who communed with the Almighty, to know the exact moment of midnight. They would have been surprised that this gallant leader was offering a hazy description. Doubts about him may have crept into their minds.

When we are expected to know, it is all the more difficult to admit that we don't. In such situations, we are tempted to bluff and offer some innocuous, often vague answer. At times, we seek to avoid the question, excusing ourselves or changing the subject. Anything to avoid having to confess to a lack of knowledge. It is in such scenarios that our sages urge us to train ourselves to say unflinchingly: "I don't know."

BERAKHOT 4A

Ideal leaders

OUR HERITAGE IS rich with leadership paradigms. It is these leaders whom we try to emulate. When we try to identify the cream of the crop, we search for the qualities that we associate with the greats of our history.

King David is, of course, among our most famous biblical leaders. It comes as no surprise that our sages sought to identify what made him so extraordinary. In doing so, our tradition depicts a timeless model for Jewish leadership.

One such passage in the Talmud (*B. Berakhot* 4a) begins with a prayer attributed to King David: *Incline Your ear, O Lord, answer me, for I am poor and needy. Preserve my soul, for I am a* ḥasid (Psalms 86:1–2). King David is requesting God's assistance on the grounds that he is a *ḥasid* – pious, steadfast and godly. Indeed, throughout rabbinic literature, David is portrayed as a virtuous king. Our sages here appear to be concerned with the question: what entitled King David to the title "*ḥasid*"?

Two opinions are offered that highlight King David's unique conduct as a ruler. The first approach spotlights David's practice of rising at midnight to sing the praises of God and to study Torah, rather than sleeping late as may have been royal custom.

A second view focuses on how David spent his waking hours. Most royals are not concerned with the day-to-day activities of the masses. King David, however, would examine bloodstains as well as embryos and afterbirths from miscarriages to determine in each instance whether they caused ritual impurity (see Leviticus 12:1–8; *B. Nidda* 24b, 26a). Thus, King David took an interest in individual couples as he determined whether they were halakhically permitted to cohabit.

The Talmud continues that after deciding how he would rule in any area of law – monetary disputes, capital cases and matters of ritual purity – King David would turn to his teacher, Mephiboshet, to seek his approval before issuing a ruling. Obviously, King David was taking a risk that Mephiboshet would not endorse his decision, thus embarrassing him before all those present. But King David was making a statement: unlike other rulers, he was not ashamed to be wrong.

A midrash offers another explanation of David's claim to piety. The passage opens by questioning David's self-appropriation of the title *ḥasid,* since elsewhere it is the Almighty who is termed a *ḥasid* (see Jeremiah 3:12). The midrash responds by declaring that one who disregards his enemies' jibes, despite having the ability to counter them, earns the title *ḥasid*. He becomes a partner with the Almighty, based on the commonality of ignoring detractors. The midrash continues by identifying David as one who exercised restraint by overlooking those who cursed him (*Midrash Tehillim* 86:1, 16:11).

All these explanations – waking early, ruling on matters of ritual impurity, humbly checking with others and overlooking hecklers – refer to conduct that is hardly characteristic of sovereigns. King David did not exploit or even take advantage of his royal status, and hence he claimed the title of *ḥasid*.

As we have seen, rabbinic literature exploring the verse in Psalms seeks to identify the behaviour of a *ḥasid*. In the context of the biblical passage, this definition describes conduct that justifies a request for Divine assistance. The Talmud here offers a model for leadership which highlights the uniqueness of the ideal Jewish leader.

Is it really the function of the ideal Jewish leader to examine bloodstains in order to determine ritual status?

A careful reading of our passage reveals that King David pored over the samples brought before him in order to "purify a woman for her husband." Undoubtedly, King David was not able to pronounce everyone ritually pure; the ritual status would depend on the nature of the particular sample. It is therefore striking that the Talmud chooses the term "purify," when King David must certainly have found the blood to cause ritual impurity at times.

The choice of language seems to indicate that King David was doing more than merely deciding matters of ritual purity. King David was actually searching for ways to rule leniently, thus allowing couples to be together.

Elsewhere in the Talmud, we hear that when reporting a halakhic debate, it is preferable to relate how sweeping the permissive ruling is rather than how sweeping the restrictive ruling is (*B. Beitza* 2b). This phrase is taken as axiomatic: it is always easy to rule stringently, thus restricting behaviour, since prohibiting something permitted does not cause obvious damage. It takes far more courage to rule leniently in cases of uncertainty (*Rashi*). It is also far more difficult, as proof needs to be presented to justify not taking the route of caution (*Tosafot*).

Refracting the model leader's demeanour through the lens of King David, the rabbis present an image of a diligent leader who does not hesitate to get his or her hands dirty. This is a leader who is connected to tradition and is sufficiently secure to take advice from those more knowledgeable. Moreover, this leader is determined to follow the proper course, even when this course is the more lenient one.

To be sure, this archetype need not rule permissively in all cases. The ideal leader is a truth seeker. At the same time, though, he is courageous enough to rule leniently when circumstances allow it.

One further talmudic passage bears quoting. With reference to the verse: *This is the generation of those who seek Him* (Psalms 24:6), our sages note the juxtaposition of *the generation* and *those who seek Him* or (taken out of context) *its seekers*, namely the leaders of the generation who pursue the welfare of their constituents (*B. Arakhin* 17a). Following one explanation of this grouping, the generation is influenced by the disposition of its leaders – a brave leader generates a brave community. An alternate approach suggests exactly the opposite. The leader parallels the generation – a valiant community produces valiant leaders.

We look to bold leaders and try to emulate their qualities. At the same time, the responsibility for producing such leaders, encouraging them and giving them support for making difficult decisions lies squarely with the community.

BERAKHOT 4A

Meriting miracles

THE SAGES PLACE in the mouths of Jacob and King David the concern that they might be unworthy of God's blessings. In both these cases, however, the Talmud appears to assume that these anxieties were groundless. Do we have examples in our tradition of inappropriate behaviour leading to a lack of blessing?

The Talmud (*B. Berakhot* 4a; *B. Sanhedrin* 98b; *B. Sota* 36a) cites a verse from the poetic Song of the Sea, sung by the Jewish people after they had successfully crossed the Reed Sea: *Until Your people will cross over, O Lord / Until this people that You have acquired will cross over* (Exodus 15:16). Though we could easily attribute the repetition to poetic licence, rabbinic tradition sees this verse as referring to two separate events. The first crossing refers to the Jews' initial entry into the Land of Israel under the leadership of Joshua. The second crossing refers to the return to the Land of Israel at the end of the Babylonian exile under the leadership of Ezra the Scribe.

The juxtaposition of these two entries into the Land of Israel leads the sages to conclude that the two were meant to be similar. As with the first entry, the Return to Zion should have been accompanied by miracles, defying the will and might of foreign rulers.

Those who returned with Ezra, however, did not benefit from such wondrous Divine assistance. They required the permission of a Persian overlord to rebuild, and continued working under his aegis. The sages account for this by saying *shegaram haḥet,* the sin caused them to lose this opportunity. What was the sin of Ezra's generation?

One approach identifies the sin with the behaviour of the Jewish people during the First Temple period (circa tenth century BCE–586 BCE). The Talmud tells us that the First Temple was destroyed because of the commission of three cardinal crimes: idol worship, adultery and murder (*T. Menaḥot* 13:22; *B. Yoma* 9b). As a result of these sins, the

Jewish people who returned to the Land of Israel did not merit entry amid miracles (*Rashi*).

This suggestion may leave us wondering: did God visit the sins of the parents on the children? Just because one generation committed heinous sins, should a subsequent generation not merit miracles?

Perhaps it is this question which leads other commentators to highlight sins that were committed by Ezra's generation. One commentator suggests that the Jews of Ezra's time were lax about certain rabbinic "fences" which were designed to prevent transgression of Torah laws. According to this approach, respecting these barriers would have reflected a commitment to retain a distinct Jewish identity, particularly during exile. As a punishment for disregarding this uniqueness, the miracles which should have been associated with entry into Israel were withheld from them (*Meshekh Ḥokhma*).

A further interpretation identifies the sin as intermarriage (*Reshit Ḥokhma; Rabbi Avraham son of the Gra; Rabbi Tzadok HaKohen of Lublin*). Intermarriage is a challenge that the Jewish people have faced throughout the ages, and we have textual evidence indicating that it was an issue during the period of the Return to Zion as well (see Ezra 10; Nehemiah 13).

Another possibility focuses on the tempered response to Ezra's call to leave the exile and return to the Land of Israel. Since the throngs did not heed the summons, those who did make the journey homeward did not merit the type of miracles that had taken place during the original mass entry into the Land of Israel (*Maharsha*).

The commentators, as we have seen, try to pin down exactly what sin made the return to the Land of Israel so different from the original entry into the Land. The use of the definite article – *haḥet,* the sin – certainly invites us to attempt to identify it.

The Talmud, however, does not seem to be concerned with identifying the exact sin, telling us only that there was one. I would suggest that this was deliberate on the part of our sages, designed to leave the question open to interpretation and to encourage us to reflect upon the nature of the misdeed.

Each generation is then able to construe the sin in accordance with its own reality and its own challenges. Against this background we can understand why the former Chief Rabbi of Israel and current political leader, Rabbi Ovadia Yosef (b. 1920), writing in our contemporary reality, chooses to underscore the lukewarm response to the opportunity to return from the exile to Israel as the reason for the lack of miracles. In addition to its relevance to Ezra's time, this explanation also resonates with our current state of affairs.

This approach may reflect the personal biography of Rabbi Yosef, who was born in Baghdad in 1920 and came to the Land of Israel at the age of four. After studying in Jerusalem and receiving rabbinic ordination from then-Chief Rabbi Ben-Tzion Meir Ḥai Uziel (1880–1953), Rabbi Yosef moved to Egypt in 1947, where he served in the senior rabbinic position in Cairo. After the establishment of the Jewish state, Rabbi Yosef himself answered the call and returned to Israel in 1950.

Thus, the passage has a timeless quality, which can be read and understood by each community over the ages. As each group reads its own story in the eternal words of our tradition, it connects viscerally to our heritage and stands fortified as it confronts its own challenges.

Our generation has been fortunate to merit an independent state, which was established with the help of many miracles. Despite this, Israel has yet to make its full contribution to the world.

I have often pondered what the sin is that has prevented the State of Israel from realising its full potential as a true light for the nations of the world. Undoubtedly, different people will suggest various possibilities. By leaving this question unanswered, however, we grant it enduring significance, while we continue to contemplate the alternatives, strive for improvement and attempt to correct the sin.

BERAKHOT 4B

Rules of prayer

In *Berakhot*, the Mishna and Talmud are filled with rules and regulations regarding prayer rites. To this day, these regulations continue to dictate the form and structure of our liturgy.

To cite but one example, the Mishna prescribes how many blessings should envelop the twice-daily reading of *Shema*. In the morning, two blessings precede *Shema* and one follows it; in the evening, two blessings again precede *Shema*, while two blessings are recited after the reading (*M. Berakhot* 1:4). The Mishna goes on to define the length of the blessings, and asserts that the ordained length is mandatory.

Despite such apparently rigid rules, we shall see that a certain malleability is revealed in the talmudic discussion (*B. Berakhot* 4b; *Yalkut Shimoni* 1:842).

The Talmud states that a mention of the ultimate redemption should be juxtaposed with the silent *Amida* prayer. One who does this successfully is guaranteed a portion in the World to Come. Indeed we are told that one of the sages smiled for an entire day after he managed to mention the redemption and continue immediately to the silent *Amida* (*B. Berakhot* 9b).

In the morning this is easily achieved, for the blessing after *Shema* deals with this very topic and concludes: "Blessed are You, God, who has redeemed Israel." Immediately after reciting these words, we launch into the silent *Amida*.

In the evening this is more problematic, for after *Shema*, as we have noted, there are two blessings; the first deals with redemption, but this blessing is followed by a second one asking for safety, peace and wise counsel. This second blessing – known by its opening word *Hashkiveinu* – separates between redemption and the *Amida* prayer, an apparent contravention of the rule requiring the juxtaposition of these two prayer elements.

The Talmud explains that since the *Hashkiveinu* blessing was instituted by the sages, it is as if all post-*Shema* paragraphs are connected to the theme of redemption, and the interruption is discounted.

In a slight variation, the same is said for the morning prayer. Even though, as we have seen, the blessing following *Shema* and preceding the *Amida* discusses redemption, before beginning the *Amida* we add a biblical verse: *God, open my lips and my mouth will say Your praise* (Psalms 51:17). The Talmud asks: Isn't this an interruption between redemption and the *Amida*? Here too, the Talmud explains that since the sages instituted this short supplication, it is considered part of the *Amida* prayer.

In both cases, the seemingly rigid rule of prayer is bent to make room for the institution of an additional rabbinic prayer. The Talmud is silent on the question of why the sages felt it necessary to flout the rules and append these passages. The service would appear to be complete without such additions. However, one thing is clear: despite the rules that at first glance are stated in unyielding terms, the sages had the authority to manipulate them.

This approach is not limited to the talmudic era. The prolific Hasidic master and halakhic authority, Rabbi Ḥayim Elazar Shapira of Munkács (1871–1937), in his commentary to the *Shulḥan Arukh*, relates to the custom of inserting various *piyutim* (liturgical poems) in the middle of the service on select Shabbatot. The Munkatcher Rebbe explains that we dare not abrogate an institution of our venerable sages, particularly considering the hidden and esoteric valence of these passages.

Once again we see that our forebears had the authority to make such changes, and once again we are left wondering what their motivation was. Licence to change the law still requires a reason to exercise that licence.

This brings us to a fourth example, also connected to prayer liturgy, this time from the responsa of the Munkatcher Rebbe. The relevant rule in this case is that biblical verses must not be recited piecemeal; entire verses as defined by tradition must not be broken up. In the words of our sages: "Any verse that was not defined as a verse by Moses, we are not permitted to define as a verse" (*B. Ta'anit* 27b; *B. Megilla* 22a). Despite this clear rule, in almost every *piyut* we find the poet using parts of biblical verses with apparent disregard for the rule. Moreover, this is often considered a laudable poetic device which ties the *piyut* to our traditional sources.

By now we should not be surprised to learn that the poet is granted poetic licence to break the stated rule. In this case, however, the Munkatcher Rebbe goes further, explicating the motive for defying the rule: the insertion of the *piyut* into the service is designed to accentuate the significance and uniqueness of the day. Each *piyut* seeks to enhance the liturgy, aiming to awaken and inspire. Faced with this noble objective, the rule proscribing breaking up biblical verses recedes, and the poet is permitted to make use of parts of biblical verses.

While the Munkatcher Rebbe's explanation relates to the flouting of a particular rule associated with the liturgy, it would appear that his reasoning is applicable to all the cases we have cited. In each case, the exalted purpose of making the prayer service more meaningful is grounds for sanctioning a departure from a stated liturgical rule.

We can therefore restate the principle that describes defined prayer rituals. Indeed, there are rules which govern the liturgy; these regulations, however, may recede in the face of other considerations that accord with the ultimate purpose of prayer rites.

There are, of course, questions that remain. Are all regulations created equal? Perhaps some rules are more pliable than others? What goals are considered worthy enough to permit breaking the rules? Who is invested with the authority to decide when a rule may be ignored? Despite these unanswered questions, the possibility of abrogating prayer rules to serve a higher purpose is evident.

BERAKHOT 5A

The shield of Torah

THE STUDY OF Torah as a cure-all for life's problems is a common theme in rabbinic literature: "If that despicable scoundrel [the evil inclination] affects you, drag him to the *beit midrash*, the house of study" (*B. Sukka* 52b; *B. Kiddushin* 30b). Not only is the Torah a tonic for spiritual ailments, it is a cure for headaches, sore throats, upset stomachs and weary bones. In fact, any physical disorder can be remedied by Torah study. Furthermore, Torah affords protection from affliction for one who studies it (*B. Berakhot* 5a).

Our experience, however, sometimes seems to indicate otherwise. Even if we understand the Talmud to be speaking of spiritual illness, we are still left wondering about the protective properties of Torah. Study of our traditional texts hardly grants immunity against the enticements of life. Torah scholars have been known to fail, despite the protective armour provided by their dedicated study. And this is not a new phenomenon. The Talmud relates anecdotes of Torah scholars who were humbled by the temptations of this world, notwithstanding their Torah study.

How are we to understand the rabbinic notion of the Torah as shield, in the face of the reality we experience, and despite the examples of human frailty cited in rabbinic literature?

One possible solution is that the scholar might have fallen to greater depths of depravity were it not for the protection of Torah. Tempting though this approach may be, it is impossible to substantiate.

In one talmudic passage we find a discussion of the extent of the protective powers of Torah (*B. Sota* 21a). Rav Yosef distinguishes between the potency of Torah and the potency of *mitzvot*. While performing a *mitzva*, one is immune from physical hardships that are incurred as punishments, and is also protected from the folly of further sin. Following the fulfilment of a *mitzva*, one continues to be protected from pain, but the *mitzva*'s powers of salvation from sin expire. In contrast, Torah provides protection from pain and salvation from transgression both during and after its study (*Rashi*).

Such a description fits the rabbinic mould: Torah as a shield against sin. What makes this passage unique is that Rav Yosef's colleague, Rabba, challenges this formulation. Citing two biblical paradigms, Rabba claims that there are those who studied Torah yet were not protected from wayward behaviour. Here we have our very question asked by the Talmud itself.

Rabba leaves the question unanswered, but his student, Rava, reformulates the rule and thus provides a solution. According to Rava, a *mitzva* affords protection from punishment during its performance and thereafter, though it never fends off the possibility of further sin. Torah, too, always provides protection, but while it is being studied it also provides salvation from sin. The underlying assumption of Rava's reformulation is that a Torah scholar sins only when not studying the holy texts.

Rava's explanation certainly mitigates the question of his master, Rabba. The Torah force field is in place only while Torah is being studied. Torah studied in the past will provide no assistance in grappling with temptations in the present. Hence, we are advised to drag the evil inclination into the *beit midrash* in order to counter its influence.

Rava's approach, however, is not easily accepted. Entering the *beit midrash* and opening our holy books is not designed to be a temporary remedy. Once that rogue is hauled into the *beit midrash*, it should be crushed or worn away by the study of Torah. Upon exiting the study hall, the scholar's burden should be lifted, and the craving for sin should dissipate. Our issue, therefore, remains: biblical, rabbinic and contemporary evidence seems to indicate that Torah is not a protection against sin.

Another talmudic passage alters the landscape of our discussion. Our sages advise that a person should incite his good inclination against his evil inclination as a means of combating the lure of sin. If this does not work, the person should study Torah. If this step proves ineffective, the person should recite *Shema*. If this too is futile, then the person should recall the day of death.

Though this passage indicates that Torah is a possible elixir of life, it also acknowledges that there are times when Torah will not suffice and other remedies should be conscripted.

The commentators offer different suggestions as to when the Torah shield may be insufficient. According to one explanation, it is when the evil inclination uses Torah itself as its tool of temptation, perhaps telling a person to study so that he or she will attain fame. In such a case, the cure becomes the disease, and an alternative tonic should be sought (*Anaf Yosef*).

Another approach highlights the particular time of day when one is challenged. Torah is a good solution during the times set for study. At night, when one has finished studying, reciting *Shema* is an appropriate counter to sin. And when one is lying in bed about to fall asleep, recalling eternal sleep – death – is the way to avoid transgression (*Riaf*).

Finally, a third approach focuses on the particular problem at hand. Not every remedy cures every illness. If a person does not perform a *mitzva* because he is fearful, he or she should ward off the evil inclination by saying it would be scarier not to perform the *mitzva*. If the vice is laziness, not fear, one should immerse oneself in Torah. If the problem is one of social propriety and pressure, one should meditate on *Shema*, recognising that nothing exists besides God. And if the challenge involves the many attractions of this physical world, one should focus on the fleeting nature of our temporal existence (*Bina LeItim*).

Whatever the case may be, it is clear that Torah should not be relied upon to provide total protection against transgression in all situations.

To be sure, a foolproof safeguard against sin – whether it is Torah study or any other elixir – would blunt the possibilities of human choice. We are confronted with challenges that must be faced, not solved by taking a swig of magic potion. The study of Torah may strengthen us in the face of life's trials, it may be the best defence we have at our disposal, but in the end we must tackle our challenges head on.

BERAKHOT 5A

The Sinai potential

AND GOD SAID *to Moses: Come up to Me to the mountain… and I will give you the tablets of stone and the Torah and the commandment that I have written, that you may teach them* (Exodus 24:12). Faced with this description, our sages identify the items mentioned in this verse: *the tablets of stone* are the Ten Commandments; *the Torah* refers to the Five Books of Moses; and *the commandment* indicates the corpus of Oral Law embodied in the Mishna. The sages go further: *which I have written* implies the remainder of Scripture – the Prophets and the Writings, and *that you may teach them* evokes the involved discussion of halakha that has reached us in the form of the Talmud. After pinpointing the meaning of each phrase, the passage concludes: "This teaches us that all of them were given at Sinai" (*B. Berakhot* 5a).

Such all-encompassing statements that declare the Sinaitic source of the entire Jewish library exist elsewhere in rabbinic literature (for example, *B. Sota* 37b). The most powerful assertion is based on the verse that precedes the Ten Commandments: *And God spoke all these words* (Exodus 20:1) – *all* includes "even that which a student will ask a teacher" (*Shemot Rabba* 47:1).

A parallel version includes not just the questions, but even the rulings of a veteran student (*Kohelet Rabba* 1:9:2; *Y. Megilla* 28a; *Y. Pe'ah* 17a). The version we find in the Babylonian Talmud includes even the laws that will be instituted at a later time in response to historical events. Thus the requirement to read the scroll of Esther in commemoration of the Purim story was revealed at Sinai (*B. Megilla* 19b).

Are we to believe that even innovations that had yet to be discovered were addressed at Sinai? Is that possible? The span of our tradition is so vast – could one person have encompassed it, even if that person was Moses? Furthermore, how would Moses have reacted when God related to him laws dealing with phenomena far from his reality, such as the halakhic status of electricity or the appropriate time to ask for rain in the southern hemisphere?

These maximalist statements become more perplexing when we note that there are voices in rabbinic literature that seem to acknowledge the concept of post-Sinaitic innovation. In one account, Rabbi Eliezer's Torah is described as "more than was said to Moses at Sinai" (*Avot DeRabbi Natan* B 13).

In another account, students came to visit Rabbi Yehoshua, who queried them: "What *ḥiddush*, innovation, was said in the *beit midrash* today?" Respectfully, the students replied: "We are your students and we drink from your waters." Rabbi Yehoshua did not let up, responding with a far-reaching claim: "There is no *beit midrash* that does not have some *ḥiddush*" (*T. Sota* 7:9–11; *B. Ḥagiga* 3a; *et al*). In one version of the story, Rabbi Yehoshua goes further, insisting on a daily *ḥiddush* in the *beit midrash* (*Y. Sota* 18d).

How can we understand the notion of *ḥiddush*? Was the entire Jewish library given at Sinai, or is there room for ongoing innovation?

This question has more than just historical and theological relevance. It touches on the very essence of what we are attempting every time we delve into our sacred texts. Are we trying to uncover that which was already given at Sinai, or are we perhaps striving to arrive at new understandings?

Many answers have been offered over the ages to this conundrum. I would suggest a synthesis of the sources quoted above. Indeed, everything was given at Sinai, albeit in potential. The encounter in the *beit midrash*, in which the veteran student discovers a fresh angle, was an event set in motion at Sinai. Reaching that *ḥiddush* is an actualisation of the Sinai potential, and as such is a real innovation.

Indeed, one midrash, noting how impossible it must have been for Moses to cover the entire Torah in forty days, states that God taught Moses the general rules (*Shemot Rabba* 41:6; *Tanḥuma, Ki Tissa* 16). Perhaps this implies that the application of those rules was consigned and entrusted to future generations.

In a famous talmudic passage we find Moses asking God why He is adding crowns to the letters of the Torah scroll. God explains that one day there will be a scholar who will derive mounds of laws from each branch of every crown. Moses asks to see this person, and, turning around, finds himself in the *beit midrash* of Rabbi Akiva. As Moses listens to Rabbi Akiva's lecture, he is baffled and distressed. After Rabbi Akiva expounds a particular law, the students ask him for the law's source. Rabbi Akiva answers: "*Halakha leMoshe miSinai* – it is a law received from Moses at Sinai."

At that moment, Moses should protest stridently; how dare Rabbi Akiva attribute some unrecognisable law to Sinai! The tale, however, takes an entirely different course – upon hearing the declaration of Rabbi Akiva, Moses' anguish subsides (*B. Menaḥot* 29b). Why is Moses calmed by Rabbi Akiva's ascription?

Perhaps Rabbi Akiva is not saying that the law was actually stated explicitly by Moses; rather he is declaring that its roots are Sinaitic. Moses is reassured when he sees the actualisation of the Sinaitic potential. Hence, Rabbi Akiva's teachings were indeed given – albeit in potential – to Moses at Sinai.

When we explore the Jewish library, we are both connecting to our past and looking to our future. We continue the traditions of old, while investigating its applications to the new.

A suitable analogy might be that of a tree which sends its roots deep into the earth in search of sustenance, while at the same time dispatching leaf-laden branches in all directions in search of sunlight. A tree with no roots will not survive, and a tree that does not bask in sunlight will not be able to nourish those precious roots.

When we sit in the *beit midrash*, we strive to grow in two directions. We cultivate the roots that connect us to Sinai, while we search for the sunlight of today.

BERAKHOT 5B

Things worth crying for

In our society, weeping is sometimes considered a weakness. We encourage our children to refrain from crying, reproving them if we deem their tears uncalled for. But there are times when shedding tears is appropriate. What is worth crying for?

This is the question that Rabbi Yoḥanan posed when he went to visit the sick Rabbi Elazar (*B. Berakhot* 5b). As he entered the abode of Rabbi Elazar, Rabbi Yoḥanan found himself in a dark, dank place. Searching for some source of light, Rabbi Yoḥanan rolled up his sleeve, revealing his legendary radiant skin (*B. Bava Metzia* 84a). The glow revealed a sorry sight; there lay Rabbi Elazar with tears streaming down his cheeks.

Seeing his colleague's tears, Rabbi Yoḥanan wondered: "Why are you crying?"

Without waiting for a response, Rabbi Yoḥanan contemplated the possibilities: "Perhaps you are crying for the Torah that you did not manage to learn during your lifetime." Rabbi Yoḥanan dismissed this, quoting the maxim: "Both the one who does much and the one who does little [are equal], as long as each person directs his heart towards heaven."

This aphorism originates in the context of sacrifices, indicating that the value of one's offering is not decisive in its acceptance; various sizes of offerings are equally welcome, provided that the intent of the giver is pure (*M. Menaḥot* 13:11). Rabbi Yoḥanan cited this dictum to comfort Rabbi Elazar. He was saying: "You may not have accumulated as much Torah as you would have liked, but since your intent was for God, you need not cry."

Rabbi Yoḥanan pondered and rejected a further possibility: "If it is because of your poverty – not everyone is fortunate enough to enjoy two daily meals." Your financial situation is not so dire. Thus it too is not grounds for tears.

Offering his final suggestion, Rabbi Yoḥanan sombrely said: "If your tears are for your deceased children" – surely you have nothing to cry about. "For this," said Rabbi Yoḥanan while producing a human bone from beneath his cloak, "is the bone of the tenth son whom I lost." What can compare to my tragedy!

Silence reigned as Rabbi Yoḥanan was lost in recollections of his own misfortune.

Having considered spiritual achievements, physical living conditions and Rabbi Elazar's progeny, Rabbi Yoḥanan looked expectantly at his friend with inquiring eyes.

Between sobs, Rabbi Elazar said in a thin voice: "I am crying for this beauty" – pointing to Rabbi Yoḥanan – "that will rot in the dust of the earth."

The words of Rabbi Elazar pierced the heart of Rabbi Yoḥanan. Acknowledging the justification for tears, he said: "For this you should certainly cry!" And he too began to weep.

Indeed, Rabbi Yoḥanan's beauty was celebrated. The thief Reish Lakish was drawn into the *beit midrash* by Rabbi Yoḥanan's attractiveness and his promise to match up Reish Lakish with his equally beautiful sister.

Nevertheless, we must wonder: Could these sages, who dedicated their lives to Torah and God, be so moved by physical beauty?

One of the renowned talmudic commentators, Maharsha, appears to be troubled by this question. Maharsha, an acronym for *moreinu* (our master), *harav* (the rabbi) Shmuel Edels (1555–1631), was born in Kraków. Following his marriage, his mother-in-law supported him and his disciples for twenty years, and in recognition he is known by her name – Edel.

Maharsha's primary contribution is in the form of two works printed in most editions of the Talmud. His novellae on legal portions of the Talmud, *Ḥiddushei Halakhot,* are characterised by their terseness. Most of Maharsha's comments in this work end with the phrase: "and weigh carefully" or "and it is easy to understand," though the meaning is often far from simple. In a parallel work, *Ḥiddushei Aggadot,* Maharsha elucidates the non-halakhic portions of the Talmud.

In *Ḥiddushei Aggadot,* Maharsha offers an explanation for our sobbing sages crying over the temporal nature of Rabbi Yoḥanan's beauty. Elsewhere in the Talmud, Rabbi Yoḥanan tells us that he is the last of the beautiful people of Jerusalem. Lying in bed and contemplating the fleeting nature of life, Rabbi Elazar sees Rabbi Yoḥanan, the last remnant of the beautiful people of Jerusalem. Realising that Rabbi Yoḥanan too would die, Rabbi Elazar was crying over the impending extinction of the beautiful people of Jerusalem.

Although Maharsha explains the sages' lament, we are still faced with our sages crying over external attractiveness. Furthermore, it appears from the text that Rabbi Elazar was crying even before the glow of Rabbi Yoḥanan's arm revealed his visitor's identity.

I would like to take Maharsha's suggestion in a slightly different direction. Our sages were not crying over physical manifestations of beauty. Rabbi Elazar was lamenting the splendour of Jerusalem: the glory of the capital city of an independent people, a religious centre for the nation where thrice yearly all men made a pilgrimage to see and be seen. Once in seven years, men, women and even young children would troop to the capital for the grand *hak'hel* gathering, a sabbatical celebration of the nation. As he lay in bed, Rabbi Elazar contemplated the loss of this majesty.

Rabbi Yoḥanan, however, stood there unmoved, unable to justify any tears. To prod his colleague, Rabbi Elazar personalised the tragedy, pointing to Rabbi Yoḥanan. You, the final vestige of the grandeur of Jerusalem, will eventually rot in the earth, signifying the end of this splendid era.

The Three Weeks between the fast of *Shiva Asar B'Tammuz* (the Seventeenth of Tammuz) and the fast of *Tisha B'Av* (the Ninth of Av) is the period when we mourn the losses of our people, our spiritual calamities and physical ruin. These tragedies still reverberate today. It is during this time that shedding tears is certainly meaningful; not only for days gone by, but for contemporary echoes of those events. As Jeremiah wrote, lamenting the destruction of Jerusalem: *For these things I weep; my eyes flow with tears, because any comforter who might revive my spirit is far from me* (Lamentations 1:16). May the comfort for our tears not be too far in the future.

BERAKHOT 5B–6A

Be nice

RABBINIC THOUGHT GENERALLY differentiates between two classes of commandments. One group encompasses interpersonal relationships – *bein adam laḥavero*. The other category, *bein adam lamakom*, refers to actions that relate to a person's bond with God.

Although stemming from a common source – the Almighty – the categories are generally seen as separate, and different rules govern the two types of laws. It is interesting, therefore, that in a talmudic passage dealing with a genuine *bein adam lamakom* pursuit – prayer – our sages inform us that it can be affected by *bein adam laḥavero* behaviour.

The Talmud records four statements of a relatively unknown sage, Abba Binyamin (*B. Berakhot* 5b–6a), the second of which relates to our topic. Two people entered a synagogue to pray. One of them finished. Without delay, he headed for the door, leaving the other person alone in the synagogue. Abba Binyamin tells us that the prayers of the person who left were torn up in front of his face. Furthermore, he was responsible for the departure of the Divine Presence from Israel.

Abba Binyamin's statement seems to reflect a reality in which places of prayer were situated on the outskirts of an inhabited district. Walking at night in these areas would have been neither a pleasant nor a safe experience. This statement is translated by the codifiers into a normative requirement to wait in the synagogue until the last person has finished praying. They do not necessarily limit the obligation to nighttime prayers in secluded synagogues.

One influential European medieval scholar – Rabbi Yitzḥak of Dampierre (died c. 1185), more commonly known by the title Ri HaZaken (the Elder) – was said to have delayed and extended his prayers until all present had left the synagogue. If despite these tactics someone were to enter the synagogue and begin praying, Ri would delve into a book until the dawdler had finished praying.

In spite of Abba Binyamin's definitive statement, the codifiers rule that if someone enters the synagogue and begins to pray at a time when it is obvious that he would be unable to finish with the others present, there is no obligation for others to wait for him. For this latecomer entered and began praying, knowing that he would not finish with the congregation. Waiting for this straggler, however, is a laudable act – as exemplified by the conduct of Ri.

The commentators point out that the punishment depicted in this passage – shredding of the prayers of the early exiter – matches the crime. Standing alone in the synagogue, perhaps wondering whether the door would be locked, perhaps considering the unaccompanied walk home, the lone supplicant would have been unable to concentrate. As the early exiter made for the door, he effectively destroyed the focus of the one left behind. Measure for measure, the prayers of the early exiter are destroyed.

The talmudic record continues, presenting the flip side. If the one who first completed praying waits, he merits the blessings described in the biblical verses: *Your peace will flow like a river, and your righteousness like the waves of the sea. And your offspring will be as abundant as the sand of the sea, and your descendants as many as its grains; their name will never be cut off or obliterated from before Me* (Isaiah 48:18–19). Surely this is a blessing worth waiting for.

The notion that a *bein adam laḥavero* infraction can impact upon a *bein adam lamakom* action is an appealing one. One might otherwise be tempted to suggest that careless *bein adam laḥavero* behaviour, such as leaving someone alone, has no bearing on a pious *bein adam lamakom* deed, such as heartfelt prayer. The clear implication of this passage is that the way we treat others indeed affects our relationship with God. Thus interpersonal behaviour must not be neglected in the pursuit of the Divine.

The idea of linking the two categories of conduct – *bein adam lamakom* and *bein adam laḥavero* – was also recognised by the influential Hasidic master, Rabbi Elimelekh of Leżajsk (1717–1787). Rabbi Elimelekh was one of the central figures in Hasidism, and he is largely credited with bringing the innovations of this revival movement to Poland and Galicia. Today his grave in the small Polish town of Leżajsk is a pilgrimage site for many Hasidim, and Hasidic tradition maintains that one who visits his tomb will not die without repenting.

Aiming to assist himself and his followers in their daily service of God, Rabbi Elimelekh composed an additional prayer that was to be recited before the set prayers. Saying this "prayer before prayer" would prepare and focus supplicants as they embarked upon the spiritual journey of communicating with God.

Though prayer is generally viewed as a *bein adam lamakom* act – an individual or community communing with God – Rabbi Elimelekh's petition is replete with references to interpersonal relationships. Significantly, his prayer concludes with a powerful request from the *bein adam laḥavero* realm: "[God,] place in our hearts, that we all see the good in our friends and not their faults. May each person speak with his peers in a straightforward manner, as is Your desire. And may we feel no hatred towards our fellows."

The implication is clear. Before approaching God, one must be beyond reproach in dealing with humans. The domain of *bein adam lamakom* is not detached from that of *bein adam laḥavero*; it casts its giant shadow on this heaven-directed sphere.

Sadly, we often neglect to pay close attention to this link as we strive for increased quality in our *bein adam lamakom* practice. If this increased quality comes at the expense of *bein adam laḥavero*, it is a price that is not worth paying, for it actually devalues the *bein adam lamakom* act. As we cultivate our connection with God, we would do well to recall that how we act towards our peers bears heavily on our relationship with the Almighty.

BERAKHOT 6A–B

Does God keep *mitzvot*?

THE TALMUD TELLS us that on some spiritual plane the Almighty adheres to the very commandments that He commands us to keep. Just as we put on *tefillin* daily, so too God puts on *tefillin* (*B. Berakhot* 6a–b). But perhaps the Almighty was not always so fastidious in His observance of His own commandments. Certainly the ministering angels felt that at times God was not following His own directives. Our sages tell us that at the time of the destruction of the Temple and the sacking of Jerusalem, the ministering angels turned to the Almighty with three charges.

First, the Torah commands that after slaughtering a wild animal or fowl, the blood must be covered with earth (Leviticus 17:13). Yet in describing the destruction of Jerusalem and the Temple, the psalmist says: *Their blood was shed like water around Jerusalem, and there is no one to bury it* (Psalms 79:3). Moreover, the prophet Ezekiel writes: *For her blood still in her* – referring to Jerusalem – *has been set on a bare rock; she did not pour it out on the ground to cover it with earth* (Ezekiel 24:7). Thus, claimed the angels, the Almighty did not fulfil the *mitzva* of covering the blood of the slaughtered.

Second, the Torah commands: *And with regard to an ox or a sheep, it and its offspring shall not be slaughtered on one day* (Leviticus 22:28). Yet at the time of the destruction, children were wantonly slaughtered together with their parents. Thus, claimed the angels, the Almighty transgressed this prohibition.

Third, when speaking about the disease of *tzara'at*, the Torah describes the procedure in the case of a building afflicted with this spiritual malady: *And the priest will order that the house be emptied before the priest will enter to examine the malady, thus nothing in the house may become ritually impure; only then will the priest enter to examine the house* (Leviticus 14:36). A house afflicted with *tzara'at* has the status of *tuma*, ritual impurity, only once it is officially declared so by the priest. At this point all the contents of the house that are susceptible to ritual impurity contract the *tuma*. To avoid an unnecessary loss of property, the contents of the house are removed before the priest makes his examination and declares his findings. If the priest declares the house ritually pure, the contents are returned; if the priest declares the house ritually impure, the house is pulled down, but the property removed from the house before the declaration is saved.

The angels argued that this biblical law was violated by the sacking of the Temple: *And they burned the house of the Lord and they tore down the wall of Jerusalem, and they burned down all its palaces in fire, and they consigned all its precious objects to destruction* (II Chronicles 36:19). Thus, claimed the angels, the Almighty should at least have saved the Temple vessels before destroying the Temple, just as a priest ensures that the contents of the house are spirited away before declaring the house ritually impure.

Our sages tell us that God responded to the claims of the ministering angels with a cryptic answer: "Is there peace in the world? Since there is no peace, there is nothing." While these Divine words are certainly powerful as well as somewhat despairing, how do they provide a response to the claims of the angels?

Rabbi Ḥayim Vital (1542–1620) was the celebrated student of perhaps the most famous kabbalist of all time, Rabbi Yitzḥak Luria (1534–1572), often referred to as the *Ari HaKadosh* (the holy lion). Rabbi Vital reported in the name of his teacher that a biblical verse hints at the three claims put forth by the ministering angels: *If a legal case baffles you, be it a controversy over blood, be it a controversy over law, be it a controversy over a spiritual malady – words of dispute are in your gates – you will rise and ascend to the place that God your Lord will have chosen* (Deuteronomy 17:8).

The biblical verse refers to three types of cases in the court system: blood, law and spiritual maladies. These correspond to the three angelic claims: blood – covering the blood of the slaughtered; law – the prohibition of killing parent and offspring on the same day; and spiritual maladies – the directive to save the contents of a stricken building. When this issue of God's flouting the law baffles you, the Ari says, know that it is because *words of dispute are in your gates* – when there is infighting, the Almighty is no longer bound by the dictates of the Torah. This is the meaning of God's succinct response: "Since there is no peace, there is nothing."

The Ari concludes his explanation with the final phrase of the biblical verse – *you will rise and ascend to the place that God your Lord will have chosen.* Only once we have overcome the infighting, the arguments that frequent our gates; only when we ascend to the holy city of Jerusalem, that place that symbolically unites our people; only when we remain steadfast in our loyalty to the tradition of our forebears – only then can we hope for peace.

BERAKHOT 6B

Space for prayer

A POSSIBLE PITFALL OF habituation is that it may breed complacency. Innovation and variation, on the other hand, lend excitement and generate interest. This reality makes the challenge of set prayer – set texts and set times – all the more formidable. It is therefore curious that the Talmud adds a third element to the fixed nature of prayer – a set place for prayer (*B. Berakhot* 6b, 7b).

Not only is there prescribed wording for prayer to be recited at fixed intervals, but our sages add: "If someone has a set place for prayer, his enemies will surrender to him." Similarly: "If someone has a set place for prayer, the God of Abraham will assist that person. Furthermore, when this person dies, people will lament: 'Woe for the loss of this humble person; woe for the loss of this pious person, this person who is of the disciples of Abraham our forefather.'"

Why is a set space for prayer linked to Abraham? The passage continues, citing biblical verses to indicate how Abraham had a designated place for prayer. One who designates a location for prayer is therefore following in the footsteps of our illustrious forefather.

Though our sages laud setting aside a place for prayer, the Talmud does not indicate *where* one should designate this space. It appears that four possibilities exist, and each possibility leads us to a different understanding of the importance of this fixed location.

First we might suggest that the sages are encouraging people to patronise a specific house of prayer. Following this line of thought, designating a particular synagogue can be seen as an act of association with a community.

A second approach sees the set place as referring to a designated seat within the synagogue, and argues for assigned seating (*Hagahot Maimoniyot*; *Rosh*). What is the advantage of having your own seat in a synagogue? On this point the commentators offer a variety of approaches.

One commentator offers a technical explanation. Our prayers replace and mirror the Temple service. Thus we pray *Shaḥarit,* the morning prayer, and *Minḥa,* the afternoon prayer, when the daily morning and afternoon sacrifices were offered. *Ma'ariv,* the evening prayer, corresponds to the nighttime burning of limbs and fats from the daytime sacrifices. Just as the Temple sacrifices had to be slaughtered and offered at a designated location, our prayers should be recited in a designated spot (*Riaf*).

Alternatively, our passage could be related to the rabbinic directive not to view prayer as a burdensome task. If the obligation to pray is considered onerous, then supplicants are likely to rid themselves of this obligation at the earliest possible moment regardless of where they find themselves. Making one's way to a designated place demonstrates that prayers are not a burden (*Riaf*).

Turning to the core of prayer, another commentator suggests that a predetermined location for prayer increases the likelihood of concentration (*Meiri*). Indeed, one is less inclined to survey the surroundings of an oft-visited place. With nothing fascinatingly new in the environs, the supplicant has fewer distractions and is more likely to focus on the prayers.

Reflecting a different aspect of prayer, another commentator maintains that a reserved place for prayer invokes awe and respect, the appropriate disposition for prayer (*Rashba*). It would follow from this that the selected location needs to evoke such feelings.

A set location for prayer also encourages regular attendance at services. People who do not have their own seat may feel less inclined to show up, knowing that they will have to contend with the challenge of finding a place to pray (*Rashba*).

As we can see, there exists a plethora of justifications for allocated seating in a synagogue. Indeed, a parallel statement in the Jerusalem Talmud supports this second approach, declaring that people should designate a particular place for prayer in the synagogue (*Y. Berakhot* 8b).

It is this understanding that receives normative expression, as the codifiers rule that not only should one choose a synagogue, but even within that house of prayer a specific seat should be selected. Practical considerations lead this directive to be tempered by a licence to pray within a four-cubit radius of one's designated place (*Shulḥan Arukh, Oraḥ Ḥayim* 90:19; *Magen Avraham*).

Let us move on to the third possibility for the location of this designated space. One scholar suggests an entirely different understanding, which is based upon an alternative version of our passage in the Jerusalem Talmud: "If someone designates a place in his house for his prayer, it is as if he has surrounded it with walls of iron."

This approach notes that the entire interior of a synagogue is designated for prayer; hence there is no significance in selecting one particular place within the four walls of this house of prayer. In a case where one cannot reach the synagogue, it is praiseworthy to set aside an area for prayer within the home. At the very least, this may minimise disruption of prayers by household members.

Lastly, we turn to the fourth and most innovative approach. Despite the existence of a synagogue filled to capacity with people, a miniature replica of the Temple, one should designate a site outside of the walls of this communal place of prayer (*Riaf*). What type of location is implied here? One might suggest that we have here a licence to leave the central synagogue and pray in a more personal and intimate setting, such as the classic *shtibel*.

Alternatively, a bolder reading of this approach might acknowledge special locations for prayer outside of any synagogue. Such personal spaces would be places that facilitate and stimulate communication with God.

Of course, the four paths offered are not mutually exclusive; an allocated seat in the synagogue does not preclude a lonely cliff top overlooking the ocean. A common theme that emerges from this passage and its possible interpretations is that spatial considerations play a role in the quality of the spiritual experience of prayer. The Talmud chooses to leave the location of that safe space unspecified. That choice challenges us to locate and frequent the area where we feel most comfortable communicating with the Almighty.

BERAKHOT 6B

Running to the *beit midrash*

Everyone has his or her own way of walking. One person shuffles along, another strides purposefully; this one has a bounce in her step, that one intently scrutinises the ground underfoot. Despite the obvious individuality of one's gait, our sages provide guidance as to how one should walk to and from a *beit midrash* or synagogue (*B. Berakhot* 6b).

Rabbi Ḥelbo says in the name of Rav Huna: "One who leaves a synagogue should not take giant strides," as this would imply that the time spent in the house of prayer was burdensome (*Rashi*). Abbaye qualifies this statement, telling us that this directive applies only to exiting; running to enter the synagogue is certainly praiseworthy.

Against this background, another talmudic scholar, Rabbi Zeira, tells of his change of heart regarding hurrying to a *beit midrash*: "At the beginning, when I saw our scholars scurrying on Shabbat to hear the sermon, I would say that they were desecrating the Shabbat." This initial reaction was based on the talmudic maxim that it is forbidden to take large strides on Shabbat (*B. Shabbat* 113b), which is derived from the biblical verse: *If you restrain your foot for the sake of Shabbat then you will delight yourself with the Lord; I will set you astride the heights of the earth, and let you enjoy the heritage of your father, Jacob* (Isaiah 58:13–14).

Rabbi Zeira, however, changed his outlook: "As soon as I heard what Rabbi Tanḥum said in the name of Rabbi Yehoshua ben Levi – that a person should always run to hear a matter of halakha, even on Shabbat – I too would sprint!"

In connection with this anecdote, the Talmud records an aphorism of the same Rabbi Zeira: "The reward for going to a class in Torah is granted for hurrying there." This statement is somewhat startling. Is there no reward for attending the study session and learning Torah? Is not the journey merely a means to the end of engaging with our traditional texts?

The passage continues with Abbaye offering another surprising adage: "The reward for attending Shabbat sermons before the festivals is bestowed for standing crammed in with other listeners in the overcrowded study hall." Again we wonder: do attendees not receive any returns for the actual act of studying Torah?

These dicta may be disheartening even for the earnest student of Torah. Is the value of the Torah we learn assessed by the difficulty and investment in getting to and attending the lecture? Is there no merit to the actual material covered during Torah classes?

Making no attempt to mitigate these statements, one classic commentator explains why reward is conferred for dashing to the *beit midrash* rather than for actual Torah study. Working with the assumption that the purpose of learning Torah is long-term recall of what was studied, this commentator states that there is no value to Torah which is studied and later forgotten. The unfortunate reality is that, as time goes by, most participants in Torah lectures are unable to recount what they studied. All that remains, therefore, is the reward for hurrying to the *beit midrash* and standing in cramped conditions during the class. Hence the talmudic axiom (*Rashi*).

This approach has serious implications for many of us who find that while we enjoy our encounters with Torah, we may not have total recall of all that we have learned. On the one hand, we may find it heartening to know that at least we get rewarded for scampering to find a seat at the beginning of the lecture. On the other hand, discounting the worth of the experience of Torah study and placing value only on the enduring result is a gloomy outlook that devalues much of our learning.

Another commentator, perhaps seeking to take the edge off these statements, focuses not on the students but on knowledgeable scholars who attend public lectures. According to this way of thinking, the talmudic dicta here are addressed to knowledgeable people who are not exposed to new laws or applications at such communal gatherings. Their reward for attending these collective study sessions is limited to their exertion in reaching the *beit midrash* and remaining there (*Maharsha*).

Another commentator, sensing the difficulty with this passage and unwilling to accept our initial reading, suggests that the maxims are not exclusionary. According to this approach, the sages intend to add to the reward for Torah study. Not only does one receive a reward for learning our sacred texts – a given – but reward is even granted for making an arduous journey to the study hall, or for choking in a stuffy, teeming room during the lecture. Lest one think that only the actual study is worthwhile, our sages tell us that the actions that facilitate this learning are laudable as well (*Ein Yaakov*).

From here we come to our last approach, a perspective suggested in the writings of the famed Maharal of Prague (1512?–1609). Maharal proposes that one who is moving towards something is, in a sense, nearer to the objective than one who is in point of fact closer to it at present, but is immobile.

To illustrate this point, let us imagine two people on a flight of stairs. One person is only a few steps from the top; the other is at the foot of the stairs. The person near the top is stationary, while the person down below is climbing the stairs intently, advancing in leaps, every so often glancing longingly up at the top. Who is more likely to reach the top?

The desire to study Torah – as exemplified by running towards the *beit midrash* or standing in uncomfortable conditions during a class – indicates more about a person's aspirations than actual participation in a lecture. Though we avidly study Torah, it is our eagerness for the encounter and our ardent striving for it which accurately reveal our commitment to our heritage.

BERAKHOT 6B

Forget-me-not

As mentioned, according to the Talmud: "The reward for going to a class in Torah is granted for hurrying there" (*B. Berakhot* 6b). In his classic commentary to the Talmud, Rashi offers a sobering explanation as to why reward is granted for the journey: "The primary reward for those who hurry to hear Torah lectures from the wise is the reward for running. This is because after a period of time most people are unable to repeat what they have learned or restate what their teachers have taught. Accordingly, they cannot receive reward for actual learning." The reward is therefore conferred for dashing to the *beit midrash*, since it appears there is no value in Torah studied and later forgotten.

How bad is it to forget the Torah you studied? Elsewhere, the sages condemn in the strongest of terms anyone who forgets Torah: "If someone forgets one word of his study, Scripture considers him to have forfeited his life" (*M. Avot* 3:8). The source for this harsh analysis is the biblical verse: *Only beware for yourself and be exceedingly careful for your soul, lest you forget the things that your eyes have seen* (Deuteronomy 4:9).

Our sages, however, acknowledge an exception. If the studies were so complicated or overwhelming that the person's memory could not encompass all that was studied, he is absolved of guilt for his forgetfulness. The source for this exception is the continuation of the aforementioned verse, *and lest they depart from your heart all the days of your life*. A person is culpable only if he deliberately removes Torah from his heart.

In the Talmud the issue of forgetfulness is recast in terms of transgression against Divine commandments: "Anyone who causes even one word of his Torah learning to be forgotten has transgressed a prohibition." Our sages debate whether the forgetful person has transgressed only one commandment, perhaps two, or even three prohibitions (*B. Menaḥot* 99b).

Alas, forgetting what we have studied is not an unheard-of occurrence; for many of us it is an all too familiar scenario. Even our heralded forebears and the sages themselves were prone to forget Torah matters. To cite but one example: in the tractate that deals with the layout of the Temple, one of the venerable sages admits that he forgot what certain offices in the Temple were used for (*M. Middot* 2:5; 5:4).

Are we constantly transgressing every time we forget? To be sure, only one of the medieval scholars places forgetting Torah on his list of the 613 commandments (*cf. Rabbeinu Yona Gerondi*). Yet, even if forgetting Torah is not one of the enumerated commandments, it is hardly a practice lauded by the Talmud.

The Talmud adds a further exception to the rule of culpability for forgetting Torah (besides forgetfulness due to the complexity of the material) – if one forgets Torah inadvertently, due to forces beyond one's control. This might include someone who forgot Torah due to illness, or because of the burden of earning a living and providing for a family (*Rashi*). Here too – as in the case of complex material – the person has not deliberately removed Torah from his heart and is therefore spared the severe talmudic censure.

Yet not all forgetfulness can be put down to *force majeure*, circumstances beyond our control. What is the measure of our responsibility and even guilt for forgetting Torah when outside circumstances cannot be blamed?

One commentator suggests that the entire prohibition applies only to rabbinic authorities and sages, for if they forget Torah it may result in incorrect halakhic decisions and instructions (*Bartenura*).

Another commentator offers an innovative approach to the entire issue of forgetting Torah. Rabbi Avraham David Wurmann of Buczacz (1771–1841) writes that forgetfulness is a problem only if we rely on memory. If we record the Torah in writing or in print, then even though we may not remember all we have learned, we can easily use our notes or books to remind ourselves. Once we take note of the Torah we have learned, the newly created external repository of our knowledge lessens our culpability for forgetfulness. This understanding recasts the prohibition against *forgetting* Torah as a prohibition against *losing* Torah. As long as Torah is not lost, even if I as an individual don't remember it at any given moment, the Torah has not truly been forgotten.

This approach reflects the importance of taking notes, transcribing Torah thoughts and printing books. Rather than rely on our frail memories, putting the idea on paper – or on the computer screen – is one way to make sure we don't truly forget our Torah.

BERAKHOT 6B

The magic of *Minḥa*

ARE ALL THE daily prayers of equal importance, or is there one prayer that demands greater commitment? Our sages seem to single out one prayer for particular attention. "Rabbi Ḥelbo said in the name of Rav Huna: A person should always be diligent with regard to the *Minḥa* prayer" (*B. Berakhot* 6b).

Commentators are quick to point out that one should not conclude that other prayers may be neglected; our sages are merely highlighting the singularity of *Minḥa* (*Maharsha*).

How do we know that *Minḥa* is preferred? The talmudic passage cites the biblical episode in which Elijah confronted the prophets of Baal on Mount Carmel with a challenge. Two animals were to be slaughtered and placed on an altar. Each of the two contestants – the prophets of Baal and Elijah – would pray for flames to descend from heaven. The true ruler – Baal or God – would consume the offering. The false prophets began calling to Baal, but nothing happened. They danced around the altar, but still no response came. At noon, Elijah mockingly told them to holler louder, lest their deity was busy or far away or asleep. Indeed the prophets shouted, gashing themselves with their spears, as was their practice, until blood streamed down their faces. There was still no reaction.

All eyes now turned to Elijah, who took twelve stones and rebuilt the altar, placing a dismembered cow upon laid-out branches. Elijah then dug a trench around the altar and ordered four jugs of water to be poured over the animal and wood. Once that was done, he ordered the emptying of a further four containers of water and then a third set of four. With the offering and the wood truly doused and the ditch forming a water-filled moat around the altar, Elijah had seemingly made his task even more difficult.

Turning to God at *Minḥa* time, Elijah beseeched: *Answer me, God, answer me.* A fire descended and consumed the offering, the wood, the stone altar, the earth and the channel of water (1 Kings 18:19–40). It is because Elijah's prayers were answered specifically at *Minḥa* time that the Talmud concludes that the afternoon prayer has particular significance.

The institution of the afternoon prayer is attributed to Isaac, who set off for the field towards evening to meditate (Genesis 24:63). One commentator suggests that Isaac went out to the field to appeal to God to send him a wife. No sooner had Isaac uttered his request than he raised his eyes and saw his wife-to-be, Rebecca, approaching (*Tur*). The implication is that *Minḥa* facilitated this match.

Despite these sources supporting the significance of *Minḥa*, we have not explained why the afternoon prayer is exceptional. I shall now attempt to do so. *Minḥa* is recited while people are immersed in earning their livelihood. Despite being engrossed in work, they need to take time from their busy schedules to pray. This prayer, therefore, requires extra commitment. It is this dedication to God that makes *Minḥa* stand out.

Let us return to the talmudic passage. Rabbi Yoḥanan adds a warning about another prayer: "One should be conscientious with the *Ma'ariv* prayer as well."

But that is not all. "Rav Naḥman ben Yitzḥak said: One should be assiduous with regard to the *Shaḥarit* prayer as well."

We have seen that praying *Minḥa* may be a daunting task, as we are asked to interrupt what we are doing and turn to God. What makes *Ma'ariv* and *Shaḥarit* – prayers that bracket our workday – so challenging that our sages also caution against their neglect?

Upon returning home from the workplace, we like to kick off our shoes, relax and eat some home-cooked food. It is quite possible that while resting, we might doze off and thus miss the evening prayer. Our sages therefore warn us to be scrupulous and guarantee that we pray *Ma'ariv* before sleep overtakes our weary bodies (*B. Berakhot* 4b).

Shaḥarit opens our day, and as such is prayed before we begin working. The vice of oversleeping, however, invariably erodes our morning prayers. Alternatively, as we rise refreshed from a night's slumber eager to approach the day's tasks, we may be tempted to say: "I will just take care of a few errands before praying." The sages urge us to commence our day by communicating with God.

In a similar vein, one sage tells us that he took pains over two matters, the first of which was that his prayer would be close to his bed. The Talmud explains that the sage fastidiously ensured that he would pray *Shaḥarit* close to the time when he arose from his slumber, before turning to his daily work (*B. Berakhot* 5b). According to some commentators, the sage would not even study Torah before reciting the morning *Shema* and *Amida* (*Rashi*).

Our sages relate to the full complement of daily prayers – *Minḥa*, *Ma'ariv* and *Shaḥarit* – highlighting the challenges that accompany our efforts to recite each of them and urging us to take care to meet these challenges (*Eitz Yosef*).

Do the warnings all carry the same weight? Indeed, each prayer is a trial in its own way, and different prayers will challenge different people. One person will find starting off his day with *Shaḥarit* to be difficult. Another person will not want to disrupt the flow of her day for *Minḥa*. A third person will be too tired at the end of a long day to invest spiritual and physical energy in *Ma'ariv*. Our sages encourage us to tackle these challenges.

Though the Talmud acknowledges the challenges of each prayer, it declares the charm of only one – *Minḥa*. With regard to no other prayer are we told that its timing is auspicious. It may be tough to start the day with *Shaḥarit* and it may be trying to end the day with *Ma'ariv*. However, inserting a conversation with God in the middle of our day has unique significance: we are bringing God into the workplace, into our everyday lives and into our livelihood. This may well account for the magic of *Minḥa*.

BERAKHOT 7A

Teaching by example

PRAYER IS ONE of the tools at our disposal to nurture our relationship with God. Regular heartfelt prayer, however, is by no means an easy endeavour. Though prayer carries with it opportunities for cultivating rapport with the Divine, it is fraught with challenges. Perhaps with the aim of encouraging one who embarks upon the journey of communing with God, the sages assume that God himself prays. They seek only a proof text to substantiate this idea, asking: "How do we know that the Holy One, blessed be He, prays?" (*B. Berakhot* 7a).

The sages respond by citing a verse from the Prophets: *I will bring them to My holy mountain and make them joyful in the house of My prayer* (Isaiah 56:7). Though the last two words – *beit tefillati* – can be translated as "My house of prayer," the Talmud renders it as "the house of My prayer." *My prayer*, says God, suggesting that God too prays.

Unsatisfied with the mere notion that God prays, the sages' inquisitive tendency leads to a further question: "What does He pray?" A stirring answer is offered to this inquiry. "May it be My will that My mercy conquer My anger, that My mercy overcome My sterner attributes, that I behave towards My children with the attribute of mercy, and that for their sake I go beyond the letter of the law."

This prayer is baffling. To whom is God praying? There is no one to override God; why does He not do as He desires? Perhaps most troubling is that this passage hints at dualism – the doctrine which holds that reality consists of, or is the outcome of, two ultimate principles. The sages, however, sharply and decisively reject dualism. To be sure, traces of dualistic beliefs can be found in various Jewish sects such as the Dead Sea Sect. However, the centrality in rabbinic literature of the *Shema* recitation – a declaration of the unity of God – affirms that monotheism is an absolute.

Thus a prayer leader who says *modim, modim* – we give thanks to You, we give thanks to You – instead of just saying the word once, is hastily silenced. This is because the doubling of the prayer suggests a belief in two deities (*M. Berakhot* 5:3). Similarly we are instructed to offer blessings for bad things just as we offer blessings for good things, since the one God is the source of all (*M. Berakhot* 9:5).

Given that there is no room for dualistic beliefs in rabbinic literature, how are we to understand God's prayer?

This puzzling prayer is the subject of lengthy discussion amongst the commentators. The Babylonian scholar and leader, Hai Gaon (939–1038), offers an innovative approach that avoids the theological difficulty. He begins by citing another talmudic passage (*B. Rosh HaShana* 17b). Following the instruction for Moses to fashion a second set of tablets, the Bible details God's attributes, commonly referred to as the Thirteen Attributes of Mercy (Exodus 34:6–7). These verses have a central place in our *seliḥot*, penitential prayers. The Talmud describes God as wrapping Himself in a *tallit*, a prayer shawl, and demonstrating for Moses how communal entreaties should be led effectively. Recognising the audacity of this image, one sage comments that were it not for the biblical verse aluding to God as the prayer leader, we would not be allowed to suggest this scene on our own.

Drawing on this image of God teaching Moses how to lead services, Hai Gaon explains our passage. God's prayer is nothing more than a pedagogic exercise. Despite the set texts of prayer mandated by our tradition, when people decide to offer their own heartfelt prayers the content of such communication is by no means obvious. God, the teacher, shows us what the substance of our prayers should be.

One medieval commentator objects to this approach not on theological grounds but on textual ones (*Rashba*). Though God's teaching by example may be an inspiring image, the commentator charges that the language of the Talmud does not support this approach. As we have seen, the passage begins by seeking a source for the notion that God prays, and it continues with a further inquiry as to the gist of that prayer. Neither question seems to signify a lesson in the particulars of human prayer.

Despite this textual objection, Hai Gaon's explanation fits nicely with the continuation of the talmudic passage.

Rabbi Yishmael ben Elisha, a *Kohen Gadol*, High Priest during the Second Temple period (c. 515 BCE–70 CE), describes his experience one Yom Kippur as he entered the Holy of Holies to burn incense. He saw a vision of God sitting on a towering, grand throne. God turned to him and said: "Yishmael, My son, bless Me." The *Kohen Gadol* acquiesced: "May it be Your will that Your mercy conquer Your anger, that Your mercy overcome Your sterner attributes, that You behave towards Your children with the attribute of mercy and that for their sake You go beyond the letter of the law." Rabbi Yishmael ben Elisha concludes his account by saying that God nodded His head in approval.

As is apparent, this blessing is identical to God's prayer described earlier. The juxtaposition of the talmudic discussion of the content of God's prayer with the *Kohen Gadol*'s blessing may support Hai Gaon's suggestion that God is instructing us as to how to formulate our prayers. This was a lesson well-learned by Rabbi Yishmael ben Elisha.

Education is not just about telling someone else what to do, how to act or when to speak. More significantly, education is about modelling worthy conduct.

In truth, educators convey part of themselves when they teach. The passion of the educator breeds enthusiasm in the student; conversely the student can "smell" an educator who lacks fervour or who has lost eagerness and conviction.

Our sages paint the picture of God passionately praying as an educator teaching by example. God does not just command: "Pray!" The pedagogic lesson that the sages suggest is more specific. God is encouraging us: "Pray as I do."

If God teaches by modelling desired behaviour, surely when we educate – as parents, as community leaders, or in any other setting – our first order of priority must be to teach by example.

BERAKHOT 7A

Who can give a blessing?

WE ARE FOREVER wishing each other well. Whether it is on joyous occasions or following sad events, we often find ourselves opening or concluding a conversation with a blessing. Are such blessings significant? Is it worthwhile to seek them? Are they effective only when given by people of stature, or are they valuable even when offered by ordinary folk?

As mentioned, one talmudic passage suggests that the desire to be blessed is not only a human need, but also a Divine aspiration. Rabbi Yishmael ben Elisha, a *Kohen Gadol* in the Second Temple, relates that one Yom Kippur as he entered the Holy of Holies to offer incense, he saw a vision of God sitting on a towering, grand throne. God turned to him and said: "Yishmael, My son, bless Me." The *Kohen Gadol* acquiesced, blessing the Almighty, Who then nodded His head in approval (*B. Berakhot* 7a). The Talmud concludes that this tale teaches that the blessing given by an ordinary person should never be insignificant in our eyes. This may be sound advice, but one might question whether the story really demonstrates this lesson. One might point out that a *Kohen Gadol* is hardly an ordinary person.

Another passage in the Talmud, however, buttresses the conclusion that a blessing given by an ordinary person should also be considered of worth (*B. Megilla* 15a). The sages cite two examples of a blessing offered by gentiles which benefited a leader of the generation. Both the blessing that David received from Arona (1 Samuel 24:23) and the blessing that Daniel received from the Persian king Darius (Daniel 6:17) were efficacious.

Indeed a further talmudic passage mandates acceptance of the blessing of a gentile (*Y. Berakhot* 12c). Quoting the biblical verse *You will be blessed above all the nations* (Deuteronomy 7:14), the Talmud renders it as "You will be blessed by all the nations." Such a blessing, our sages say, should be graciously accepted with an *amen* response.

The talmudic passages complement each other, each offering a different insight. God's request to the *Kohen Gadol* for a blessing shows that one may actively seek and solicit blessings. Such blessings are valuable and may be effective when uttered by any and all, even someone who has a belief system that runs contrary to our tradition. One who is fortunate enough to receive a blessing should accept it warmly and openly.

This brings us to the story of a disciple who travelled to spend the holy day of Yom Kippur with the famed Hasidic master, Rabbi Yaakov Yitzḥak Horowitz (1734–1815), better known as the *Ḥozeh* (seer) of Lublin. The Ḥozeh was renowned for being able to look at a person's face and see deep into his or her heart.

When the disciple reached the city of his master, he went straight to the Ḥozeh's *beit midrash*. The Ḥozeh took one look at him and ordered him to return to his family. Confused and crestfallen, the disciple turned around and began the journey home.

That night he lodged at a small roadside inn. While he sat in a corner drowning his sorrows in a glass of tea, the door swung open and in trooped a group of his friends making their way to Lublin for Yom Kippur. When they spied their friend sitting gloomily in a corner, they excitedly called him over and exclaimed: "So you too are going to Lublin!"

With a long face, the unhappy disciple replied: "No, I will not be joining you. The Ḥozeh instructed me to return home."

Trying to cheer him up, they replied: "No need to be sad. Let's drink *Leḥayim,* to life!"

They filled their glasses and blessed their downcast friend: "May you merit to live a long life! *Leḥayim*!"

Glasses were quickly refilled. "May you have much joy from your children! *Leḥayim*!"

Another round was called for. "May you merit to spend other festivals in the presence of our master! *Leḥayim*!"

One by one, they drank *leḥayim,* and each friend blessed the dejected disciple.

When the sun rose, the wagon driver entered the inn and found his passengers slouched over and under tables amid empty bottles. The driver could not wait for the revellers to rise and ready themselves for travel, so he picked them up one by one – including the homeward-bound disciple – and threw them in the back of his wagon. He then continued towards Lublin. Hours later, the disciple awoke as the wagon bumped its way into Lublin. With horror, he realised what had transpired. His horror quickly turned to dread as he grasped the implication. That night was Yom Kippur; he would not be able to reach home before sunset as his master had directed!

The disciple devised a clever plan. He would stand in the back of the *beit midrash*, wrap himself in his *tallit* and bury himself in his *maḥzor*, the festival prayer book. After Yom Kippur, he would travel home. The Ḥozeh would never know!

That evening, the Ḥozeh entered the packed *beit midrash*. Instead of making his way to his usual seat, the master made a bee-line for the disciple tucked away in the corner and greeted him: "What a pleasure to have you with us for this holy day! May you be sealed in the book of life."

As the service commenced, the disciple stood there bewildered.

Following the service, the befuddled disciple approached the Ḥozeh seeking an explanation. With a kind smile, the Ḥozeh explained: "When you first arrived, I realised that you were destined not to live out the year. I therefore told you to return home so that you would spend your final days with your family. When your simple friends heaped earnest blessings on you, the heavenly decree was reversed. Naturally, I was overjoyed to see you."

Blessings may come from unusual quarters. Regardless of the stature of the one offering the blessing, we should accept any blessing proffered with an open heart. For we cannot know which blessings will truly bring us good fortune.

BERAKHOT 7A

Chances to encounter the Almighty

WHAT WOULD YOU do if God suddenly appeared before you? How would you react – would you bow low or stand straight? Look directly at the Almighty or avert your eyes?

The Bible recounts how Adam and Abraham conversed with God and how Jacob experienced the Almighty in his dreams and wrestled with God's messenger. Moses at the burning bush, however, was the first biblical hero to encounter God directly in a very dramatic fashion (Exodus 3:1). While herding the sheep of his father-in-law, Moses was lured by a strange sight – a bush that was burning but was not consumed. Amazed, Moses drew closer to investigate. At that moment he heard his name being called, and God identified Himself. What was Moses' response when faced with such an intense Divine experience? Scripture tells us: *Moses concealed his face, for he was afraid to look upon God* (Exodus 3:6).

Our sages are divided as to whether God approved or disapproved of Moses' reaction (*B. Berakhot* 7a; *Shemot Rabba* 3:1).

According to some of the sages, Moses' response was appropriate, as if to exclaim: "The God of my fathers is standing here. How can I not hide my face?!" This approach goes further, identifying the reward Moses was granted for averting his eyes. Later in the Bible, God's interaction with Moses is described as *face to face, as a person would speak to his neighbour* (Exodus 33:11). The sages note that in the merit of hiding his face, Moses conversed with God face to face. In context, it was this habitual face to face relationship that allowed Moses to plead before God and gain forgiveness for Israel's crime at Sinai with the Golden Calf.

Indeed, seeing God face to face is no insignificant matter; after Jacob wrestled with the messenger of God, he was surprised to have survived such an intimate and direct encounter with the Divine. He described this meeting with the words: *I have seen God face to face and my life has been spared* (Genesis 32:31).

Another sage suggests that Moses was rewarded for hiding his face by being granted a unique glowing countenance. Similar to the other sages, this sage plays on the word *face*. He cites the verse that *the skin of Moses' face radiated* (Exodus 34:35), such that he would speak to the Jewish people through a veil, removing it only when he interacted with God.

A third approach focuses on each detail of the verse describing Moses' reaction, and describes parallel rewards for each of his actions. As a reward for concealing his face, Moses was granted a shining countenance; for expressing awe at his encounter with God, the Jewish people were awestruck by Moses when his face became radiant; and for voluntarily averting his gaze, he was permitted to see the image of God (Numbers 12:8).

All of these sages agree that Moses acted correctly when he chose not to look upon God, despite being afforded the opportunity, and for this course he was granted a suitable reward.

Our tradition also records an entirely different line of thinking which describes Moses' course as mistaken and faults him for averting his eyes. God presented the future leader of the Jewish people with a golden opportunity for beholding the Divine. Instead of taking advantage of this prospect, Moses chose to hide his face.

The price of Moses' blunder did not end there. Later, when Moses beseeched God, *Show me Your glory* (Exodus 33:18), God refused his servant's request. The sages give voice to God responding to Moses' request: "I came to let you experience the Divine, and you hid your face, declining the opportunity. Now that you want to perceive godliness, I say to you that *no person can see Me and live* (Exodus 22:20)."

Although this response may be understandable, it seems to paint a vengeful, perhaps even childish, portrait of God. It is as if the Almighty is spitefully saying: "You missed your chance!" This is especially difficult to stomach since we are instructed to walk in God's ways (Deuteronomy 28:9), and we are also commanded to steer clear of revenge and to resist holding on to anger or harbouring a grudge (Leviticus 19:18).

According to at least one rabbinic understanding of this approach, God's response need not be cast in a rancorous light. God was not retaliating against Moses for his hesitation and reluctance at that first meeting. Rather, God's refusal to reveal His mystique was grounded in the new post-Golden Calf reality. It is as if God was saying: "I wanted to reveal all, but now I cannot be fully perceived by people. The opportunity for purity of vision has passed, and now no person can see Me and continue living a physical existence."

This explanation presents a powerful lesson. Windows of opportunity regularly open before us. We choose whether to make the most of such prospects or whether to ignore them and continue on our current path. It is important to bear in mind that such windows also close, and that portholes into other realms, once viable possibilities, may be sealed.

Perhaps this lies behind Hillel's adage: "Do not say 'When I have free time, then I will study,' lest you never have free time" (*M. Avot* 2:4). When we are presented with the chance to delve into the texts of our heritage, Hillel advises us not to squander this opportunity. It is noteworthy that Hillel does not base his dictum on the notion that our tradition contains a wealth of precious jewels that can augment and enhance our lives. Rather, Hillel advocates an immediate encounter with Torah for fear that the window of opportunity may slip away.

Chances present themselves before us daily. Just as quickly, the gates to new realities close and possibilities disappear. Based on the behaviour of Moses, our sages are cautioning us against hiding our faces when such opportunities present themselves, lest we miss the chance of a face to face encounter with the Divine.

BERAKHOT 8A

Sacred space

THE HEAD OF the talmudic academy in the Land of Israel, Rabbi Yoḥanan, was astounded to learn that there were elderly people living outside Israel, in Babylonia (*B. Berakhot* 8a).

Rabbi Yoḥanan's amazement was born of his reading of the biblical verse that forms part of the daily *Shema* prayer: *In order that your days be multiplied and the days of your children in the land that God swore to your ancestors to give them* (Deuteronomy 11:21). Focusing on the words *in the land,* Rabbi Yoḥanan understood that the only location that afforded the prospect of growing old was the Holy Land. Outside this unique space, the Divine blessing of longevity was not even a possibility, and hence Rabbi Yoḥanan's astonishment at the Babylonian elderly.

Rabbi Yoḥanan was mollified only when he was told that the elderly of Babylonia were people who would rise early to attend morning services and stay late to participate in the evening service, thus spending extended time in the synagogue. "That is the merit which is responsible for their longevity," he declared.

An obvious question arises from this exchange. What is the connection between longevity and lingering in the synagogue?

According to one commentator, staying longer in the synagogue or *beit midrash* is rewarded measure-for-measure by having life prolonged. The time invested in prayer and Torah study is repaid with a life extension (*Rabbi Yehonatan HaKohen of Lunel*). This approach teaches that despite the scriptural promise of longevity conditioned on living in the Land of Israel, there may be other deeds that warrant this gift. Indeed, the Bible and the sages detail a number of acts that merit long life.

An alternative approach refers us to a fascinating image. Elsewhere in the Talmud, our sages teach that in the future, the synagogues and houses of study that are located in the Diaspora will be uprooted and replanted in the Land of Israel (*B. Megilla* 29a). In light of this future relocation, these institutions carry a certain Land of Israel quality, even while they are still located throughout the world. In a sense, time spent in the synagogue and the *beit midrash* is time spent in the Land of Israel. Hence the blessing of longevity, particular to those dwelling in the Land of Israel, extends to those who habituate the confines of the synagogue or *beit midrash* (*Maharsha*).

The idea that someone can be standing in one place physically, and yet be considered to be in another locale, is recognised in secular international law. Countries have extra-territorial jurisdiction over their embassies abroad, even though strictly speaking, the embassy compound is on the land of the host country. Similarly, a vessel or aircraft bearing the flag of a particular country is bound by that country's laws, even when it leaves the territorial waters or airspace of that country.

Despite the parallel between international law and the image our sages present, there is a clear difference. International law creates a legal fiction that is limited to questions of jurisdiction. In contrast, our sages teach that despite physical location, a particular space may have an added spiritual dimension.

Not so long ago, in pre-war Poland, a similar notion was invoked in the famed Yeshivat Ḥakhmei Lublin (written in Polish as Jeszywas Chachmej Lublin), the grand institute of higher learning built in Lublin during the inter-war period. Following the death of Rabbi Meir Shapira (1887–1934), the Yeshiva was bereft of its founder and illustrious leader. Determined to keep this fine institution of higher learning viable, a spiritual governing board was formed. This body was comprised of the greatest talmudic scholars in Poland, and its function was to conceive and direct the education policy of the Yeshiva. At any one time, at least one member of this board was present in the Yeshiva. The stately Hasidic leader and scholar Rabbi Moshenu Friedman of Boyan-Kraków (1881–Auschwitz 1943) served on this body.

Another central personality who led the Yeshiva at the time was the talmudist Rabbi Aryeh Zvi Fromer (1884–Majdanek 1943). Besides authoring important responsa that were collated under the title *Eretz Tzvi*, Rabbi Leib Hirsch – as he was known – innovated a programme of *Mishna Yomit*, daily study of Mishna.

One Friday night, when both scholars were spending Shabbat in Yeshivat Ḥakhmei Lublin, Rabbi Moshenu began to dance, together with some of his disciples. Rabbi Leib Hirsch, however, was known to view dancing on Shabbat as rabbinically proscribed lest it lead to repairing musical instruments, a biblical transgression. Many of the students stood rooted to their places, torn between the pull of Rabbi Moshenu's dance and the ruling of Rabbi Leib Hirsch. Bewildered, the students turned to Rabbi Leib Hirsch, who raised his eyes and responded: "Go, go dance; in the Temple there are no such rabbinic restrictions." With that the students joined the dancing circle (*Pardes Yosef HeḤadash*).

Jewish law dictates that in the Temple, where the atmosphere was saturated with awe of the Almighty, cautionary provisions such as the prohibition against dancing on Shabbat were unnecessary. The Levites, for instance, played musical instruments on Shabbat, though outside of the Temple such an activity is forbidden lest the musician be tempted to fix a broken instrument. The sages explained that in the holy sanctuary, one need not fear a lapse of awareness in which a musician might unthinkingly repair a broken instrument.

Rabbi Leib Hirsch – probably driven by respect for his colleague and a strong desire to avoid strife in the institution – felt that the holy space of Yeshivat Ḥakhmei Lublin qualified, at least for the issue of dancing on Shabbat, as sacred Temple space.

Certain spaces encompass far more than their physical borders. The synagogue and the *beit midrash* are such sacred spaces that, no matter where they are physically located, they contain a trace of the holiness of the Land of Israel.

BERAKHOT 8A

Doorways to prayer

WHEN WE ENTER a synagogue, our first impulse is generally to find a seat. Where do you like to sit in the synagogue? Do you enter and quietly try to find a seat in the back rows, or do you try to blend in with the congregation by sitting in the middle of the sanctuary? Or maybe you prefer not to sit, hanging about the door and leaning on the back wall? Perhaps you enter and stride purposefully to the front so that you can "have a seat by the eastern wall," in the words of Tevye, Sholem Aleichem's milkman?

The Talmud tells us that upon entering a synagogue, a person should pass through two doors (*B. Berakhot* 8a; *Y. Berakhot* 9a). The sages base this directive on the verse: *Happy is the person who listens to Me, who comes quickly to My doors every day, to guard the doorposts of My entranceways* (Proverbs 8:34). Daily entrance is understood to denote the daily prayer services in the synagogue, and the use of the plural – *doors* – is interpreted as the need for two doors.

The Talmud, however, questions this directive, assuming that the sages could not be giving architectural advice about the requisite number of doorways of a "kosher" synagogue. The prescription is thus elucidated: when entering a synagogue we should walk the measure of two doors and subsequently pray.

The instruction remains cryptic: what is meant by "the measure of two doors"? The commentators grapple with this guideline, and two main schools of thought emerge. The medieval scholars interpret "the measure of two doors" as referring to this-worldly dimensions of space or time, while the Hasidic masters understand these doorways in spiritual terms.

Rashi explains that we should not sit near the entryway of the synagogue. Rather, we should walk a distance of two door widths in. This is so it does not appear that we are anticipating a hasty exit to liberate ourselves from the burdens of prayer. Apparently, Rashi would not approve of those of us who choose to stand near the door.

There is a caveat, however, to the proscription of sitting near the door. If you sit in your assigned seat in the synagogue, which happens to be near the exit, this is unobjectionable, since you are not planning a quick escape; it is simply your seat (*Rabbeinu Yona Gerondi*).

Spanish commentators from the late twelfth and early thirteenth centuries prefer to understand the talmudic passage as relating to time rather than space. They explain that we should allot the time it takes to pass through two doors before we begin praying, to allow our minds to settle and focus. Dashing into prayer gives the impression that we wish to be rid of a burden, and such rushing hinders heartfelt, quality service of God (*Rashba, Rosh, Ritva*).

Unlike the medieval commentators, the Hasidic masters understand traversing two doors to be a spiritual formula. One master suggests that the two doors are the paths of awe and love of God. Meaningful prayer can be achieved only by opening both the gate of awe and the gate of love (*Maor VaShamesh*).

In 1997, the present Boyaner Rebbe, Rabbi Naḥum Dov Brayer,

suggested that the sages are referring to the two "doors" that guard our speech – our teeth and our lips. As we enter the synagogue we cross these two gates, closing them behind us, and ensuring that time spent in prayer is not mingled with idle conversation.

Looking at the words of the Boyaner Rebbe from a different perspective, we can suggest that before praying we must enter deep inside ourselves, beyond our teeth and lips. This ensures that we are not merely offering lip service. When we turn to God we aim to offer prayer from deep within our hearts.

Let us turn from the words of the medieval and Hasidic greats back to the sages. A parallel passage in the Midrash seems to offer insight into this talmudic directive (*Devarim Rabba* 7:2). Why, ask our sages, should you pass through a door beyond a door when entering the synagogue? "Because the Holy One, blessed be He, counts your steps and rewards you for them."

Although this exchange does not explicate the meaning of the two doors – for that we must look to the commentators – it provides an overarching framework for understanding the instruction to enter through two doors. The further our entry into the synagogue – physically and perhaps spiritually as well – the more significant it is.

In 1901, Zalman and Ryfka Nożyk built a synagogue in Warszawa – *Synagoga Nożyków*. With six hundred seats, it was not the largest synagogue in this culturally rich city, but it was intended to host great cantors for Warsaw Jewry's elite. Today, it is the only surviving synagogue in a city that once contained countless houses of prayer, and daily prayer services are still held there. Before the Holocaust, seats in the Nożyk Synagogue were sold an entire year in advance, and the price of each seat was determined by its distance from the ark. The more expensive seats were at the front, while places near the exit were cheaper. Though this policy was not rooted in the Midrash's urging us to step further into the synagogue, it seems to be in sync with it: the further into the sanctuary we go, the dearer our steps become.

Each step into the synagogue is a show of commitment. This Midrash presents a vivid image: like an expectant lover, God waits to see how close His beloved will come, counting the steps and perhaps hoping for intimacy. Each movement through a door is an advance in our relationship with God. Opening the door to enter into the synagogue is not just a matter of finding a seat to recite the prayers. It is a step in building our relationship with God.

BERAKHOT 8A

Opportunities for starting afresh

WHAT DO YOU say to a bride and groom when you see them on their wedding day? Undoubtedly you wish them *mazal tov*. Perhaps you also ask how they are feeling on this exciting day. The Talmud reports a simple yet cryptic question that people would ask grooms in the Land of Israel: "*Matza* or *motze*?" (*B. Berakhot* 8a; *B. Yevamot* 63b).

The Talmud elaborates. Each of these two words is referring to a verse. *Matza* is taken from the verse: *He who has found* (matza) *a wife has found goodness and obtains favour from God* (Proverbs 18:22). *Motze* hints at the verse: *And I find* (u'motze) *to be more bitter than death the woman, whose heart is snares and nets, and her hands are fetters; he who pleases God shall flee from her, but the sinner shall be caught by her* (Ecclesiastes 7:26). Essentially, the groom is being asked whether he has married a worthy bride.

This is indeed a strange question to pose to a newlywed. First, we would hope that every groom would unhesitatingly affirm the praiseworthiness and goodness of his bride. We might be justified in questioning whether a groom who finds a woman *more bitter than death* should enter the marriage in the first place.

Second, even if we can find some justification for the question, is the groom really qualified, in the midst of the joy of the wedding, to assess his bride? Such a determination can be made only over time, once the couple has begun to build a life together. If indeed he finds his bride lacking, then comfort, encouragement and wise counsel are in order, not declarations of a preference for death.

Third, what is the purpose of seeking this interim report? It would appear that posing such a question would succeed only in sowing the seeds of doubt in the mind of a young groom, urging him to scrutinise his bride with zeal.

The Ḥafetz Ḥayim, Rabbi Yisrael Meir HaKohen of Radin (1838–1933), probes this practice from the perspective of his special interest: guarding one's tongue. He points out that in all likelihood this question and the groom's answer could be considered *lashon hara,* slander. The prohibition of *lashon hara* can be transgressed even by hinting to something negative – and certainly by using code-words such as *matza* and *motze.* Giving the answer "*motze*" would be a transgression even if it were the solemn truth. How could the sages condone such behaviour?

Rabbi Yoshiya Pinto (1565–1648), a talmudist and kabbalist, addresses these difficulties. Rabbi Pinto spent his life serving as a rabbi in Damascus, excluding the time that he spent in the Land of Israel. He arrived in Jerusalem in 1617 and moved to Safed in 1625, but left a year later following his son's death. Among Rabbi Pinto's writings, some of which remain in manuscript, is a popular commentary on the aggadic portions of the Talmud, compiled in the wake of his son's untimely death.

Rabbi Pinto begins by citing the rabbinic tradition that a person's sins are forgiven on his or her wedding day (*B. Yevamot* 63b). The source of this tradition lies in the resolution of a biblical discrepancy. One of the wives of Esau was the daughter of Ishmael. In one place her name is recorded as Basemath (Genesis 36:3); yet earlier, when Esau marries her, she is referred to as Mahalath (*Ibid.* 28:9). Noting this, the sages read the name Mahalath as a descriptive term rather than a proper noun. "Mahalath" comes from the Hebrew root meaning forgiveness. Since she is known as Mahalath only when she marries Esau, the sages conclude that the sins of newlyweds are pardoned on the occasion of their marriage (*Y. Bikkurim* 65c–d; *Midrash Shmuel* 17:1).

A newlywed, therefore, has two possible paths stretching into the future. Past misdeeds are cast away and a new life begun. In this case, the groom has truly found – *matza* – goodness by marrying. Alternatively, follies of life as a single are not abandoned and the prospect of wiping the slate clean is squandered. In this scenario, the wasted opportunity of a fresh start makes the chosen transition to married life objectively worse than the transition of death. Thus Rabbi Pinto suggests that the question "*Matza* or *motze*?" was more of a warning or reminder than a query.

The Ḥafetz Ḥayim hints at this approach as well. First, he points out that the prohibition of *lashon hara* does not apply when the matter is already known to all. We must assume that all know whether the bride is worthy, and hence asking the groom for his thoughts would not be a violation of the purity of speech. Though this explanation solves the *lashon hara* issue, it does not address the other difficulties with the passage.

In a second explanation, the Ḥafetz Ḥayim subtly notes that *lashon hara* is permitted when there is a distinct utility in relaying the truth. He does not, however, specify what the purpose might be in this case. An oral tradition expands the Ḥafetz Ḥayim's second explanation as follows. The questioners did not wait around for an answer. They were intent on asking the question and letting the impact sink in as they made a hasty exit. The idea was to remind the groom of the opportunity that lay before him – to choose between a life of *matza* or a life of *motze*.

This choice, according to the Ḥafetz Ḥayim, is not a one-time decision. A path that in the past may have been *matza* – filled with goodness – can too quickly turn to *motze* – a life bereft of spiritual fulfilment, whereby even death is preferable.

Any chance to start afresh is a precious opportunity which should not be squandered. Jewish tradition teaches that when a couple embarks upon life together, they are presented with the prospect of a clean slate. This is not the only juncture at which we are afforded such an opportunity. Yom Kippur also focuses on starting afresh. In many communities the bride and groom treat the lead-up to their marriage as a private Yom Kippur, and thus they fast on their wedding day. We should make a point of taking full advantage of these valuable opportunities to start anew.

BERAKHOT 8A

Gates of halakha

FOLLOWING THE DESTRUCTION of the *Beit Hamikdash,* the central Temple in Jerusalem, our people were forced into an exilic existence which led to extensive change in our modes of Divine service. Gone was the central place of worship; the sacrifices were no more. Adjustments had to be made as we coped with this new reality. We sought alternate centres for communion with God, to assume the former role of the *Beit Hamikdash* in our lives. The *beit knesset* – the house of gathering for prayer, together with the *beit midrash* – the house of study, now became religious focal points.

With this background we can understand the talmudic preoccupation with delving into the significance of the *beit knesset* and *beit midrash.* In one talmudic passage we find a scholar turning to a colleague and respectfully beseeching: "Would the master share with us some of the excellent lessons you taught in the name of Rav Ḥisda regarding the synagogue?" (*B. Berakhot* 8a).

The colleague obliged, opening with the biblical verse: *God loves the gates of Zion more than all the dwelling places of Jacob* (Psalms 87:2). He went on to interpret the Hebrew word for Zion, *Tziyon*: "God loves the gates that are *metzuyanim,* distinguished by Jewish law, more than synagogues and houses of study."

The hierarchy offered in this passage is unexpected. In the post-Temple reality of the sages, there is generally no place more sanctified or more highly regarded than the *beit knesset* and *beit midrash.* Entry into either of them was the nearest one could get to the residing place of the Holy Presence. It is therefore striking to find something more beloved than the familiar and celebrated *beit knesset* and *beit midrash.*

A further more perplexing enigma also arises from this passage. We are familiar with the *beit knesset* and the *beit midrash,* but what and where are the "gates distinguished by Jewish law"?

Given that these gates are God's most favoured location, it behooves us to do our best to identify them. Once we define the "gates distinguished by Jewish law," perhaps we will be able to comprehend the sages' veneration for them. Commentators throughout the ages have sought to illuminate the meaning of this appellation, which appears nowhere else in the Talmud, in an attempt to understand the ranking of holy places presented in our passage.

Let us begin by focusing on gates as opposed to houses. In biblical terms, the gates were where judges accepted cases, deliberated and arbitrated. Why at the gates? Would it not have been more appropriate to adjudicate in a sanctified structure such as a house of worship or house of study?

The gates were a public place that afforded equal access to all. By using this unrestricted area as a courthouse, the judicial system ensured that all people had the opportunity to have their cases heard, without being intimidated by hallowed halls. Justice was not removed from the people. Justice was available in the marketplace, together with the everyday goods and services on offer, and together with the inevitable business disputes that would crop up.

Yet from the judge's perspective, exiting the synagogue or study hall may not have been appealing. For the Jewish scholar, one of the most spiritually fulfilling pursuits is exploring the intricacies of the word of God in the *beit midrash* itself. For the Jew steeped in prayer and meditation, the synagogue is a haven for communion with God. Leaving these sacred locations might be experienced as a descent from Divine space to the mundane market, where two people might be grasping tightly to a shred of material, each relentlessly claiming ownership.

The talmudic passage corrects such an attitude, instructing the judge that arbitrating between litigants is a more than worthwhile quest. Serving justice in the public eye for the masses is more beloved by God than being holed-up in ivory towers, meditating on the Divine through prayer or study. Thus "gates distinguished by Jewish law" refers to the courthouses found in the markets, souks and bazaars, where cases were decided on the basis of Jewish law.

A careful reading of the talmudic passage, however, reveals that the intended recipient of this lesson – the judge – is only alluded to (by the use of the term "gates"). The teaching is phrased in general terms, so that even those who do not sit in judgment can draw some nourishment from the timeless words of our sages.

Let us return to the image of gates and houses. Gates have one face towards private property and the other towards the public domain. It can be said that gates define the threshold between the personal and the communal realms.

Our sages may be suggesting that Jewish tradition flourishes when it straddles this threshold, thereby keeping one foot in each world. Indeed, Jewish law and genuine spiritual experiences may well be personal encounters, yet they should also be shared in the public sphere. Rather than remaining in the synagogue and study hall, the light and warmth generated while encountering our tradition in these sacred places should radiate outward from the houses of worship and study to the gates facing the public.

A gate, however, is a two-way opening. At the same time that the glow from our sacred places should light up the area outside, ideas from beyond the synagogue and study hall should make their way into the melting pot of Jewish tradition, enhancing the flavour of its final product. Thus the synagogue and study hall should not barricade themselves in an attempt to shut out the reality of life beyond the gates. Jewish tradition remains eternal when it retains its relevance.

In the words of Balaam: *How good are your tents, O Jacob, and your dwelling places, O Israel* (Numbers 24:5). The dwelling places of Israel may indeed be fair, but the sages warn us against the insularity of keeping this goodness within the tents of Jacob. The wealth of our heritage should not be limited to the confines of the synagogue and study hall. Our tradition should *come forth from Zion* (Isaiah 2:3; Micah 4:2) towards the gates that guard our hallowed spaces. There it will hover as it draws both from the source and from life beyond the gates, permeating both realms with godliness.

BERAKHOT 8A

Communal learning

ON THE FIRST momentous Rosh HaShana, after the wall around Jerusalem was reconstructed by the returnees from the Babylonian exile, everyone gathered to hear Ezra the Scribe read from the Torah: *And Ezra opened the scroll before the eyes of all the people, for he was [on a platform] above all the people; and when he began, all the people stood* (Nehemiah 8:5). Citing another biblical verse, our sages conclude that the standing mentioned here signifies silence (*B. Sota* 39a). From this our sages infer that it is forbidden to converse, even regarding halakhic matters, once the Torah scroll has been opened.

The reinterpretation of standing as referring to silence leads to a further halakhic conclusion. There is no requirement to stand during the reading of the Torah; people may sit or stand as long as they follow attentively (*Tur*). Nevertheless, there are meticulous individuals who respectfully stand while the Torah is being read (*Mishna Berura*).

Ambiguity surrounds the meaning of one of the words in this verse – *kefitḥo*, translated above as "when he began." This ambiguity gives rise to differing opinions as to the onset of the prohibition against talking. When did the masses attentively fall silent – when Ezra opened the scroll or when he began reading? If the ceremony began with the opening of the Torah scroll, we can conclude that the prohibition against conversing begins as soon as the scroll is opened for Torah reading, and remains in force until the scroll is closed at the end of the reading (*Rabbeinu Yona Gerondi*). If, however, the people rose only when Ezra began to read, then the prohibition applies only during the reading (*Maimonides*). An alternative verse is offered as an additional source for the ban on conversation during Torah reading: *And the ears of all the people were attentive to the Torah scroll* (Nehemiah 8:3).

A talmudic passage from our tractate offers another angle on the mores of Torah reading (*B. Berakhot* 8a). Our sages tell us that the prophetic words *And they who forsake God shall be consumed* (Isaiah 1:28) refer to people who exit the synagogue while the Torah scroll is open and being read. This statement is qualified to permit a quick exit during the short intervals when people are being called up to read from the Torah.

A further question is raised: is it permitted to leave during the even shorter gap between verses, while the translator renders the verse in Aramaic? This query is left unanswered by our sages, and is theoretical for most communities today, since we no longer translate each verse into Aramaic. (Yemenite communities are the exception.)

The passage concludes with a surprising report about the practice of one sage. Rav Sheshet would turn away during the public Torah reading and study the Oral Torah. Explaining his actions, Rav Sheshet said: "We are occupied with our domain, and they are occupied with theirs!"

Rav Sheshet's practice and justification causes quite a stir amongst the commentators. Given the prohibition against talking during the public Torah reading – even about weighty Torah matters – how could Rav Sheshet literally turn his back on the service to study Torah?

A number of explanations are offered by the commentators. Their common denominator is an attempt to explain why Rav Sheshet was exempted from the general rule that proscribes conversing.

An early approach suggests that the rule against chatter during Torah reading does not apply to those whose Torah study is their profession. Thus Rav Sheshet and his colleagues were permitted to excuse themselves (*Rabbeinu Ḥananel*). According to this approach, Torah reading is designed for the masses. The privileged who are fortunate to spend their days engrossed in Torah study are permitted to continue their lofty pursuit, even while the rest of the members of the congregation attentively listen to the Torah reading.

Another approach limits the exception to Rav Sheshet himself. Rav Sheshet was blind and hence was not obligated to read the Torah. He alone was permitted to turn away from the public Torah reading (*Tosafot*).

Other explanations redefine the prohibition of talking during the reading of the Torah. Thus according to some commentators, the ban is only against disturbing chatter; talking inaudibly would not contravene the injunction. Additionally, Rav Sheshet was not making a point of turning away; he merely sought to facilitate his concentration (*Rosh*).

Alternatively, the prohibition can be circumvented by beginning to study prior to the Torah reading. Rav Sheshet thus turned away to show clearly that he had begun his Torah study before the Torah reading commenced (*Rabbeinu Yona Gerondi*).

It is of course entirely possible that the sources reflect two conflicting approaches amongst the sages as to the importance of the public Torah reading. One source gives voice to its centrality, prohibiting any conversation even about Torah matters; the other gives primacy to personal Torah study.

It must be said that, in general, commentators strive to present the Talmud as a unified text such that passages in one tractate complement parallel passages in other tractates. Faced with an apparent contradiction – as in our case – the commentators attempt to distinguish between the two cases and demonstrate that the texts complement rather than contradict each other. Here too, the commentators, as we have seen, try to reconcile the two passages rather than suggest that there is a disagreement.

In addition to the goal of presenting a unified text, there may be a further reason in this case for avoiding conflicting views. The public Torah reading is an act of communal study. It is difficult to entertain the idea that a sage – in our case Rav Sheshet – would deny the value of this communal endeavour. Hence distinctions are offered that acknowledge exceptions but keep the rule intact, even according to Rav Sheshet.

Torah reading is an unmediated encounter with our foundational text, without commentators and without recourse to legal arguments. Thus it is designed to be accessible to all, and it reflects the communal value that we place on joint study.

BERAKHOT 8B

Torah coursing through our veins

According to tradition, Moses ascended Mount Sinai on the first of Elul to receive the second set of tablets. Moses spent forty days atop the mountain, descending on Yom Kippur with two new complete tablets in hand once the schism between God and the Jewish people had been mended (*Tanḥuma, Ki Tissa* 31). We might wonder: what happened to the fragments of the first set of tablets? Were they left lying in the dust at the foot of Mount Sinai?

The Talmud declares that the remains of the first tablets were placed in the Holy Ark together with the second tablets (*B. Berakhot* 8b; *B. Menaḥot* 99a). This conclusion is based on the verse: *I will write on the tablets the words that were on the first tablets that you smashed, and you are to put them in the ark* (Deuteronomy 10:2). While the pronoun at the end of this verse – *them* – apparently denotes the new set of tablets, the sages tell us that the instruction *to put them in the ark* refers to the remains of the first smashed tablets.

Drawing on the image of the broken pieces being accorded a place of honour in the Holy Ark, the Talmud derives a lesson. Wise people who involuntarily forget their learning should not be treated disdainfully; such people should still be accorded honour.

At first blush, the analogy between scholars who cannot recall their Torah and the fragments of the first tablets would seem imprecise. We could argue that the first tablets were the handiwork of God and thus retained their sanctity even in their fragmented state. In contrast, the uniqueness of scholars lies in the Torah they study; without this Torah, perhaps their holiness dissipates. In fact, we could argue that another talmudic passage provides a more apt comparison. The sages rule that if a Torah scroll's letters have been erased, such that the cream-white parchment is all that remains, that scroll loses its sanctified status (*B. Shabbat* 116a). Perhaps this is the appropriate paradigm for scholars who once had the words of Torah etched on their hearts, but are now like blank parchment. The once-holy parchment loses the sanctity it had gained when the scribe meticulously blotted the page after writing each word of the Torah. So too, perhaps Torah scholars, if they forget the words of our tradition, lose the holiness they had gained when they painstakingly delved into it.

Why then do we compare Torah scholars who forgot their learning to the fragments of the broken first tablets?

In an entirely different context, a medieval scholar asserts that in the future an angel will come and remind the righteous people of all the Torah they studied (*Tashbetz Katan*). While this statement does not refer to our passage, we might suggest that wise people who forget their Torah must still be revered because at some time in the future they will be reminded of what they once knew. At that time, these people will once again be the proud bearers of Torah knowledge. As such, they continue to command our respect in the interim. This suggestion is buttressed by a later scholar's assertion that one day, God will restore the first tablets to their former, unbroken state (*Rema MiFano*).

This approach suggests an interesting paradigm. Honour is not accorded only on the basis of current status; great potential should also be considered. This may be particularly relevant to youth, whose potential is yet to be realised. We may be tempted to treat youth irreverently in light of their lack of experience, yet this approach suggests that they too deserve our respect. Furthermore, by showing regard for young people, we are more likely to instil in them feelings of self-worth and confidence, which will in turn spur them to maximise their potential.

Chief Rabbi Avraham Yitzḥak HaKohen Kook (1865–1935) suggests another approach to the comparison between fragments and scholars. In his commentary on this passage he implies that an encounter with Torah has two outcomes. The first and more obvious is the increase in knowledge that results from delving into the texts of our tradition, from creative readings of those texts and from exploring and expounding new ideas.

A second, perhaps more important, by-product of the experience of studying Torah is the indelible impression it makes on our lives. This deep-rooted and enduring imprint remains with us, even after we have forgotten the minutiae of a lecture or the nuances of a text. It is this lasting characteristic of Torah that commands our attention long after the details have been forgotten.

Many of us find ourselves swept up by ideas we encounter when studying Torah, yet soon afterwards we forget what exactly it was that stimulated us so. A lecture may have been inspiring, yet when we try to recall how the teacher wove together disparate sources, we find ourselves at a loss. We seem to be left with mere broken fragments. Despite this natural tendency, we continue to carry with us the enduring impression of the Torah encounter. As we grow older, details that we studied in our youth may become blurred; yet the overall experience of the Torah encounter remains vivid and significant.

BERAKHOT 9A–B

Plundering Egypt

THE BIBLICAL VERSES in which Israel is instructed to despoil Egypt as part of the Exodus have provoked – and indeed continue to trigger – discomfort among readers (Genesis 15:13–14; Exodus 3:20–22, 11:2–3, 12:35–36; Psalms 105:37). Was the Almighty sanctioning deception when he instructed the Jewish people to *borrow* gold and silver utensils? Was the fledgling nation justified in carrying off Egyptian goods? To be sure, this may have been standard practice during the biblical era (see II Chronicles 20:25). Nevertheless, we may question whether such actions are worthy paradigms to be lauded and imitated.

There is a long and robust exegetical tradition of grappling with these verses. Our sages suggest that the key to understanding the Almighty's instructions to Moses is His use of the beseeching *please* or *I beg of you* (Exodus 11:2). The Talmud paraphrases God's charge to Moses: "I beg of you, go and tell Israel; I beg of you, borrow from Egypt silver utensils and gold utensils, so that that righteous person, Abraham, will not say [to Me] 'You fulfilled *and they will enslave them and they will afflict them,* but you did not fulfil *and afterwards they will depart with much property* (Genesis 15:13–14).'" The exhortation was necessary because at that time the enslaved Jewish people were solely concerned with swiftly escaping Egyptian custody. The sages continue with the response of Israel: "We wish only to leave ourselves!" Property issues and Divine pledges to Abraham were of no interest to the trapped, freedom-desiring people. The Talmud concludes the passage with a short parable. "A person is incarcerated in prison and is told, 'Tomorrow you will be taken out of gaol and be given vast wealth.' The prisoner responds to these tidings: 'I beg of you, take me out today, and I will desire nothing more'" (*B. Berakhot* 9a–b).

One commentator on this talmudic passage acknowledges that the despoiling of Egypt in this manner was a necessary part of the Divine plan. The commentator goes further, suggesting that the Jewish people felt that the task at hand was alien and repugnant. It was the odious nature of what Israel was being asked to do that necessitated the Almighty first beseeching Moses to pass the directive on to Israel and further imploring Israel to fulfil the request (*Ran*).

Scholars throughout the ages have grappled with this issue, providing us with a range of perspectives on the plundering of Egypt. The common denominator among the approaches is the attempt to justify the deed and show its legitimacy.

For instance, many commentators note that the Egyptians gave items to the Jewish people willingly, acknowledging their debt and wishing to repay them. In this light, the act can hardly be termed plundering or despoiling, and the moral cloud hanging over the biblical episode dissipates (*Rashi*).

Other commentators cite a grand Divine rule of property rights: *The earth and all that is in it belongs to God* (Psalms 24:1). The Almighty, Who is the rightful owner of everything, allocates temporal ownership with infinite wisdom. The Exodus included a justified redistribution of God's assets (*Ibn Ezra*).

Another approach relies on the legal maxim that under certain circumstances, a person may carry out judgment without recourse to the court system (*B. Bava Kamma* 27b). Egypt unlawfully held assets of

Israel, and the despoiling was aimed at affecting lawful restitution. What debt did the Egyptians owe Israel? On what grounds was redistribution from Egypt to Israel equitable? What Jewish-owned assets were being held by Egypt? Various suggestions have been offered.

First, during his tenure at the helm of Egypt, Joseph had amassed great wealth (Genesis 47:14). When Joseph died, his assets were seized and appropriated by the Egyptians. It was these property interests that were now being returned to Jewish hands as Israel prepared to leave Egypt (*B. Pesaḥim* 119a).

Alternatively, the departing Jewish people were forced to abandon their unmovable property. In exchange for what they were leaving behind, the Egyptians handed over moveable goods that could be taken on the journey to the Promised Land. In this way, the despoiling of Egypt was in fact legitimate exchange of property, not unlawful plunder (*Ḥizkuni*).

A third possibility is that this was a recovery of the unpaid wages of the Jewish workers for the lengthy duration of their enslavement. Furthermore, according to Jewish law a freed slave is granted an entitlement by his master as a parting gift (Deuteronomy 15:13–14). The utensils were given in lieu of these wages and gifts (*Rabbeinu Baḥya*).

Other commentators shy away from a discussion of financial rights and obligations. They read the verses through a universal moral lens. Thus one commentator suggests that the entire biblical episode teaches us that the Almighty does not forsake the oppressed, the exploited and the abused. Reading the verses should make us realise that God will do whatever is necessary to ensure that the ill-treated are looked after and cared for (*Shadal*).

An honest appraisal of the explanations offered above may reveal that some approaches sound more apologetic than intrinsic to the text. Certainly the Bible uses terms here that are not normally employed to describe repaying debts or upholding lofty moral principles. Thus coming to grips with the verses remains a challenging endeavour.

The sheer number of commentators who grapple with the issue, however, provides some comfort. Our forebears understood that whatever the secrets of the verses, one thing is clear. Our tradition cannot be suggesting a paradigm of wily, devious behaviour; despoiling an enemy under the pretence of "borrowing" utensils is unacceptable. Reading the commentators, we may conclude what the biblical lesson *cannot* be. It remains for us, however, to reveal what the verses are trying to teach us. In this way we continue the quest to unlock the mysteries of the ancient texts of our heritage.

BERAKHOT 9B

I just can't wait to be king

SHEMA, THE QUINTESSENTIAL declaration of Jewish faith, is recited twice a day – once in the morning and once in the evening. This follows the biblical instruction to speak about Torah *beshokhbekha* – when you lie down, and *bekumekha* – when you arise (Deuteronomy 6:7, 11:18). Our sages attempt to define the parameters of these times, and ask: when exactly are *beshokhbekha* and *bekumekha*?

The Mishna presents two opinions regarding the earliest time for the recitation of the morning *Shema* "when you arise" (*M. Berakhot* 1:2). According to the first opinion, the time for the morning *Shema* begins when one can distinguish between white and blue – that is, the white wool of *tzitzit* strands and the single blue thread. This fits with the third paragraph of *Shema,* where we are instructed to see the blue strand of *tzitzit* (Numbers 15:39). The second opinion gives a different time: when one can distinguish between blue and a greenish leek colour. These two colours are similar, and hence more light is needed to determine which is which. This opinion, therefore, proposes a slightly later time. The thrust of both opinions is that people rise at daybreak, and that is when the obligation to recite *Shema* begins.

The Mishna continues with the latest time for reciting *Shema* in the morning, and once again two opinions are offered. According to one opinion, the window for *Shema* is very short. It should be read by sunrise, since most people arise by this time. The second opinion provides more latitude for this morning obligation, stating that *Shema* may be recited until the end of the first three hours of the day.

Why may *Shema* be recited until the end of the third hour, long after most people have risen from their slumber? The Mishna explains that it is the custom of kings to get up three hours into the day. Since some people are still rising at this late hour, it is still considered *bekumekha* and the morning *Shema* may be read.

Why is such an extended licence for reading *Shema* granted to royalty? Are they not obligated, just like ordinary people, to acknowledge the Almighty each morning? We may understand the licence as a privilege of office; the monarch has certain dispensations by virtue of his position. Alternatively, the licence may be seen as a necessity, not as a privilege. The ruler must deal with affairs of national importance, and while he is not granted a reprieve from his religious obligation, he is given greater flexibility in fulfilling this obligation. A third possibility – and the one that sounds most likely from the language of the Mishna – is that the extended time is an issue of practicality. In point of fact, kings sleep late. What is fascinating here is that the codifiers accept "three hours" as the latest time for anyone to read *Shema,* and they do not limit the ruling to kings!

In systems of law – Jewish law included – rules generally apply equally to all. The discussion in the Mishna, therefore, is what should be the rule. The first opinion suggests that the rule as defined by *bekumekha* should follow the prevalent practice. Most people rise early in the morning, and hence *Shema* should be said by all – presumably kings included – early in the morning.

The second opinion suggests that the rule should follow the practice of kings. Why should *bekumekha* be defined by the practice of kings, who are a clear minority compared to the masses?

I would like to suggest an answer to this question in light of a Mishna from another tractate. Our sages discuss care of the sick and use of medicine on Shabbat (*M. Shabbat* 14:3–4). It is permissible to violate Shabbat for someone who is dangerously ill, but taking medicines if the ailment is not serious is prohibited. This prohibition is due to the concern that in preparing the medicine, ingredients will be crushed – a violation of the injunction against grinding on Shabbat.

The Mishna raises a question in connection with this limitation. On Shabbat, is it permitted to eat regular foods that also have medicinal properties? Despite the general Shabbat ban on taking medicine to treat non-dangerous ailments, the sages rule that if an item serves as food or drink for healthy people, it may also be given on Shabbat to a person in discomfort in order to alleviate pain.

In the list of various remedies discussed in the Mishna, the sages deal with someone who feels pain in his loins and wishes to alleviate this discomfort with an ointment. Smearing the loins with a wine or vinegar ointment is prohibited, since such liquids are used only for therapeutic purposes; people do not regularly put wine or vinegar on their bodies. Smearing with oil, however, is permitted, for healthy people as well as sick people anoint themselves with oils.

What about rose oil, a rare and expensive oil that most people do not use except for therapeutic purposes? Two opinions are recorded in the Mishna. The first opinion prohibits using rose oil, since its cost prevents most people from using it except in cases of medical necessity. Princes, however, may apply rose oil to their wounds on Shabbat, for they have the means to use it even when they are healthy.

The second opinion in the Mishna rejects the idea of two classes, one that is permitted to use rose oil on Shabbat and the other that is banned from such use. What, then, should be the rule? Since the masses do not use rose oil when they are healthy, we might think that the rule follows the majority and bans rose oil. However, Rabbi Shimon succinctly states: "All Israel are princes." According to Rabbi Shimon, smearing rose oil on Shabbat is permitted for all, and the reason for this licence is that every Jew is considered royalty.

Returning to the morning *Shema,* we now understand why *bekumekha* is defined by the practice of kings. While most people do not have the royal privilege of sleeping late each morning, and many of us cannot afford a daily rose oil massage, our tradition views us all as nobility. Indeed, we are the children of a king – the King of Kings.

BERAKHOT 10A

Bearing the children of redemption

THE FAMED TORAH scholar Beruria was once challenged by a heretic, who sought to undermine her steadfast allegiance to the tradition (*B. Berakhot* 10a). Citing the biblical verse *Sing out, O barren one who has not given birth* (Isaiah 54:1), he queried: "Surely barrenness is a cause for sadness, not for rejoicing! Why does the prophet describe the childless woman as joyfully singing out?"

Beruria swiftly responded: "Fool! Go down to the end of the verse, where it is written *for the children of the desolate one* – referring to Jerusalem – *are more numerous than the children of the espoused one* – referring to the powerful Edomites." Clearly the so-called *barren one* does not remain childless, and therefore has good reason for singing.

Beruria's retort to the non-believer contains a hint of criticism. In instructing him to "go down" and examine the end of the biblical verse, she employs the word *shefil*, which also carries the connotation of lowering oneself, retreating from haughtiness. Not only was Beruria directing the heretic to go to the end of the verse, but she may have also been exhorting this troublemaker to subordinate himself to the words of Scripture.

Beruria, however, was not finished. She felt that the verse – or, more accurately, the heretic – deserved more attention. She continued: "If Jerusalem is to be filled with children, why then is she described at the beginning of the verse as being barren?" Without hesitating, Beruria offered a stinging answer, divorced from the biblical context: "Let the Congregation of Israel rejoice, for she is like a barren woman in that she has not given birth to children destined for Gehenna like you!" Indeed, Jerusalem is barren, but only from uncouth progeny like you, and that is certainly a cause for joy.

The central issue in this exchange – the barren woman eventually bearing children – is a common biblical motif. Three of the four Mothers – Sarah, Rebecca and Rachel – were barren (Genesis 11:30;

16:1–2; 25:21; 29:31; 20:1–2, 22–24), and a close reading of the text suggests that even Leah was at first unable to bear children. Other biblical heroines, such as the mother of Samson (Judges 13:2–3) and Hannah the mother of Samuel (I Samuel 1:2, 5–6), were also barren until God granted them offspring. How are we to understand the phenomenon of barrenness among women of the Bible?

The sages cite God's deep-seated desire for the prayers of such righteous women as a possible reason for biblical barrenness. Before granting the gift of children, God seeks the sincere prayers of virtuous women (*Bereshit Rabba* 45:4). A careful reading of this rabbinic passage reveals that the Almighty is not pining for introspective prayer or earnest supplications. Rather, the sages tell us that God craves the *siḥa*, speech or discourse, with these heroines. The term *siḥa* implies an interaction that is less formal, less structured and less ritual – an exchange that features a strong personal element. Thus our sages may be suggesting that the Almighty is providing an opportunity for cultivating a relationship. God may be saying: "First let us develop our personal relationship; after that has been secured, we can move to the miracle and challenge of raising a new generation."

This approach presents an appealing paradigm for developing relationships – interpersonal relationships as well as relationships with God. A relationship should be cultivated, strengthened and shored up before it is expected to bear fruit.

Though we may appreciate the wisdom in this lesson, the means by which it is presented – heartbreaking barrenness – is troubling. Surely there are other ways to develop relationships without making women barren and causing so much distress?

One commentator suggests that the barrenness of the Mothers was natural (*Radak*). Could such widespread barrenness really have been a natural occurrence? While this is a difficult question to answer, we should bear in mind that the four Mothers were all related, and could possibly have shared a genetic inability to have children. According to this approach, the miraculous ability to suddenly have children reflects the wondrous capabilities of God. Moreover, this was not a cynical display of God's might, since the barrenness was not a Divine ruse but a natural occurrence.

Another commentator proposes that childbearing in the wake of barrenness signals the Almighty's direct involvement in the development of our nation. The offspring of barren biblical figures arrive as Divine gifts. Thus, Isaac, Jacob, the tribes, Samson and Samuel would not have been able to contribute to the building of our people were it not for Godly intervention (*Rabbi Samson Raphael Hirsch*).

Looking at this approach from a different angle, we can suggest that by granting children to our heroines, God takes the first step in forging a unique connection. The Almighty extends a hand in an offer of relationship, placing the onus on us to respond in kind. Hannah understood this before Samuel was even born, and therefore she vowed to dedicate the life of her yet-to-be-conceived son to the service of God, in gratitude for his birth (I Samuel 1:11).

Let us return to the prophetic words of Isaiah that portray the redemption and return of the exiles in terms of a barren woman bearing children. This image may indicate that just as God responded to the heartfelt yearnings of the barren woman, so too God will respond to the sincere prayers of our people for a return to our former glory as a proud nation.

The parallel, however, does not stop here. The new mother must raise her child in a manner that will validate the granting of such a precious gift. So too, the return to Zion is the beginning of a new stage with new responsibilities. A homecoming to the Land of Israel is not an end in itself. The return is an opening of the door to a new reality, a reality infused with the challenge of cultivating holiness in this world.

BERAKHOT 10B

Book of Remedies

OUR SAGES CREDIT the righteous monarch King Hezekiah, ruler of the Kingdom of Judah for twenty-nine years, with a number of achievements. One of these accomplishments was the hiding of a certain "Book of Remedies" (*M. Pesaḥim* 4:10; *B. Pesaḥim* 56a). This feat is so valued by the Talmud that it is offered as one of two possible merits that Hezekiah invoked when he was beseeching God to be healed of his fatal illness. Thus he said: *I have done that which is good in Your eyes* (Isaiah 38:3) – that which is good, namely the suppression of the Book of Remedies (*B. Berakhot* 10b).

What is this Book of Remedies? Who authored the work? And perhaps most importantly, what is so commendable about its censorship? The commentators have long debated these questions.

In terms of who the author of this work is, there are those who credit the wise King Solomon (*Radak, Ramban*). Others attribute the book to one of Noah's sons, who procured the information from an angel (*Tashbetz Katan*). One commentator sees the book's remedies as dating back to Moses and the desert years, when the loyalty of the wandering Jewish people was tested, since knowledge of these cures could lead people to feel independent of God. According to this approach, the Book of Remedies was a compilation of natural tonics, describing the healing properties of plants, herbs and the like found in nature. In Hezekiah's time, the people had come to rely on these cures instead of turning to God, perhaps praising and expressing their gratitude to the Book of Remedies rather than extolling the Almighty. The monarch hid the book that was leading people astray, so that the ill would be compelled to recognise God (*Rabbeinu Baḥya*). Hezekiah's act was, therefore, a demonstration of his faith in God and was acclaimed as such by the sages.

This approach may have profound implications for modern medicine. Would Hezekiah advocate the suppression of the vast, and often life-saving, medical knowledge we are fortunate to possess, because some people do not acknowledge God's hidden hand?

Maimonides, himself a well-known and much sought-after physician, harshly criticises this reading. Branding this approach as one that befits fools, Maimonides incredulously asks: If people are famished and eat bread to conquer their hunger, would we say that they have lost their faith in God because they have turned to food for sustenance rather than to the Almighty? Rather, Maimonides explains, people should thank God for the medicine, just as they thank God for bread. Maimonides accordingly presents a different understanding of the Book of Remedies. He suggests that this work was a book of magical healing that prescribed incantations for the sick. Written originally for permissible academic purposes (*B. Shabbat* 75a; *B. Sanhedrin* 68a), it was later put to practical use – an act forbidden by Jewish law. To combat this crime, Hezekiah censored the book.

Despite the strident protest of Maimonides, the talmudic sages may indeed be relating to the pitfalls of medical knowledge. Elsewhere in rabbinic literature, we find a harsh and unusual statement: "The best of the doctors is destined for Gehenna" (*M. Kiddushin* 4:14).

Jewish scholars offer various explanations for this harsh verdict. They all limit the judgment to a certain class of doctors: doctors who cause death when they could save lives (*Rashi*), doctors who act in bad faith (*Ri*), doctors who act recklessly and callously (*Ramban*), doctors who pretend to be experts when they are truly ignorant of the profession (*Kalonymus ben Kalonymus*) or doctors who act when there are others with greater expertise (*Rashbatz*). One commentator, himself a recognised physician, applies this adage to doctors who perform internal operations, perhaps reflecting the state of medical knowledge in his day (*Paḥad Yitzḥak*).

We might offer another possible understanding of this unforgiving declaration. The best of doctors may be inclined to credit their own acumen for their medical achievements. Such foolishness, say the sages, leads one away from the path of God. The faculties with which we are endowed and the opportunities we are granted should not be seen as resulting from "the strength of our own hands." Rather, it behooves us to remember God and His role behind the scenes as the playmaker and facilitator (Deuteronomy 8:17–18).

An oft-recounted parable tells of a person drowning at sea. As he struggles in the water, gasping for breath, he fervently prays to God for salvation. Seemingly out of nowhere a boat approaches him and throws a buoy in his direction. The man refuses the proffered assistance. "I am waiting for God to save me!" he calls, and he continues to gallantly tread water, praying for redemption through God's mighty hand.

A helicopter miraculously appears and offers the drowning man a rope ladder to climb out of the clutches of the ocean. Once again the help tendered is rebuffed. "God will save me!" he shouts, and he continues valiantly to keep afloat, passionately beseeching the Almighty to save him.

As his strength wanes and death approaches, the man lets out one last heartfelt prayer, and a piece of driftwood slides within reach. Instead of clutching it, the man pushes it aside, thinking: "Surely, God will not forsake me."

Alas, the waters finally overtake him, and the man appears in heaven before God. "Why did You not heed my heartfelt prayers? Where were You in my time of need?" he complains.

In a booming voice God responds: "Who do you think sent the boat, the helicopter and the piece of driftwood!?"

Seeking medical advice is not folly. The challenge is to recognise that professional medical assistance attained is truly a gift from God. As such, the doctor is a messenger of God, charged with the momentous task of saving lives. It is not the doctor who heals, nor is it the medicine or tonic; God is the true healer.

BERAKHOT 10B–11A

Hillel's Hasidic court

THE SAGES DEBATE the appropriate posture for the recitation of *Shema* (*M. Berakhot* 1:3; *B. Berakhot* 10b–11a). The School of Shammai maintains that there is a prescribed stance for each reading of *Shema*. In the evening we are instructed to recline while reading *Shema*, and in the morning we must stand while reading the passage. The School of Shammai reaches this conclusion based on its understanding of the biblical verse that is the source of the twice-daily *Shema* recitation: *And you should teach them to your children [recite them] when you stay at home and when you walk along the way, when you lie down and when you arise* (Deuteronomy 6:7). The verse refers both to the time of day and the appropriate stance. Thus *Shema* should be read once when you lie down, that is, while reclining in the evening, and once more when you arise, that is, while standing in the morning.

Basing itself on the same biblical verse, the School of Hillel rules differently. According to the School of Hillel, the cited verse relates only to the time of day when *Shema* should be recited – in the evening when you lie down, and in the morning when you arise. There is no requirement regarding posture. The appropriate pose is given by a different phrase in the verse: *and when you walk along the way* – everyone should read *Shema* in the position that they happen to be in, even if they are in the middle of a journey. Thus according to the School of Hillel there is no mandated posture.

The Mishna continues with a tale related by Rabbi Tarfon: "I happened to return by road. [In the evening] I lay down to read [*Shema*] in accordance with the view of the School of Shammai, and I endangered myself [by lying down] because of bandits."

Rabbi Tarfon's peers responded without sympathy: "You deserved to forfeit your life, for you transgressed the words of the School of Hillel!" Indeed, normative law follows the opinion of the School of Hillel; no particular posture is mandated for the reading of *Shema*.

The Jerusalem Talmud notes that the vehemence of the sages' response is surprising and seems overly harsh (*Y. Berakhot* 3b). Had Rabbi Tarfon not recited *Shema* at all, he would have forfeited the chance to fulfil one of the positive commandments. Regrettable though such a missed opportunity may be, this infraction does not carry the death penalty. Rabbi Tarfon, however, did recite *Shema*, but he did so in a manner contrary to normative law, and as such he was deserving of death.

The insistence on following the opinion of the School of Hillel seems to indicate that this school's position, is not just normative, but fundamental to Jewish thought. Such an interpretation can be found in the writings of one lesser-known Hasidic master.

Rabbi Shlomo Ḥayim Friedman (1887–1972) was a scion of the regal Ruzhin dynasty of Hasidic masters, born in the Ruzhin stronghold of Sadagóra. His father and predecessor died when Rabbi Shlomo was only 19 years old. Together with his four brothers, Rabbi Shlomenyu – as he was affectionately known – began serving as a Hasidic leader. With the outbreak of the Great War, Rabbi Shlomenyu fled to Vienna together with many others. In Vienna, Rabbi Shlomenyu concluded that there was no need for another Hasidic master in the city, and he valiantly relinquished his title.

After the German troops entered Austria to enforce the Anschluss in 1938, Rabbi Shlomenyu made *aliya*. He settled first in Jerusalem, but soon moved to Tel Aviv where other Ruzhin Rebbes resided. In Tel Aviv, Rabbi Shlomenyu continued to refuse to serve as a leader of a community. He left the title of Sadigora Rebbe to his older brother Rabbi Avraham Yaakov (1884–1960), known as the *Avir Yaakov*, and later to his nephew Rabbi Mordekhai Shalom Yosef (1896–1979), known as the *Knesset Mordekhai*. Rabbi Shlomenyu apparently did not even wear the customary *shtreimel*, the fur headcovering donned by Hasidim. After his brother passed away, he agreed to sit at the head of the table at Hasidic gatherings which were held in honour of his forebears' *yahrtzeits* (the anniversary of their death). It was at such a talk in 1962, in honour of his ancestor Rabbi Dov Ber (d. 1772), the *Maggid* (preacher) of Mezrich

(Międzyrzec Korecki), that Rabbi Shlomenyu used the opinion of the School of Hillel in this Mishna to explain the thrust of the Hasidic movement.

The School of Hillel is giving voice to the idea that Divinity permeates our entire world. In every place, at every moment, in every situation – whether we are lying down, standing still or walking – godliness is present. Whatever the scenario, the Divine should be sought and the yoke of heaven accepted.

The danger that Rabbi Tarfon found himself in was a spiritual danger. He mistakenly thought that accepting God's presence required a certain physical posture particular to the time of day – standing in the morning and reclining in the evening. In truth, God's presence permeates the world under all circumstances and without interruption. Rabbi Shlomenyu's interpretation illuminates a basic tenet of Hasidic thought. The Almighty is not confined to a particular location; indeed there is no place that is empty of the Divine Presence.

There are times and places in which connecting to that unlimited Divine Presence may be easier – perhaps when learning the hallowed texts of our tradition, or perhaps when praying with a congregation and using the very same words that have been on the lips of our people for generations. The challenge is to connect to God even in places that (at least at first glance) are not holy – the home, the workplace, the street. According to Rabbi Shlomenyu, the School of Hillel teaches us that the Almighty can be found in any situation; the Hasidic challenge is to embark on this quest for God.

BERAKHOT 11B

Abundant and everlasting love

THE FAMED TALMUDIST, Rabbi Meir Simḥa HaKohen of Dvinsk (1843–1926), was renowned for his erudition and rabbinic leadership. For forty years, he served the community of Dvinsk (today Daugavpils, Latvia). In 1906, Rabbi Meir Simḥa was offered a rabbinical post in Jerusalem. He declined the offer, following the desperate entreaties of the Dvinsk community members, who felt that his departure would destroy their city. During the First World War, most Jews of Dvinsk fled, leaving behind only the poor and infirm. Rabbi Meir Simḥa remained with these inhabitants, declaring that if there were nine Jews in the city, he would be the tenth, in order to make up the requisite quorum for communal prayer.

Rabbi Meir Simḥa's commentary on Maimonides, *Or Same'aḥ*, reflects his scholarship. His commentary on the Torah, *Meshekh Ḥokhma*, which was published the year after his death, displays his breadth of knowledge of Jewish sources, and sparkles with originality. We also have his novellae to various tractates of Talmud, some responsa and other notes, all published posthumously.

The story is told of how Rabbi Meir Simḥa once penned a letter to a friend, signing off the letter with the unusual ending: "The one who signs according to Shmuel and the Rabbis, Meir Simḥa of Dvinsk" (retold by Asher Bergman in his biography of Rabbi Meir Simḥa).

When the letter reached the addressee, this unusual signature puzzled him. Not being able to fathom its meaning, he took the undecipherable line to a rabbinic acquaintance. The rabbi was also initially baffled; finally his eyes brightened as he figured out the meaning of this curious signature.

In the entire Talmud there is only one disagreement presented between Shmuel and the Rabbis. The Mishna indicates that two blessings must be recited before the morning *Shema* (*M. Berakhot* 1:4). The

Talmud discusses these blessings and inquires as to the precise wording of the second blessing, the one that immediately precedes *Shema* (*B. Berakhot* 11b).

The first opinion presented is that of Shmuel, which is supported by other sages and earlier traditions. He says that the blessing opens with God's affection for His people, reflected by the words *ahava rabba*, abundant love. The Rabbis, however, offer an alternative rendition. They state that the blessing begins with the words *ahavat olam*, everlasting love. They offer scriptural support for this version: *And with an eternal love* (ahavat olam) *I have loved you, therefore I have drawn kindness to you* (Jeremiah 31:2).

The talmudic discussion focuses only on the opening words of the blessing – *ahava rabba* or *ahavat olam*. The remainder of the paragraph is not the subject of dispute (*Baḥ*). To be sure, in the various traditions that have reached us there are minor differences in the syntax of the blessing, but the content is basically uniform.

Returning to Rabbi Meir Simḥa's signature, the decipherer explained its meaning to the addressee. "Rabbi Meir Simḥa wanted to convey his deep love for you. Instead of writing of it openly, he encoded his thoughts by signing off in this unique manner. Now choose for yourself one of the two opinions – Shmuel or the Rabbis – and know that Rabbi Meir Simḥa loves you either with everlasting love or with abundant love."

I would suggest a slightly different conclusion. Rabbi Meir Simḥa was conveying that his love for the addressee was both abundant and everlasting, which was why he signed "according to Shmuel and the Rabbis." Indeed, when describing God's feelings for us, we would hardly want to be forced to choose between His abundant love and His everlasting love. Certainly we yearn for both forms of love. This dual desire is reflected in the opinion of some halakhists as well as in the Ashkenazi prayer rite, as we shall see.

Many codifiers had before them a version of the talmudic passage which preserves an earlier tradition supporting the opinion of the Rabbis that *ahavat olam* should be said. Consequently, these halakhists ruled that *ahavat olam* should always be said. This is the accepted ruling in the Sephardi rite and the practice in Hasidic communities (*Rif*). Others follow the version of the talmudic discussion that we have before us, which sees the earlier tradition as supporting the view of Shmuel, and hence they prefer the alternative formulation – *ahava rabba* (*Rashba*).

One Provençal halakhist suggests that a combination may be said: *ahavat olam rabba* (*Sefer HaManhig*). Other authorities opine that while both versions – *ahava rabba* and *ahavat olam* – are valid, a hybrid rendition should not be recited. Instead, they recommend alternating: *ahava rabba* before the morning *Shema* and *ahavat olam* before the evening *Shema* (*Geonim*). Indeed, this is the accepted practice in Ashkenazi communities.

Though the Talmud does not offer a scriptural basis for the *ahava rabba* view, the biblical verse *They are new each morning; abundant* (rabba) *is Your faithfulness* (Lamentations 3:23) has been suggested as a source. Since in this verse *morning* is juxtaposed with *abundant*, it is appropriate to say the phrase *ahava rabba* before the morning *Shema* (*Perisha*).

In addition, one commentator – Rabbi Yeḥezkel Landau (1713–1793) – explains why *ahavat olam* is particularly appropriate before the evening *Shema*. This is because *ahavat olam* ends with the words "And may You never (*le'olamim*) take away Your love from us." Hence, both the beginning of the blessing and its end refer to an everlasting relationship with God. Rabbi Landau thus concludes that the Ashkenazi practice of alternating is proper. He does validate the Sephardi custom. However, he is highly critical of European Jews who departed from their Ashkenazi custom and adopted the Sephardi rite instead. This would seem to refer to Ashkenazi Jews who were drawn to Hasidism.

Using the wrong formula is not considered a serious error. Mistakenly referring to God's everlasting love in the morning or His abundant love in the evening does not invalidate the prayer (*Mishna Berura* 6:2). This ruling reflects our longing for a compound signature bearing God's mark – a signature that expresses the Almighty's abundant love and His everlasting love, regardless of the rite of our community.

BERAKHOT 11B

Divine teacher of Torah

THE STUDY OF our sacred traditions is central to Jewish life. Early in our history as a nation, Joshua was instructed to be engaged day and night in Torah study (Joshua 1:8). It therefore comes as no surprise that the central *Shema* prayer includes the injunction to learn and teach Torah (Deuteronomy 6:6–7).

The study of Torah should be a conscious enterprise; students of Torah should be aware that they are not merely garnering knowledge from books. Though Torah study shares some elements with academic pursuits, it strives for more. When delving into the texts of our heritage, we hope to forge lasting connections with our traditions and infuse our existence with meaning and purpose. With this insight we can appreciate why Torah study should be undertaken only once we have focused our thoughts by reciting a blessing prior to it. Thus the Talmud asks (*B. Berakhot* 11b): what is the blessing that should be recited before the study of Torah?

The first response offered is a blessing that concludes: "Who has sanctified us with His commandments and has commanded us to engage with the words of Torah." This parallels other benedictions recited before fulfilling *mitzvot,* and concludes with an insightful phrase that reflects how occupied with Torah we should be; it is insufficient to peruse Torah leisurely while dozing in a comfortable armchair. This blessing signals the lofty goal of poring over the sacred texts of our tradition, delving into every turn of phrase.

The Talmud goes on to report that another sage would conclude the above blessing with the words: "Now sweeten, Lord our God, the words of Your Torah in our mouths and in the mouths of Your nation, the House of Israel. And may we – we, our descendants, and the descendants of Your nation, the House of Israel, all of us – be amongst those who know Your name and who engage with Your Torah."

In this blessing we have a unique request. There is no other *mitzva* whose performance is preceded by the expression of the hope that future generations will do as we are about to do. Today, the concern with continuity draws attention from Jewish leadership across the board. Communal resources are often channelled in directions that are expected to bolster the chances of our children continuing in our path. Yet only with regard to the study of Torah do our sages mandate a prayer for continuity.

The blessing concludes with the enchanting words: "Blessed are you, God, Who teaches Torah to His nation, Israel." Is God really the teacher of Torah today? Wouldn't it would be more appropriate to thank God for providing talented educators who teach Torah?

This is an interesting concept. Those whom we refer to as teachers are not the true educators; they are transmitters and, more importantly, facilitators. The true educator is God, Who speaks through the voice of Torah. To be sure, it is challenging to hear the Divine voice, and at times it is challenging for teachers to let this voice be heard. Torah teachers, however, do not aim to teach their version of Torah; they hope to convey faithfully God's message.

Clearly this is an impossible task, for everything in this world is tainted by subjectivity. Yet the challenge remains for the human teacher to be as objective a mouthpiece as possible for the Divine teacher. Thus, when we walk into a Torah lecture – whether as a student or a teacher – we hope to encounter that still, silent voice of the Divine Torah teacher Who educates His people.

The talmudic passage continues by citing another version of the blessing: "Who chose us from amongst all the nations and gave us His Torah." Here too, we see that the Torah we study is not the earthly teacher's Torah, but the Torah of the Almighty. It is this gift of Torah that delineates the contours of our distinct mission in this world.

The Talmud then states that this benediction is "the best of the blessings." However, it does not elaborate on what gives this blessing its preferred status.

One commentator proposes that the blessing praises God while referring to the Torah and the Jewish people. This star-studded lineup – God, Torah and the Jewish people – gives the blessing its distinction (*Rashi*).

Perhaps we could suggest that the eminence of this benediction is connected with the captivating words that conclude it: "Blessed are You, God, Who gives the Torah." The present tense usage – "gives" – cries out for explanation. Wasn't the Torah given long ago at Sinai? One commentator points out that in a sense, the Torah continues to be given. When we delve into our sacred texts, God grants us fresh understandings (*Taz*). Once again we have the sense that God continues to teach Torah actively. Indeed, the Talmud tells us that there is no *beit midrash* that does not include something innovative (*T. Sota* 7:9). One version of this statement even declares that every *beit midrash* has an innovative insight every single day (*Y. Sota* 18d).

Faced with these different proposals for the appropriate blessing before the study of Torah, our passage concludes: "Therefore, you are to recite them all."

This is an appealing, normative ruling that is paralleled elsewhere in the Talmud (*B. Sota* 40a). The sages discuss the appropriate congregational response to the leader's *Modim* prayer in the repetition of the *Amida*. Five suggestions are proffered, whereupon the passage concludes with the ruling: "Therefore, we are to recite them all." This prayer is known as *Modim DeRabbanan*, the *Modim* prayer of our rabbis, since it was composed by a group of sages.

Normative practice in all communities is to recite *Modim DeRabbanan*, albeit with minor differences from the talmudic version. Likewise, we recite all the suggested blessings upon the Torah daily, notwithstanding minor changes from the talmudic text.

Thus, we pray for all the elements included in the various Torah blessings before we consciously embark upon the pursuit of Torah study. We strive to be absorbed in Torah study that will be continued by our children, to learn from the Divine teacher Who continues to grant us innovative insights into our tradition, and to engage in all this while endeavouring to fulfil our mission in this world.

BERAKHOT 11B

Sweet Torah study

IN HASIDIC COMMUNITIES, the formal education of children begins at the age of three. For boys, this is marked by their first haircut, which leaves the youngsters' *pe'ot* (sidelocks) while cutting the rest of their hair. Some have a custom that girls begin to light a solitary candle on Friday eve from the age of three, as a mark of their entry into the world of Jewish education.

Since children embark on the lifelong pursuit of Torah at age three, it is also customary for them to mark this auspicious birthday with their first official encounter with our texts and traditions. Yet the Torah that children study on this day does not involve books; there is no grappling with difficult texts, no exploring lofty ideas. Instead, children are offered an *alef*-shaped biscuit. As they successfully identify the Hebrew letter, it is then dipped in honey, and the child joyfully partakes of this treat. Thus we bless our children that their Torah study should always be as sweet as honey. We do our best to provide appealing religious experiences for our children, even at this tender age. We try to ensure that their encounters with Torah are engaging and alluring. This is an approach we can adopt – or adapt – even if we are not of Hasidic descent.

Is this, however, the ideal for Jewish adult life? Do we seek sweetness whenever we delve into our texts? At least one Hasidic master felt that enjoying Torah study was not the ideal. Rabbi Yeraḥmiel Yisrael Yitzḥak Dancyger (1853–1910), from the town of Aleksandrów Łódzki just outside the Polish city of Łódz, quoted his father, Rabbi Yeḥiel Dancyger (1828–1894) as deploring those who seek pleasurable Torah study. True Torah acquisition can be achieved only through struggling, toiling over texts while probing the depths of our traditions. Anything less is an act done for the individual's pleasure, not out of devotion to the Almighty or commitment to our heritage. True service of God, concluded Rabbi Dancyger, entails simple faith and fidelity, whether or not we identify with the inner meaning of the Almighty's commandments. We are fortunate that God allows us to engage with His Torah, and this alone should suffice as a cause for satisfaction. Thus according to Rabbi Dancyger, the honey-dipped letters are a childish experience that preferably should not be echoed in adulthood.

A contemporaneous Polish Hasidic master, responding to this notion, disputed the ideal of not enjoying Torah study. Rabbi Avraham Bornsztain of Sochaczew (1839–1910) felt that the epitome of Torah study is a pleasurable encounter with the tradition. Only through such an idyllic experience would Torah enter our bloodstream, becoming part of our essential nature and infusing us with life.

This notion – that the apex of Torah study is an enjoyable experience – seems to be based on the words of our sages that have been canonised in our daily prayers. In the talmudic discussion of the blessing over Torah study, one sage opines that it should include the words: "Now sweeten, Lord our God, the words of Your Torah in our mouths and in the mouths of Your nation, the House of Israel" (*B. Berakhot* 11b).

This formulation, beseeching God that what we are about to embark upon should be sweet, is unique. We do not precede the fulfilment of any other *mitzva* with such a request. We pray, take the *lulav* and partake of *matza*, but we never beseech God that the experience of prayer should be pleasant, that shaking the *lulav* should be fun, that the *matza* should taste sweet! Why are we so concerned that the study of Torah should be enjoyable?

This request may give voice to the supreme place of Torah in Judaism. Torah is the soul of our people. As such we hope that we can integrate it into our lives and absorb it in our bones without undue hardship. Distaste for a particular *mitzva* is a challenge that does not jeopardise the identity of our people; in contrast, aversion to Torah, the life force of our nation, may be spiritually life-threatening.

This leads us to the other unique aspect of this blessing – the mention of future generations. "And may we – we, our descendants, and the descendants of Your nation, the House of Israel, all of us – be amongst those who know Your name and who engage with Your Torah."

We may wish for our children to follow in our footsteps, yet we also know that as individuals they need to walk their own path. The desire for continuity needs to focus only on matters that reflect our essence. Even if our favourite colour may be blue, we do not hope that our children will continue in our path by preferring this colour; we have no hallowed tradition of revering the colour blue, and our preference for blue is not part of our core being. Torah, however, is *sine qua non* for a meaningful Jewish existence, and as such we pray that our children will also find the words of Torah sweet.

Thus the blessing before Torah study appears to support the notion that the encounter with our heritage should be a gratifying experience, as voiced by Rabbi Bornsztain. How are we then to understand the position of Rabbi Dancyger, who maintained that the ideal is non-enjoyable Torah study?

Perhaps we can read these two Hasidic masters as presenting complementary concepts of the Torah encounter. Certainly the pinnacle is to enjoy the sweetness of Torah study; this ideal is embodied in the words of the sages and enshrined in our daily prayers. Temporal life and our human frailty, however, necessitate an awareness of an opposing reality. As our experience makes evident, not every passage in the Torah stirs our emotions and stimulates our intellect. There are times when – despite our daily request for a Divine sweetening of our Torah encounter – the text does not come alive, and learning is a laborious chore that carries no joy. It is at such gloomy junctures that the words of Rabbi Dancyger offer encouragement. Today we may not be excited about Torah study, yet that exact feeling makes the experience all the more valuable!

Indeed, these contradictory philosophies are handy tools to carry in our mental satchel. We enter the *beit midrash* with the prayer and the hope of enjoying our Torah study, together with the knowledge that at times this encounter may not be as sweet as a honey-coated biscuit.

BERAKHOT 12A

The core of our people

THE RECITATION OF *Shema* followed by the *Amida* is the focus of both the morning and evening prayers. Yet, perusing the Torah, we might be inclined to suggest an additional passage that could be considered essential – the Ten Commandments. Indeed, our sages recount that the original Temple service included the recitation of the Ten Commandments (*M. Tamid* 5:1). Each morning an appointed *kohen* would turn to his colleagues with the instruction: "Recite one blessing," and his peers would comply. They would then proceed to read the Ten Commandments and *Shema*. Three further blessings would be recited. First was the blessing of *Emet VeYatziv* (true and certain), a paragraph that we say today after reading the morning *Shema*. Second was a blessing over the Temple service, a variant of which is recited today as the seventeenth blessing of the daily *Amida*. Third, the *kohanim* would recite the priestly benediction, raising their hands and blessing all those present (Numbers 6:24–26). With much work to do in the Temple, the *kohanim* did not recite the entire *Amida* at this time.

Thus the Ten Commandments were a central part of the prayer service in Temple times. Moreover, though *kohanim* were pressed for time and did not recite the entire *Amida*, nevertheless they did read the Ten Commandments.

It is easy to understand why the Ten Commandments should be at the core of our prayers. At the moment of Divine revelation at Sinai, these were the words that our people heard. Furthermore, these statements represent the soul of our faith (*Maimonides*). One scholar went further, authoring a work in which he showed how the source of each of the 613 commandments could be found in the Ten Commandments (*Sa'adia Gaon*).

Despite the obvious centrality of the Ten Commandments, this key scriptural passage is generally not recited as part of our daily liturgy.

Nowadays, we hear the Ten Commandments as part of the Torah reading at certain junctures during the year. These critical biblical verses that recall the Sinai covenant and reflect our very essence seem to have disappeared from our prayers. What happened to this cornerstone of revelation?

The Talmud recounts that sages in various places in the Land of Israel originally followed the Temple rite and recited the Ten Commandments as part of the daily prayer service. However, this practice was abolished as a result of heretics. Several similar Babylonian initiatives to institute the practice of appending the Ten Commandments to *Shema* were also abandoned for this reason (*B. Berakhot* 12a).

What was the quarrel that brought about the elimination of this fundamental passage from our liturgy? It appears that the central place accorded to the Ten Commandments led – or could lead – agitators to claim that *only* these statements were Divine; the remainder of the Torah, which was not heard directly from God at Sinai – so the argument goes – was merely a human invention and as such has no right to make any claim on our lives. The rabbinic response to this threat was to excise this passage from the liturgy (*Y. Berakhot* 3c).

Attempts to reinstate the Ten Commandments as a focal point of the daily service did not end during the talmudic period. In the thirteenth century, some people in a certain community sought to re-establish the public recitation of the Ten Commandments. The question as to its advisability came before the famed Barcelonan respondent, Rashba (1235–1310). Following talmudic precedent, his answer was firm: it is forbidden to institutionalise the Ten Commandments as part of the liturgy.

The Rashba appears to be responding to the suggestion that the Ten Commandments be restored to their former place of glory at the hub of the service. In his responsum, the Rashba does not relate to the possibility of reciting the Ten Commandments elsewhere in the service. Such a suggestion had already been made centuries earlier.

During the ninth century, the Jews of Spain wrote to the contemporary authoritative Judaic centre in Babylonia, asking for an accurate version of the liturgy. The leader of the Torah academy in Sura, Amram Gaon (d. 875), compiled a work that was to become the basis for all prayer books thereafter, contributing much to the relative uniformity of our liturgy. In this influential work, Amram Gaon wrote that the Ten Commandments should be recited daily, not as part of the central portion of the service but following the *Amida*, together with other key Torah portions. Thus a compromise position had been arrived at: the Ten Commandments would no longer form part of the centrepiece of the daily liturgy, yet they would be recited as a postscript to the service.

This tempered position became the normative one. Thus it was recommended that the Ten Commandments be recited daily (*Tur*), while at the same time any public reading was proscribed. It was determined that a private reading would not arouse the pesky questions of dissenting heretics, and furthermore, daily recital would recall the national Sinai experience and strengthen belief in the Almighty (*Shulḥan Arukh*). This private recital was further limited. It was to take place before or after the principal prayers, but not as part of them (*Mishna Berura*).

In fact, we have a fascinating testimony of one Polish rabbinic leader, Maharshal (1510–1573), regarding the liturgical place of the Ten Commandments. In response to a question regarding prayer, Maharshal bemoans the fact that he was unable to preserve the prayer rituals of his forebears, for in his youth he had focused solely on Talmud and the hair-splitting study of this text, neglecting the study of liturgy. Even the prayer book of his father was not available, for it had been destroyed by fire. Maharshal proceeds to share the snippets of tradition which he recalled, and then details his own innovative prayer practices, including the daily custom of reading aloud the Ten Commandments before the opening *Barukh She'amar* prayer.

The Ten Commandments no longer assume a strategic place in our public prayer. They are relegated to a place of secondary importance, and at times neglected entirely. Nevertheless, their seminal contribution to our tradition should not be ignored. For when we read this passage we evoke the foundations of our heritage.

BERAKHOT 12A

Halakha and aggada: Inseparable sisters

THE TALMUD IS a work rich in both halakha – Jewish law, and aggada – Jewish lore. These two fields are masterfully interwoven, creating a singular text that stimulates the legal mind while stirring the imaginative soul. Perhaps not fully recognising the significance of this unique feature, various scholars over the ages have valiantly tried to isolate one discipline from the other. These attempts have produced great works, though the capacity to truly split these interlocked branches remains questionable.

One such work is the popular *Ein Yaakov*, compiled by the Spanish scholar Rabbi Yaakov ibn Ḥabib (c. 1450–1516). The author was born in Castile, Spain, but upon the expulsion of the Jews in 1492 made his way to Portugal and then on to Salonika. In Spain he was already a renowned scholar, and when he reached Salonika he continued his rabbinic and scholarly work, playing a significant leadership role in the community. His halakhic works were widely quoted in his day and after his death. Alas, much of what he wrote has not survived. His fame, however, is associated with the *Ein Yaakov*, a collection of the non-legal portions of the Babylonian Talmud and some of those from the Jerusalem Talmud. With the *Ein Yaakov*, Rabbi Yaakov ibn Ḥabib complemented his halakhic and communal efforts, as he sought to provide direction and guidance in his turbulent times. The *Ein Yaakov* has endured as a treasure trove of talmudic aggada. The work's popularity has been bolstered by editions of the *Ein Yaakov* printed with later commentaries to the aggadic passages.

Thus when opening the *Ein Yaakov* we expect to find talmudic aggada, without halakhic deliberations and normative conclusions. It is therefore surprising to find the talmudic discussion concerning the recital of the Ten Commandments during the prayer service (*B. Berakhot* 12a) – apparently an issue of normative practice – in the *Ein Yaakov*.

As mentioned, in Temple times, the priests' daily prayer service would begin with a blessing. It continued with the recital of the Ten Commandments, the reading of the three passages of *Shema* and the recitation of an abbreviated *Amida*. It concluded with the priestly blessing (*M. Tamid* 5:1). This abridged service allowed the priests to go about their daily Temple duties. Later, the service was further condensed when the recital of the Ten Commandments was abandoned, due to troublesome heretics suggesting that only the Ten Commandments were the word of God, while the rest of Torah was not of Divine origin (*Y. Berakhot* 3c).

When we look at this talmudic discussion, it appears to be a *bona fide* legal text. We have a report of the prayer rite in the Temple, a recounting of events that precipitated a change to this practice and a rule for prayer services that is observed to this day. Thus we would not expect to find this text in the *Ein Yaakov* anthology of aggadic passages. Fortunately Rabbi Yaakov ibn Ḥabib complemented his work with a commentary entitled *HaKotev* (the writer), where he addresses this very question.

Striking a personal note, he begins: "I cited this passage because of what it taught me with regard to faith and particularly with regard to the distinct value of prayer." Rabbi Yaakov ibn Ḥabib then details the non-legal lessons that can be derived from this halakhic passage. First, he notes that the priests, despite being busily engaged in Temple service and in a rush to offer the morning sacrifices, nevertheless understood that there was no substitute for prayer. The abbreviation of the service was a concession due to the required Temple service, yet once the Temple service had been completed – opines Rabbi Yaakov ibn Ḥabib – the priests would dedicate appropriate time to prayer. To support this contention, he describes how when King Solomon completed the construction of the Temple, after dedicating it with numerous sacrifices offered by the priests he added his personal petitions, raising his hands heavenward in heartfelt prayer (1 Kings 8).

Rabbi Yaakov ibn Ḥabib continues, offering other lessons that can be derived from this passage, lessons that do not fall under the purview of normative law. In this manner, he justifies the inclusion of a halakhic passage in his aggadic compilation.

From his discussion it is apparent that despite his gallant attempt to separate the aggada from the halakha in the Talmud, such a dissection is nearly impossible, for aggadic messages can be derived even from halakhic passages.

Let us move to another area of the Diaspora some years later. The Polish talmudist Rabbi Shmuel Edels (1555–1631), more commonly known by the acronym Maharsha, set about writing a commentary on the entire Talmud. Maharsha divided his commentary into two separate works, one on the legal portions of the Talmud and the other on the non-legal, aggadic passages. Maharsha realised that some texts have both halakhic significance and aggadic import, so for the sake of brevity his commentary on such passages appears in only one work but with a cross-reference in the other work.

Upon completion of his works, Maharsha bemoaned his chosen path. In the introduction to his halakhic commentary, he writes: "In truth I see now that the sages of the Talmud made one work of legal and non-legal material, for our Torah is one." He goes on to explain that the words of the sages contain morals, wisdom and instruction, and therefore cannot be split into two separate disciplines. Thus he regretted dividing his commentary, poetically describing the two types of material as sisters.

Maharsha tells us that he was unable to repair the damage he had wrought and make his two commentaries into one holistic work. He concludes by requesting that his readers ignore the separation and probe both works: "For [the reader] will see that in the case where this one hides, that one reveals; this one closes, that one opens – and they will both be complete together."

Initially Maharsha's works were published separately. Students had to classify a talmudic passage as halakhic or aggadic before they could find Maharsha's relevant comments. Later, after his death, the printers in Metz recognised the truth of his lament and published his two commentaries as one work. To differentiate between the two, a slightly larger font was used for the halakhic commentary. To this day, Maharsha's commentaries are published in this manner at the back of standard editions of the Talmud.

Thus we see that Jewish law and Jewish lore are inextricably intertwined. As Maharsha points out, what could serve as a better example than the Talmud itself, where halakha and aggada are masterfully and seamlessly woven together into one text! Any attempt to split the inseparable will perforce leave us lacking.

BERAKHOT 12A

The price of passion

THE JEWISH COMMUNITY in Istanbul, Turkey, has an engaging custom. Moments before beginning the *Amida* prayer, worshippers apologetically wave to each other, silently asking for forgiveness for any wrongs committed. Prior to our standing before the Almighty in solemn prayer – the principal act in the realm of *bein adam lamakom* (between a person and God) – the *bein adam laḥavero* (interpersonal) realm must be repaired. This appealing custom reflects the desire to bridge the *bein adam lamakom/bein adam laḥavero* divide, ensuring that our relationship with God is not at the expense of our relationship with fellow human beings.

The Turkish practice echoes a Temple ritual described by our sages. After the morning Temple service began, the *kohanim* would enter the Chamber of Hewn Stone for an abbreviated prayer service. Once a week, on Shabbat, an extra blessing was recited by those *kohanim* who were completing their tour of duty in the Temple (*M. Tamid* 5:1).

The *kohanim*, as well as the Levites, were divided into twenty-four *mishmarot* or watches. Each *mishmeret* would serve in the Temple for one week twice a year (1 Chronicles 24–25). On festivals when the entire nation came to Jerusalem, there was no specific *mishmeret*. During the Second Temple period, this system was still employed; however, a new internal division of *mishmarot* was used. Each *mishmeret* was divided into six families, and each family was responsible for one day during the week. On Shabbat the entire *mishmeret* served together, offering the morning sacrifices. After that, the incumbent *mishmeret* would pass the baton to the next week's *mishmeret*, who would complete the

Shabbat Temple service. At the completion of the term of the incumbent *mishmeret*, a special blessing for the changing of the guard was recited (*B. Sukka* 56b). The Talmud relates the content of this additional Shabbat blessing. The outgoing *mishmeret* would turn to the incoming *mishmeret* and say: "May the One Who has caused His name to dwell in this House cause love and brotherhood, peace and friendship to dwell among you" (*B. Berakhot* 12a).

This is indeed a beautiful benediction. Before entering the ultimate *bein adam lamakom* realm and embarking on God-centred Temple service, the new *mishmeret* was given a blessing in the realm of interpersonal relationships.

This blessing, however, may not have been introduced in a vacuum; it is entirely possible that awful events surround its institution.

Each morning at dawn, a shovel of burning ashes was taken from the Temple altar and deposited on the floor (Leviticus 6:3). This act, known as *terumat hadeshen*, was initially done by whichever priest rose sufficiently early. Later, many priests wished to perform this service, and a daily footrace up the ramp of the altar was conducted. The winner of this race was accorded the honour of *terumat hadeshen*.

This practice, however, was terminated following a wretched episode. One morning, two *kohanim* sped up the altar ramp, each vying for the honour of *terumat hadeshen*. Neck-and-neck they raced until one *kohen*, desperate for the privilege to remove the smouldering ashes, pushed his fellow, who fell and broke his leg. When the court saw the danger involved in the race, they cancelled the competition and instead enacted a lottery – as was the custom for other Temple tasks – for the right to perform *terumat hadeshen* (*M. Yoma* 2:1–2).

A more tragic calamity that occurred during one of these races is also related. Two *kohanim* were racing up the ramp. (In one version of the account, they were actually brothers.) At the finish line, one *kohen* pipped his colleague, winning the contest and the right to perform *terumat hadeshen*. At this point, the loser took a knife and drove it into the winner's heart. The callousness that this zeal betrayed was matched by that of the father of the dying boy, who, running to the scene, found his child in his death throes on the floor of the Temple. Indifferently, the father declared: "My son is still writhing and therefore the knife has not become impure!" He was implying that the knife should quickly be removed before the death of the young *kohen* could render it impure. Apparently the impurity of utensils was of greater concern than murder (*T. Yoma* 1:12; *T. Shavuot* 1:4).

The Talmud questions the chronology of these two appalling episodes, and concludes that the murder occurred first. However, at the time it was presumed – perhaps in a further show of apathy – that this was a freak occurrence that would not repeat itself. Following the second episode, in which a *kohen* sustained a comparatively mild injury, the trend towards violent zealousness (even if the intent was not to maim) could not be ignored, and the lottery was legislated (*B. Yoma* 23a).

In light of these accounts, the benediction of the outgoing *mishmeret* to the incoming *mishmeret* may have been a charge and a caution more than a blessing, as if to say: "Beware that your eagerness for Divine service not be at the expense of peace and friendship between you." Alternatively, one commentator suggests that the blessing comes from the pre-lottery period and reflects the deplorable but acute and life-threatening bickering that was commonplace in the Temple (*Maharsha*).

Perhaps there is an inherent danger when our focus turns too intently to the *bein adam lamakom* sphere. With our eyes keenly directed to God, we are liable to forget our fellow humans who may be running next to us or standing beside us. The quest for a relationship with the Almighty should not be at the expense of our relationship with other humans. Rising before dawn and eagerly racing to perform the Temple service is certainly laudable, but when it entails pushing another aside, the fervour is misdirected. Our tradition indicates that a tame, insipid lottery is preferable to passionate competition, if that competition exacts a price on the *bein adam laḥavero* front.

BERAKHOT 12B

Whom can we ask for help?

OUR SAGES TEACH: "Whoever has the opportunity to beseech the Almighty for mercy on behalf of another, yet refrains from doing so, is called a sinner" (*B. Berakhot* 12b). To buttress this declaration, the Talmud cites the words of the prophet Samuel to the People of Israel: *I too, far be it from me to sin against God, to refrain from praying on your behalf* (1 Samuel 12:23). Praying on behalf of another is thus a praiseworthy, even obligatory, pursuit.

While the proof text cited comes from the words of the prophet Samuel, the Talmud uses more general language – "whoever has the opportunity." This suggests that praying for others is not the exclusive province of a certain class of people. Earlier in the tractate we are told that the Almighty asked the *Kohen Gadol,* Rabbi Yishmael ben Elisha, to bless Him. From the fact that the Almighty was interested in the blessing of a mortal, the Talmud concludes that the blessing of an ordinary person should not be unimportant in our eyes (*B. Berakhot* 7a).

Are we permitted to initiate this process by turning to others and requesting that they pray on our behalf? The Talmud appears to advocate this very course. It states: "Whoever has a sick person in his house should go to a sage and have the sage plead for mercy on his behalf" (*B. Bava Batra* 116a).

Need the person we turn to be alive, or can we perhaps even approach the deceased and beseech them to pray for us? In talmudic times it was customary to go to the cemetery on fast days at the conclusion of the prayer service. The Talmud asks what the purpose of this cemetery visit was. Two explanations are offered. First, we may go to the cemetery as a symbolic act to remind ourselves of the temporal nature of life on earth, as if to recognise that in the Almighty's eyes we are nothing more than corpses-to-be. Such a visit to the cemetery will hopefully spawn a feeling of humility that can serve as a motivation or catalyst for repentance. The second explanation is that we visit the cemetery in times of need so that the deceased will beg for mercy on our behalf (*B. Ta'anit* 16a).

From this passage it is unclear whether we need – or for that matter are even allowed – to ask the deceased to pray for us. Perhaps our mere presence in the cemetery leads them to pray on our behalf? One German halakhic authority, Maharil (c. 1360–1427), unequivocally condemns any thought of beseeching the deceased when visiting the cemetery. The reason to visit the cemetery, according to Maharil, is to ask the Almighty to heed our prayers in the merit of the righteous people of past generations.

Maharil's position is widely quoted. However, another talmudic passage clearly indicates that there is no problem with asking the deceased to pray on our behalf. The Talmud notes that when the spies reached the Land of Israel, the biblical passage says: *And they ascended in the south and he came to Hebron* (Numbers 13:22). *They ascended* refers to all the spies who came from the south; however, *he came* – evidently only one went to Hebron. Who was this lone traveller to the city of our forebears?

The Talmud explains that Caleb disengaged from the spying party and went to Hebron, to the Cave of Makhpela, to prostrate himself at the graves of the Patriarchs and Matriarchs. When he reached his destination, Caleb said: "My forebears, beseech for mercy on my behalf that I may be saved from the machinations of the spies" (*B. Sota* 34b). It appears that Caleb – or at least the sages who report his Hebron visit – advocated asking the deceased for help.

What about asking for a blessing from an angel? In his encounter with a mystery angel, Jacob refused to release the assailant until he agreed to grant a blessing (Genesis 32:27). Later in his life, Jacob blessed two of his grandchildren, Joseph's sons, saying: *The angel who redeemed me from all evil, let him bless the lads; let them carry my name and the name of my fathers Abraham and Isaac, and let them grow into a multitude in the midst of the earth* (Genesis 48:16). Moreover, each week when we return home from the synagogue and gather around the table before reciting *kiddush*, it is customary to say or sing *Shalom Aleikhem*, greeting the angels who accompany us. In the first and second stanzas we welcome the angels, inviting them to come in. In the final stanza we grant them leave, but before we do that, in the third stanza we ask the angels to bless us with peace.

At first blush, turning to angels or other people – dead or alive – and asking them for a blessing would seem to contradict one of the Thirteen Principles of Judaism as rendered by Maimonides. In many prayer books, where these Thirteen Principles are paraphrased, the formulation given for the Fifth Principle is: "I believe with perfect faith that it is appropriate to pray only to the Creator, may His name be blessed, and it is inappropriate to pray to anyone besides Him." How then can we pray to anyone besides the Almighty without finding ourselves outside the boundaries of Jewish faith as delineated by Maimonides?

The answer to this conundrum may be simple. The text of the Principles of Jewish Faith in the prayer book is a concise rewording of Maimonides' original formulation. In the original, Maimonides decries not *prayer* but *worship*; not asking for help, but assuming that reaching the Almighty is only possible through the agency of others. Worshipping other humans, the deceased or angels is idol worship and as such a cardinal transgression. Asking for assistance – though some authorities criticise this path – should not be considered beyond the pale of our tradition.

BERAKHOT 12B–13A

What's in a name?

OUR TRADITION SEES names as more than mere functional labels, necessary in order to call people or refer to them. Biblical names are often accompanied by an explanation which reflects the recipients' appearance or deeds, or more significantly, their essence or destiny.

Thus Esau, who was born with a full head of hair, was given a name that in Hebrew might refer to his mature physical appearance (Genesis

25:25). Moses' name reflects how the daughter of Pharaoh drew him from the Nile (Exodus 2:10). More meaningful are biblical names that include an element of foreshadowing. Noah's birth was accompanied by the explicit aspiration that the newborn would provide comfort *from our work and from the toil of our hands, because of the ground which God cursed* (Genesis 5:29).

With this background we can understand the import of biblical name changes (*B. Berakhot* 12b–13a). The first biblical hero to have his name changed was Abraham, formerly known as Avram. Our sages explain that originally his name denoted that he was the *av* (father) of his native country, Aram. His new title reflected the future of his progeny, as he was to become an *av* of many nations. The Talmud proposes that the name Abraham designates our forefather as the *av* of the entire world, perhaps reflecting the monotheism that Abraham bequeathed to society. In a similar vein, the matriarch Sarah was originally known as Sarai, meaning "my princess," but the name was altered to signal her greater role as part of the duo who bequeathed monotheism to humanity.

What happens to a former name? Is it abolished entirely or merely relegated to secondary status? In the case of Abraham, the biblical verse indicates that his previous name was superseded, as God directed: *Your name shall no longer be called Avram; your name shall be Abraham* (Genesis 17:5). According to one sage this verse is actually a positive commandment for us to use the name Abraham instead of the former name Avram. Another sage concludes that there is even a prohibition on using the old name. Appropriately, once Abraham was granted his new name, Scripture does not employ his previous one. The Talmud dismisses a verse that makes reference to Abraham's previous name – *You are God, the Lord Who chose Avram* (Nehemiah 9:7) – and explains that the verse is recounting what happened in earlier times, rather than referring to our patriarch by his previous name.

Interestingly, almost no codifiers, enumerators of commandments or commentators make mention of the restriction on using the name Avram (*cf. Magen Avraham*). One commentator explains that normative law does not accept this stricture; rather the norm is reflected by the verse *Avram who is Abraham* (1 Chronicles 1:27), which preserves the former name (*Tzlaḥ*).

The objection to employing the name Avram is somewhat tempered when it comes to the use of the name Sarai. In this case, our sages conclude that only Abraham was prohibited from using his wife's former name. Nevertheless, as a general rule, new names supplant former ones.

A notable exception is Jacob, who was promised a new name following his struggle against a mysterious assailant (Genesis 32:28). Indeed this pledge was realised, as God later directed: *Your name shall no longer be called Jacob, but Israel shall be your name* (Genesis 35:10).

The language of God's instruction to Jacob and His directive to Abraham are strikingly similar: *Your name shall no longer be called.* Yet Jacob's name change is never entirely complete. Numerous biblical passages use his birth name, Jacob. Even God continued to call Jacob by his former name: *And God spoke to Israel in a vision of the night, and He said: "Jacob, Jacob…"* (Genesis 46:2). Thus the sages conclude that Jacob's original name was not entirely uprooted; it merely became secondary to his new name. Given this data, we might ask *why* Jacob's name change was not complete.

Following the biblical approach that names are more than mere labels, we can suggest a greater significance to Jacob's partial name change. The birth name "Jacob" initially denoted the tight grip he had on Esau's *ekev* (heel) as the twins emerged from Rebecca's womb (Genesis 25:26).

Later, Esau saw a different significance in his brother's name. As Jacob cunningly acquired the birthright and later the blessings from Isaac, Esau cried out: *Is he not rightly named Jacob* (Yaakov), *for he has tricked me* (va'ya'akveni) *these two times* (Genesis 27:36), using the Hebrew word with the same root as his brother's name. After engaging in this initial trickery, Jacob spent much of his life being tricked by others. After he fled the wrath of his brother, Jacob was outmanoeuvred by his father-in-law, Laban, and woke up after his wedding with an unexpected bride (Genesis 29:25). His years spent with Laban were marked by dubious business arrangements imposed by his father-in-law. Later in his life, Jacob was tricked by his sons, who presented the blood-stained coat of his beloved Joseph. As the brothers planned, Jacob reached his own tragic conclusion: *A horrible beast has devoured him; Joseph has surely been torn to pieces* (Genesis 37:33). Finally, towards the end of his life, Jacob was forced to endure the manoeuvrings of Joseph, who conspired to bring the family to Egypt.

Jacob's scheming as he clashed with his brother, his wheeling and dealing with Laban and the troubles he bore at the hands of his children can be contrasted with the name he is granted – Israel (*Yisrael*). It contains both God's name, *El*, and the word *yashar*, upright. Jacob's destiny was to be a paradigm of honesty; as the prophet says: *Grant truth to Jacob* (Micah 7:20). Alas, the journey to this ideal was fraught with trickery which needed to be overcome.

Jacob's journey may reflect the voyage of our people as we seek our destiny on the world stage. Our challenge as a nation remains to overcome the wily characteristics associated with the name Jacob and to strive to be a people distinguished by uprightness and morality before God. Indeed, the prophet foretells that the pride of Jacob will be restored as the pride of Israel (Nahum 2:3).

Perhaps this ideal is within arm's reach of our generation. A ray of hope shines forth from the name chosen for our modern state, *Yisrael.*

Berakhot
Chapter Two

Where will you go for community?

WHY IS THE synagogue our locus of prayer? Is it always the ideal place for genuine meditation? Being on a lonely mountaintop watching a stunning sunset reflect off calm waters might be more spiritually uplifting. Synagogues and the societal norms they perpetuate may stifle our inner voice, as our focus is often diverted from earnest conversation with the Almighty. Despite the challenges, the sages insist on sincere intent during communal prayer. Placing particular emphasis on the final word of the first verse of *Shema* – *eḥad* (one) – our sages declare that "Those who prolong the pronunciation of the word *eḥad* have their days and years prolonged" (*B. Berakhot* 13b; *Y. Berakhot* 4a).

The Talmud elucidates the procedure for protracting the articulation of the word *eḥad*. The final letter – *dalet* – should be drawn out while intoning the word. Extending the final letter should not be done at the expense of the middle letter – *ḥet* – which need not be hurried. Stretching out this final word of the opening line of *Shema* provides ample opportunity to ponder the oneness and omnipresence of the Almighty and to meditate on the aspiration for a time when all will recognise God's unity (*Semak*).

The common Ashkenazi pronunciation of the letter *dalet* makes it practically impossible to lengthen its articulation. Thus halakhic authorities caution against adding an extra vowel to give the *dalet* a longer sound, such as *e-ḥa-de*. They add that it is the meditation that should be protracted, not the articulation of the word (*Shulḥan Arukh HaRav*). The Yemenite tradition preserves a different articulation of this consonant, pronouncing the *dalet* as a hard "th" as in the word "this." Hence

Yemenites are able to elongate the final word with the fricative th-th-th-th until they run out of breath.

The Talmud proceeds to tell us of a sage who followed this rabbinic directive by protracting the *dalet* as he articulated the word *eḥad,* but the anecdote highlights the limitations of this instruction. Rabbi Yirmiya was sitting before his teacher, Rabbi Zeira, while reciting *Shema*. Rabbi Zeira saw that his disciple was excessively prolonging the pronunciation of the final word of *Shema*. The master turned to the disciple and said: "Once you have acknowledged God's rule over the heavens above and the earth below and the four directions, no more is required."

What was Rabbi Yirmiya's mistake? Surely intense meditation on the unity of the Almighty cannot be faulted. In light of the rabbinic dictate we would have expected Rabbi Zeira to praise his student for his heartfelt recitation of this quintessential prayer.

Faced with this twist in the flow of the passage, one commentator opines that Rabbi Zeira did not approve of Rabbi Yirmiya falling behind the congregation. The congregation was about to continue to the silent *Amida* prayer, and Rabbi Zeira chastised his pupil for lengthening his own personal prayer at the expense of communal participation (*Maharsha*). This highlights an important aspect of synagogue prayer – being part of a community. Indeed, the synagogue experience is not just about prayer, it is also about community.

There are synagogues that boldly display signs cautioning worshippers: "If you come here to talk, where will you go to pray?" Entering the synagogue, one could respond, tongue-in-cheek: "Pray? I can pray at home; I come here to talk!" While no one would seriously advocate chatting during services, nor earnestly suggest that the synagogue is the locale for catching up with friends and discussing current events instead of praying, the role of the synagogue as a community centre should not be overlooked.

The Hebrew term for the synagogue – *beit knesset,* the house of gathering – indicates that this institution is more than just a place for prayer; it is a meeting place for the community. In reality, while we go to the *beit knesset* to commune with God, we also go to commune with our fellow worshippers.

Stressing the importance of communal prayer, the Talmud relates how the sage Rabbi Yitzḥak inquired about the whereabouts of Rav Naḥman: "Why have you not been coming to the synagogue to pray with the congregation?" Rav Naḥman responded that he was too weak to attend the service. Rabbi Yitzḥak offered to assemble a quorum in the home of the infirm scholar so that he could pray with a congregation. Rav Naḥman balked at the offer, saying that he was uncomfortable with the prospect of burdening people. Rabbi Yitzḥak was not through, and suggested: "Why don't you ask a messenger to inform you when the congregation is worshipping so that you can pray at the same time?" Seeing that his colleague was not to be deterred, and perhaps somewhat puzzled, Rav Naḥman asked: "Why are you being so adamant?" At this point Rabbi Yitzḥak relayed a rabbinic tradition which accords special significance to the time of communal prayer. The talmudic passage then continues to extol the virtues of communal prayer (*B. Berakhot* 7b–8a).

A cursory look at our prayers reveals that almost the entire service is said in the plural. Our prayers were not composed to be uttered in a cloister; they were designed to be recited by a group coming together to connect with the Almighty. Our desires are phrased as requests for the well-being and improvement of the whole community, not as self-centred wishes for our own betterment. Moreover, we join a community of worshippers so that our prayers will be accepted based on the merit of the community, even if as individuals we may not have earned favoured status.

Beyond our own synagogue experience, our participation in communal prayers may create the conditions necessary for others to engage in heartfelt supplications and facilitate their spiritual journeys. One Hasidic master, Rabbi Menaḥem Naḥum of Ştefăneşti (1823–1869), asserted: "The worst prayer recited with the congregation is better than the best prayer recited while alone."

Intent concentration on the oneness of God is unquestionably laudable and is truly the hub of prayer. Awareness of our fellow worshippers and attentiveness to their needs, however, is a parallel focal point of the *beit knesset*.

BERAKHOT 14A

To sleep, perchance to dream

DREAMS, NIGHTMARES, VISIONS while we sleep – all are part of the nightly regimen. Sometimes we recall our dreams in the morning; other times we remember that we had a nightmare but cannot recall what scared us so. Some visions are vivid or recurring, others frightening. Though attributing significance to dreams dates back to biblical times, not dreaming would seem to be neutral. It is therefore surprising that our sages state: "Whoever sleeps for seven days without having a dream is called wicked." This homiletic teaching is derived from a re-vocalisation of the verse: *A person will rest in contentment* (save'a) *and not be visited with evil* (Proverbs 19:23). This verse can be re-vocalised so that it reads: *A person who rests for seven* (sheva) *without being visited is evil* (*B. Berakhot* 14a). What is so dire about a week of restful sleep without dreams? Many of us yearn for one quiet, peaceful night and would rejoice at not being disturbed by night visions for an entire week!

The great commentator Rashi reverses the sequence of the talmudic statement. Instead of saying that one who does not dream is called evil, Rashi explains that it is because a person is evil that he is not visited by dreams. Following the biblical paradigm, Rashi understands dreams to be veiled Divine communiqués. The wicked forfeit the privilege of a godly message, as the Almighty does not deign to visit evil people.

An alternative understanding of dreams sees them as windows into the subconscious. Thus our sages tell us that dreams reflect the deepest thoughts and feelings in a person's heart (*B. Berakhot* 55b). Continuing with this line of thought, one commentator soberly states that we all sin in some way, perhaps only in thought. But deep down even the most sinful people regret their misguided actions. These misgivings surface while we sleep and find expression in our dreams. Fitful sleep, therefore, is a positive indicator of the regret that lies in the heart of the sinner. Not dreaming for a full week – despite the inevitability of sin – is a bleak gauge which indicates that thoughts of repentance have not entered even the deepest recesses of the subconscious. It is for this reason that the undisturbed sleeper is called evil (*Iyun Yaakov*).

Missing from both these explanations is the significance of specifically seven days without dreams. The great Hasidic master, the regal Rabbi Yisrael of Ruzhin (1797–1850), creatively endows this teaching with contemporary significance. Unabashedly departing from the obvious meaning of the passage, he offers an ingenious reading. He points out that in the High Holy Days service, human life is likened to a fleeting dream. Since the Hebrew term for "days" in Scripture sometimes refers to years (Leviticus 25:29), "seven days" may reflect the seven decades of human life (Psalms 90:10). We can live life in a trance-like state, frittering away opportunities and wasting our potential. However, our sages call upon us to appreciate and seize the opportunities offered by our seventy years in this world. Thus, one who slumbers in a dream-like state for seven days – that is, seventy years – is called evil.

Considering the notion of a seventy-year slumber reminds us of the Second Temple sage Ḥoni, who pondered how the psalmist could describe the Babylonian exile as a seventy-year dream (Psalms 126:1). "Could one really dreamily slumber for seventy years?" he queried (*B. Ta'anit* 23a).

One day Ḥoni chanced upon a person planting a carob tree. He asked the person planting it: "How many years will it take for this tree to bear fruit?"

"Up to seventy years," came the nonchalant reply.

"Is it obvious to you that you will live for seventy years, so that you will benefit from the fruits of this tree?"

Once again the response came in an unflappable tone: "I found this world with carob trees that my ancestors planted for me, and so too I am planting for my descendants."

Having satisfied his curiosity, Ḥoni sat down to eat, and sleep overtook him. A rocky overhang hid him from view, and he slumbered for seventy years. When Ḥoni awoke he found a man gathering carobs. Ḥoni asked him: "Are you the one who planted the tree?"

"I am his grandson," the man answered, and Ḥoni realised he had slept through two entire generations.

The Talmud does not expound on the connection between Ḥoni's seventy-year slumber and the seventy-year Babylonian exile. The retribution visited upon Ḥoni would have demonstrated to him how seventy years could be as fleeting as a dream. For those who merited the return to Zion after seventy years in exile, the past would have seemed like a dream, or rather a nightmare. Awakening from this exilic nightmare, those returning to the Promised Land sought to resettle our ancestral terrain and rebuild the Temple. Israel was not a new entity; rather it had merely fallen asleep and was now reawakening from a national slumber.

In the case of the Babylonian exile, a seventy-year sleep is cast in positive terms: since it was only a fleeting dream-like encounter, the Jewish people were able to connect to their past, and reconnect to their national destiny. Living in this post-exile reality, Ḥoni could not understand how the years of exile could just be disregarded. Perhaps in his Second Temple reality he yearned for the miraculous First Temple existence. Ḥoni was taught a harsh lesson. Yes, seventy years can be described as a dream – but only when that notion serves the goal of communal continuity with a distant past. Since you, Ḥoni, doubted this possibility, you will feel the harsh consequences of a seventy-year dream.

Ḥoni then made his way home. "Is the son of Ḥoni alive?" he asked.

"No, the son of Ḥoni is no more, but his grandson is alive," came the reply. Two generations had vanished.

Without pause, Ḥoni responded: "I am Ḥoni!" But no one believed him. Perhaps seeking solace in a safe space, Ḥoni made his way to the *beit midrash*.

Upon entering this familiar realm, he heard the sages commenting: "The laws are as clear as they were in the days of Ḥoni." They continued to reminisce of that bygone era: "For when Ḥoni entered the *beit midrash*, he would solve any problem that the sages raised."

Encouraged by this memory, Ḥoni announced: "I am he!" Again he was shunned and not accorded the respect he deserved.

In the case of Ḥoni, the lost seventy years left him bereft of family and community. A later talmudic sage applied this adage to the plight of Ḥoni: "Either a *ḥavruta* or *mituta*, death." A *ḥavruta* is literally a study partner or peer; more broadly, it can mean a community. Ḥoni's fate was tragic: having lost everything, he asked for Divine mercy to take him from this world. With that, Ḥoni died, though in truth his existence in this world really ended when he began to slumber.

Rabbi Yisrael of Ruzhin concludes his comment on a sleepy existence as follows. Our role and purpose in this physical world is to repair its fragmented reality for the sake of the Creator. If we dreamily slumber through our seventy years in this world, waiting to wake up, then we miss the meaning of life. If we do not take any action, if we do not fulfil our destiny, if we do not contribute to society, we indeed deserve to be called evil, for we have squandered the opportunities our existence proffers.

BERAKHOT 14A–B

Seeking Truth

TRUTH – with a capital T – is a certainty we crave. At times we may feel that we have achieved this elusive ideal, only to sober up to the fact that any Truth we identify is at most a truth – with a lowercase t – as viewed through our own subjective eyes. To a religious mind, Truth is associated with the indefinable Almighty. The pursuit of Truth, therefore, is the quest for knowledge of the Divine.

Emet, truth, is the word that opens the passage that immediately follows the twice-daily recitation of the *Shema* prayer. Our sages disallow any interruption or even any pause between the conclusion of *Shema* and the beginning of the next paragraph. This position is explained as being based on the verse: *But the Lord is the true God* (Jeremiah 10:10). Jeremiah here is juxtaposing a reference to God – similar to that in the final two words of *Shema* – with the word *emet* (*M. Berakhot* 2:2; *B. Berakhot* 14a–b).

Thus the word *emet* in the post-*Shema* prayer serves a dual function. It concludes the recitation of *Shema* and simultaneously launches the following passage. This twofold purpose leads to an uncertainty. Is a single recitation of the word *emet* sufficient, or should the word be uttered twice – once for each role? The talmudic sages are divided on this issue.

Insisting on a repetition of the word *emet* is a readily understandable position, as each recitation serves a different passage of prayer. This opinion, however, is not accepted as the halakhic rule (*Shulḥan Arukh, Oraḥ Ḥayim* 66:6). It is somewhat more difficult to fathom why the normative ruling is that a single recitation suffices to fulfil a dual purpose. Some commentators explain that duplicating the word *emet* would be akin to repeating other key words in the service that might indicate a belief in dualism – the doctrine that reality consists of, or is the outcome of, two ultimate principles.

Our tradition resolutely rejects dualism, and hence a prayer leader who implies dualistic empathy is swiftly silenced. The sages call for the ejection of a leader who says "*modim, modim*" (we give thanks, we give thanks) instead of just saying the word once. This rule is also applied to one who opens *Shema* by saying "*shema, shema*" (hear, hear) or who repeats the first verse (*M. Berakhot* 5:3; *B. Berakhot* 33b). Along the same lines, duplicating the word *emet* may intimate a belief in two Truths and hence two deities. Therefore, a single recitation is mandated (*Rabbi Yehuda Arye of Modena*).

A careful comparison, however, reveals a striking distinction between the two repetitions. While repetition of *modim* or *shema* leads to the hushing of the prayer leader, no such sanction is advocated for duplicating *emet*. What's more, one sage even promotes repeating the word. The Talmud relates the tale of an unnamed prayer leader who dared to repeat the word *emet* in the presence of Rabba, the proponent of the single recitation/dual use position. Instead of summarily gagging the leader, Rabba tolerantly and somewhat cryptically responded: "This person was seized by *emet*."

Thus it appears that the duplication of the word *emet* is not of the same negative valence as the repetition of other key words in the service.

The discussion regarding the word *emet* and its repetition may reflect a fundamental question: is there indeed a single, absolute Truth? Jewish scholars over the generations have pondered this critical issue and its corollary: if there is indeed such an ultimate Truth, what is our duty and accountability vis-à-vis this reality?

According to Maharal of Prague (1512?–1609), Truth is the only genuine unity in this physical world. Maharal identifies this singular, unchanging Truth with God. Following this definitive stance may provide us with a new understanding of the hesitation in duplicating the word *emet*. Such a repetition might smack of manifold truths and hence imply multiple deities.

Despite Maharal's absoluteness in declaring the existence of a single Divine Truth, we are still bereft of a means of accessing it.

The Spanish poet-scholar Yehuda Halevi (c. 1075–1141) claims that we can rest assured that rabbinic leadership – with endowed and earned wisdom, with piety, with safety in numbers and with Divine assistance – will reach the coveted objective of absolute Truth.

Cynics may be sceptical of such an assertion, which provides a guarantee that can never be proved or tested. Moreover, the prevalence of disputes among the sages appears to call this notion into question.

A creative approach to the Truth conundrum is suggested by one Galician halakhist, Rabbi Aryeh Leib HaKohen Heller (1745–1812), in the introduction to his legal treatise, *Ketzot HaḤoshen*. The Ketzot, as he is often known, champions the existence of an absolute Truth, but denies our obligation to align ourselves with it. The Torah's legal system, he argues, is entrusted to our fallible human hands, and we are charged with operating this system with integrity. At the same time, any correlation between our mortal conclusions and Divine Truth are fortunate and valuable, but cannot be proved. Hence absolute Truth is not essential to our existence; we are obligated to act in accordance with the earthly perception of truth, not by the exalted Divine Truth.

A maverick position that leaves room for the possibility of multiple Divine Truths is proposed by the Spanish talmudist Ritva (1250–1330) in the name of unidentified French scholars. Building on the oft-quoted rabbinic adage "These and these are the words of the living God" (*B. Eruvin* 13b), Ritva suggests that there is no such thing as a mistaken halakhic position in the eyes of the Almighty. In the gamut of possible outcomes, all are Divinely legitimate, and truth is simply an earthly notion relevant for normative practice. Therefore, any ruling arrived at by legitimate authority reflects Truth, albeit one Truth of many possible Truths.

As we conclude *Shema* with the declaration that God is True, it is uncertain whether the quest for absolute Truth bears tangible fruit. Nevertheless, the longing for a greater understanding of the Divine and our consequent place and role in this world is certainly valuable, as we continue to strive to find meaning in our existence.

BERAKHOT 15A–B

Audible prayer

THE MISHNA RECORDS a disagreement as to whether a person reading the twice-daily *Shema* should do so aloud. "If someone reads *Shema* so quietly that he himself is unable to hear it, he has discharged his obligation; Rabbi Yose says that he has not discharged his obligation" (*M. Berakhot* 2:3). The Talmud notes that the approach of Rabbi Yose is also the opinion of other sages, including Rabbi Yehuda the Prince (or Rebbi, as he is commonly known), the author of the mishnaic text which has reached us.

The Talmud further explains that these sages reach their conclusion based on the first word of the prescribed text – "*shema*" meaning "hear." The word "*shema*" is understood as setting down the requirement that the passage must be read loudly enough so that it can be heard by the reader (*B. Berakhot* 13a, 15a). In contrast, the majority opinion as expressed by the first anonymous opinion in the Mishna understands the word "*shema*" to indicate that the passage can be read in any language, and therefore concludes that there is no audibility requirement.

What about other *mitzvot* that also require the recitation of texts, such as the *Amida* and the Grace After Meals? Must they be said audibly? Later sages note that the mishnaic argument exists specifically with regard to *Shema* since there is the possibility of understanding the word "*shema*" as indicating a requirement that what is being said must be heard. All sages agree that other *mitzvot* that require speech need not be said audibly. With regard to the Grace After Meals, there is an opinion that it should be recited audibly; however, this is not seen as a requirement which if not met invalidates the recitation (*B. Berakhot* 15a–b).

Elsewhere in our tractate we find a statement regarding the audibility of the so-called "silent" *Amida*. As we have noted, there is clearly no requirement to recite the *Amida* aloud. The issue raised is whether it *may* be said aloud if the supplicant so wishes. The Talmud states: "If someone makes his voice heard in his prayer" – referring to the *Amida* – "behold he is lacking in faith" (*B. Berakhot* 24b). The logic behind this would seem to be that a person who finds it necessary to pray out loud might think or lead others to think that God can hear only supplications pronounced audibly. This statement makes it crystal clear that the Almighty hears our prayers, even when they are inaudible to the human ear.

The rule that the *Amida* must be said silently is immediately qualified. Those who cannot focus when reciting the *Amida* silently are permitted to pray audibly as long as they are praying alone. Praying audibly with a congregation, however, might disturb fellow supplicants and therefore is not permitted, even for those who have difficulty concentrating when praying silently.

Here too, we find exceptions. Codifiers note that for educational purposes, the prohibition against praying aloud in public is relaxed (*Tur*). Praying aloud on the High Holy Days is also treated as a different category. Since there are some people who make extra effort to attend services on Rosh HaShana and Yom Kippur, in consideration of them we allow audible prayer in order to facilitate their participation. Also, prayers on these significant days are often of a different calibre, and audible praying may facilitate greater concentration and focus.

It should be noted that praying silently does not mean visually scanning the words. Rather, supplicants are encouraged to mouth the words that they are reciting inaudibly. This follows the paradigm of Hannah's heartfelt prayer for a child, in which her lips moved but her voice was not heard; her prayer was answered with the birth of the prophet Samuel (I Samuel 1).

Codifiers discuss how silent the "silent" *Amida* must be. According to the classic codes, "silent" means that fellow congregants cannot hear the recitation. The supplicants themselves, however, should be able to hear their own hushed tones (*Shulḥan Arukh, Oraḥ Ḥayim* 101:2). Others, particularly those who follow the Jewish mystical tradition as expounded by the Ari, Rabbi Yitzḥak Luria (1534–1572), rule that the silent *Amida* should be just that – recited in silence such that no one can hear, not even the supplicant.

The Hasidic master Rabbi Ḥayim Elazar Shapira of Munkács (1871–1937), himself an ardent follower of the Ari's teachings, reported that while visiting Germany he heard his fellow supplicants pray the *Amida* in hushed tones, and he was rather taken aback. The Munkatcher Rebbe, however, pointed out that there was sound halakhic basis for such conduct, strange though it seemed to his ear.

When discussing the rules of any ritual such as prayer, there is always the danger that we will get lost in the minutiae of the law. Instead of focusing on the big picture, we get bogged down in the details. To be sure, the details come together to give the form, and we endeavour to fulfil each element of the law. Yet it is regrettable to focus solely on the details without so much as a glance in the direction of the larger issue that the details seek to address.

The discussions regarding the audibility of our prayers must be about more than setting an appropriate decibel level for our supplications. It would appear that the tension surrounding the audibility of prayers turns on the two distinct yet interwoven concerns of the prayer venture: the individual's personal and heartfelt supplications on the one hand, and the community's joint, collective effort on the other hand.

The most effective medium for an individual may indeed be to pray aloud. When reading aloud we are often able to focus not only on what we read but also on what we hear. Alas, an individual muttering his prayers can easily distract another person trying to pour out her heart to the Almighty. Moreover, if everyone in the community were to pray aloud, the result would be cacophony. When we gather as a community, individual silent prayer may be preferable in order to provide space for each supplicant, though the cost may be that some community members cannot concentrate.

The challenge that stands before any community is how we create a space that allows individuals to pray as part of a group. The audibility of prayers is one of the issues that must be addressed when trying to find the most appropriate balance between the personal prayer endeavour and the joint communal effort to commune with the Almighty.

BERAKHOT 15B–16A

Immersion in the *mikveh* of our heritage

ACQUIESCING TO THE pleading of Balak, king of Moab, the prophet Balaam attempted to curse Israel. From his vantage point, Balaam saw the encampment of Israel and could not but bless what his eyes beheld. Using poetic imagery, Balaam praised the Israelite tents that lay before him: *How goodly are your tents, O Jacob, your dwellings, O Israel. Like brooks stretched out, like gardens beside a river, like aloes planted by God, like cedars beside the water* (Numbers 24:5–6).

Our sages comment on Balaam's use of simile, focusing on his comparison between tents and water: "Just as brooks serve to advance people from impurity to purity, so too tents serve to advance people from being guilt-laden to being meritorious" (*B. Berakhot* 15b–16a). The change of status from impurity to purity is effected by immersion in a *mikveh*, a body of water – such as a brook (Leviticus 11:36) – that serves as a ritual bath. Which *tents* are being referenced in this talmudic passage? A parallel version of the analogy makes it abundantly clear: "Just as the impure descend into this brook and arise pure, so too with the Temple – one enters with sin and exits without sin" (*Midrash Tehillim* 5:1).

In the post-Temple reality, these tents – and other tent references in our tradition – were reinterpreted to refer to the places which serve as Temple substitutes: the *beit midrash* and the *beit knesset*. These would now be the tents of Torah study (*B. Sanhedrin* 105b).

Unpacking the connection between a tent and a sacred space –

whether Temple, *beit midrash* or *beit knesset* – one commentator explains that tent dwellers are people who distance themselves from areas of settlement, pitching their tents away from mundane, worldly existence. So too, choosing holy space as an abode is also choosing a path that departs from an unsanctified physical existence, and reflects a consecration of life (*Maharsha*).

Thus, decoding the talmudic analogy, we arrive at the following. Just as immersion in a *mikveh* elevates a person from impurity to purity, so too plunging into the depths of our heritage by "residing" in the *beit midrash* and *beit knesset* can raise a person from being guilt-laden to being meritorious.

Our sages offer this comparison between ritual immersion on the one hand and study and prayer on the other, but take it no further. Scholars over the generations pondering this talmudic passage offer additional insights.

If not for Balaam's analogy, would we be unaware of the power of the *beit midrash* and the *beit knesset* to convert fault to merit? In countless places our sages reflect on the effectiveness of our tents of Torah. For example: "If that despicable scoundrel" – referring to the evil inclination – "affects you, drag him to the *beit midrash*" (*B. Sukka* 52b; *B. Kiddushin* 30b). What, therefore, does Balaam's analogy add? This question illuminates the power of the tents of Torah study. Ritual purification can be effected even without the intent to go through the purification process. Thus, if a person ready for ritual cleansing is thrust unwillingly or unknowingly into a *mikveh,* that person emerges purified (*B. Ḥullin* 31a). So too, if people enter the *beit midrash* or *beit knesset* even without proper motives – whether social pressures dictate their involvement or their desire for honour leads them to participation – the tents of Torah have the ability to convert their guilt to merit (*Ḥida*; *Torah Temima*).

Though intent is not necessary, other regulations do exist. Just as the utility of the *mikveh* is limited, so too the power of the *beit midrash* is circumscribed. Partial submersion in a *mikveh* is not considered a valid immersion; the entire body, with no intervening objects, must be enveloped by the waters. The potency of the tents of Torah is also dependent on total immersion. Entering the *beit midrash* in body but not in spirit can negate the power of the experience (*Penei Menaḥem*).

Furthermore, not every puddle can be considered a *mikveh*. Just as there are benchmarks for categorising a body of water as a *mikveh*, there are yardsticks by which a place of learning can be considered a legitimate tent. To be sure, the parameters of a *mikveh* are clearly delineated; defining a tent of Torah study is somewhat more nebulous.

These comparisons lend substance to the sages' understanding of Balaam's poetic blessing. Nevertheless, our contemporary concept of ritual purity is far removed from the understandings of the bygone Temple era. The analogy between bathing in a brook and dwelling in the tents of Torah might also be expressed via current notions of hygiene, giving it an accessible and relevant meaning.

Extricating dirt that is embedded in the folds of our skin can require vigorous scouring. At times, it seems that we are not removing the dirt but the skin itself. While we attempt to return to our former, pristine state we cry out in pain, only later appreciating the scrubbing as our skin glows. At the end of the process we realise that we have in fact removed the foreign bodies that concealed our true self.

An encounter with our tradition can also be a painful experience. As foreign bodies are pried from our existence we cry out, feeling that we are being dismembered, that our very identity is being peeled away layer by layer. Only later do we see that our true self has not been eroded but revealed. We can then appreciate the return to our pristine state as cleansed individuals.

Our tradition, however, is like no other cleansing agent. Ordinary soap cleans the dirt that has piled up; Torah supplies a protective coating that endows our souls with a veneer that repels spiritual dirt. In the words of the Talmud: "While one is involved in Torah study, the Torah protects from punishment and saves from sin" (*B. Sota* 21a).

Balaam noticed how fortunate our people are to have the rivers of Torah flowing through our communities. They stretch before us enticingly, and tender an opportunity for the spiritual cleansing of our souls by immersion in our heritage.

BERAKHOT 16A

Broadminded activism

WHAT DID YOU do on your wedding day? At a guess, you were rushing around making last minute preparations, hairdresser, make-up; perhaps a quick moment for personal prayer. Then to the hall for family photos, and the guests began to arrive. In contrast, the Talmud describes the remarkable wedding day conduct of Rabbi Elazar ben Pedat, a Babylonian scholar who after his initial education made his way to the Land of Israel (*B. Berakhot* 16a).

Two of the groom's junior colleagues – Rabbis Ami and Assi – were fastening the canopy for their friend's wedding. With preparations for the big night underway, the groom turned to his busy peers and said: "In the meantime, I will go and hear something in the *beit midrash,* and I will come back and relate it to you." With that, Rabbi Elazar ben Pedat made his way to the *beit midrash* where the head of the academy – a position the groom would one day fill – was teaching.

When he reached the *beit midrash,* a *tanna* (someone who memorised and recited vast amounts of rabbinic material) was standing before the famed Rabbi Yoḥanan, transmitting an earlier source verbatim, perhaps without fully understanding its meaning and import (*Rashi, Sota* 22a). The lesson was about mistakes during *Shema* prayer, and four scenarios were brought up.

First, if a person forgets a word or sentence in *Shema,* but does not know precisely where the mistake occurred – the reader must return to the very beginning of *Shema.* Second, if the reader knows in which of the *Shema* passages the mistake occurred – he need only return to the beginning of that passage. Third, if the reader knows that he was in between paragraphs, but cannot recall whether he was in between the first and second or whether he had in fact completed the second paragraph and needed to begin the third – he must assume that the blunder was in the first break, and should continue from the second paragraph (*Rashi*; *cf. Maimonides*).

The fourth case refers to the verse containing the commandment to write *mezuzot* to affix to our doorposts. This instruction appears with identical wording in the first and second paragraphs of *Shema* (Deuteronomy 6:9 and 11:20). If a reader, having intoned this verse, cannot recall whether he was in the first or second paragraph – he must return to the verse's first occurrence and continue from there.

Hearing this account of the law, Rabbi Yoḥanan qualified the last scenario. The fourth case applies when the reader has yet to begin the verse that follows the *mezuza* commandment in the second paragraph – *In order to prolong your days* (Deuteronomy 11:21). If the reader has already continued with this verse, we may assume that he continued in his habitual manner of reciting *Shema* without getting muddled, and any uncertainties are dismissed. In this case, we assume the reader has completed the second paragraph and he is permitted to continue reading (*Rashba*; *cf. Rashi*). Having heard this lecture, Rabbi Elazar ben Pedat returned to the wedding hall.

The unique character of Rabbi Elazar ben Pedat is immediately apparent. On his own wedding day, amid the panic and excitement, he had the strength of conviction to put all aside and journey to the *beit midrash*.

The material discussed in the *beit midrash* on that day and the framing story of Rabbi Elazar the groom provide us with a stark comparison and perhaps a hidden critique. On the one hand, we have cases of people reciting *Shema* who are unable to focus and thus err while reciting *Shema*. In contrast, we have a sage who is able to apply his faculties of concentration on his very own wedding day, the eve of a time when a groom is even released from his nightly obligation to recite *Shema* because he is unable to focus (*M. Berakhot* 2:5).

It is no wonder that commentators laud the behaviour of Rabbi Elazar ben Pedat. Never again can a person proffer an excuse for not learning. Whether it be troublesome times or joyful occasions, there is no justification for losing even one moment of Torah study, for indeed each learning session holds some inestimable innovation more precious than gems (*Rabbi Yehuda Arye of Modena*).

Commenting on this passage, the first Chief Rabbi of the Land of Israel, Rabbi Avraham Yitzḥak HaKohen Kook (1865–1935), highlights an additional dimension of the groom's behaviour. Indeed, Rabbi Elazar ben Pedat demonstrated the importance of studying Torah even when one is extremely busy. Yet a greater lesson can be learned. His trip to the *beit midrash* did not result in the learning of foundational laws or the hearing of wondrous tales. Rather, rules relating to mistakes made when reading *Shema* were given and clarified – hardly the most stimulating material. Rabbi Elazar ben Pedat, nevertheless, saw value in his visit, and when he returned to his two colleagues he excitedly recounted what he had learned. Thus, at this hectic moment, Rabbi Elazar ben Pedat was so excited about what he had learned that he wished to share it with his friends.

Rabbi Kook adds yet another dimension to this story. Turning from the groom, Rabbi Kook focuses on Rabbis Ami and Assi, who were industriously erecting the wedding canopy when their colleague left. The Talmud relates that when Rabbi Elazar ben Pedat returned, he relayed what he had just learned during his short excursion to the *beit midrash*. Rabbi Ami and Rabbi Assi exclaimed: "If we had come only to hear this matter, it would have been enough for us!" Despite the fact that these two sages were occupied with the grand *mitzva* of doing kindness for another, and its particular application in taking part in wedding preparations, they nonetheless responded, with genuine excitement, to the laws of which they were now apprised. It takes broadmindedness to be able to acknowledge and appreciate a valuable cause, even while you are diligently involved in a different worthy enterprise.

Rabbi Kook describes such a person as having an expansive heart that is filled with love of God and His Torah. Small-minded people cannot see beyond the cause they have embraced. Activists should be lauded for their committed work, but dedication and devotion to one worthwhile cause should not preclude recognition of other commendable endeavours.

One need not champion every valid venture. However, donning blinkers and waving the flag of a single mission, oblivious and uncaring about any other issue, reflects an insular approach that may be more concerned with self-fulfilment than with the betterment of society. Though we need not undertake every project, we must strive for broadmindedness as we validate and appreciate multiple causes.

BERAKHOT 16A

Success in tough economic times

WHEN THE TIME for prayer arrives, we occasionally find ourselves in locations that are hardly conducive to communion with the Almighty. An employer may be standing over us waiting for us to complete a task, or perhaps we are speeding along a highway. When we are under time constraints due to our profession, different rules are set down for *Shema* and the *Amida*. Workers atop a scaffolding or up a tree may read *Shema* where they find themselves; for the *Amida*, however, they must descend (*M. Berakhot* 2:4).

The difference is that reading *Shema* is a declaration of faith which can be expressed in any situation. The *Amida* is a heartfelt supplication which requires a level of concentration that cannot be achieved when balanced precariously above the ground (*Rashi*). A parallel source further notes that if a person finds himself in an olive tree or a fig tree – trees laden with branches that provide ample place to stand firmly – even the *Amida* may be said without descending (*T. Berakhot* 2:8).

Besides the ability to concentrate, there is another consideration when deciding whether workers must descend from their workplace to pray. An employee is hired to work. To what extent is the employee permitted to divert his attention, time and energy to pursuits other than the tasks at hand? Is the prayer requirement a valid reason to take a break from work?

According to one commentator, the olive and fig tree labourers should not descend for prayer, for they would be unjustly taking a break from the task for which they were employed. In contrast, other trees are easy to climb down, and therefore the descent for prayer is a less significant encroachment on the employee's responsibilities (*Rabbeinu Yona Gerondi*). This explains why the employer – as master of his own time – must always descend for prayer, regardless of the type of tree he has climbed.

A further source discusses the performance of other rituals during working hours. While on the job, workers must read *Shema* together with its introductory and concluding blessings, recite the *Amida* and eat bread with the appropriate benedictions before and after the meal. Employees should not, however, serve as the leader of the prayer service, for this takes away too much time from their work (*T. Berakhot* 2:9).

Analysing these passages, the Talmud further regulates the rights of employees to take breaks for rituals, noting that the above guidelines apply only to workers who are rewarded with meals alone – a minimum wage of sorts. Workers who in addition to receiving food also collect wages are limited in the time they may take for rituals while working, as their relatively lucrative contract precludes liberal breaks. According to the original talmudic law, wage-receiving employees were to recite a shortened form of the *Amida*, were not to recite the blessing over bread and needed say only the abridged Grace After Meals (*B. Berakhot* 16a).

The talmudic law evolved over the years. In the codes of Jewish law, workers' rights to take breaks for prayer were broadened under the assumption that expectations and common practice have changed since talmudic times (*Shulḥan Arukh, Oraḥ Ḥayim* 110:2; *Mishna Berura* 191:2). The principle, however, remains intact: employees have a responsibility to their employers and they must honestly fulfil their contractual obligations.

When presenting these laws, Maimonides offers a biblical paradigm for honest employees. Before leaving his father-in-law's employ, Jacob turned to Rachel and Leah and said: *As you know, I have served your father with all my strength* (Genesis 31:6). Citing this source, Maimonides rules that just as an employer must not cheat an employee, so too the employee must not cheat the employer. In what way does an employee cheat an employer? By wasting a bit of time here and a bit of time there, until the entire day has passed with little or no productive work done. An employee should be like the righteous Jacob, who worked with all his might for his employer.

It is worth noting that Jacob was working for Laban, who was hardly the paradigm of an honest employer; it is doubtful whether Laban fulfilled all his moral obligations as an employer. Jacob could, perhaps, be excused for cutting corners, yet he chose to work hard and not shirk his employee responsibilities. Maimonides' biblical proof text is particularly surprising in that he adds a title to Jacob's name – *Yaakov HaTzaddik* (Jacob the righteous). Jacob is normally referred to as *Yaakov Avinu* (Jacob our forefather), even in Maimonides' writings. The only biblical personality in Jewish literature to be regularly accorded the epithet *hatzaddik* is Joseph, who earned the appellation with his display of fortitude in resisting the advances of his Egyptian master's wife. Joseph is called *hatzaddik* because despite the opportunity to sin, and perhaps the utility in acquiescing to the overtures of Potiphar's wife, he courageously refused (Genesis 39:7–20).

Pondering Maimonides' unexpected designation – *Yaakov HaTzaddik* – we can surmise that there are two paradigms of the *tzaddik*. One path of righteousness is taken by the *tzaddik* who resists temptations of the flesh. A parallel virtuous path is followed by the *tzaddik* who withstands the lure of money. In light of this, we can understand another talmudic passage, where the holiness of two sages is extolled (*Y. Sanhedrin* 29c). The famed Rabbi Yehuda the Prince was known as *Rabbeinu HaKadosh*, our rabbi the holy one, because he never focused on his sexual organs. Another sage was known as Naḥum *Kodesh HaKodashim*, Naḥum the holy of holies, for he never looked upon money. Again we have two paradigms of righteousness, and in this talmudic source it would seem that withstanding the vice of money is more praiseworthy.

Maimonides' conclusion is even more relevant in difficult economic times, when markets are crashing and when economic depression looms. Maimonides maintains that Jacob the *tzaddik* merited wealth in this world because of his honest, upstanding and hardworking attitude as an employee. Maimonides appears to be providing sound financial advice: a prerequisite for economic success is hard, honest work.

BERAKHOT 16B

Class differences

THANKFULLY, OWNING *AVADIM* – servants, bondsmen or slaves – is not an accepted norm in our society. We would be burying our heads in the sand, however, if we claimed that slavery was never an accepted norm. Ignoring this fact would not only be denying history, but would also result in a lost opportunity – the opportunity to see how our sages relate to those whom society saw as being of lower status.

The Mishna describes Rabban Gamliel's response to the demise of Tavi, his servant (*M. Berakhot* 2:7). Following the burial of the deceased, funeral attendees would customarily pass before the mourners and offered their condolences. Thus after the interment of Tavi, Rabban Gamliel sat ready to be offered words of comfort, and those present complied (*Rabbi Shlomo Sirilio*). Students of the sage looked on in surprise and exclaimed: "But you, our master, have taught us that one may not accept condolences for the loss of a gentile slave!" Commentators explain the reason for this rule – lest onlookers mistakenly assume that the deceased was a Jew (*Tosafot*).

Turning to his students, Rabban Gamliel succinctly responded: "My bondsman Tavi is not like other gentile slaves, for he was a worthy individual." Elsewhere in the Mishna, we find Rabban Gamliel proudly announcing that Tavi was a Torah scholar (*M. Sukka* 2:1). Moreover, when the sages discuss the long-term effects of our actions, they refer to Tavi. The righteous not only merit favourable treatment for their deeds, but also bequeath merit to their descendants. In contrast, evil people not only render themselves culpable, but also pass on hereditary liability to their descendants. Highlighting the enduring consequences of the deeds of our forebears, the sages note that Tavi was worthy of rabbinic ordination, but because of his lineage he was denied this opportunity and never achieved this status (*B. Yoma* 87a). Let us return to Tavi's funeral.

In honour of Tavi's accomplishments in the field of Torah scholarship, Rabban Gamliel felt it appropriate to accept condolences for his loss.

It is important to note that achievement in Torah alone would not justify accepting condolences, a practice normally reserved for family members. Commentators remark that there is often a familial relationship between master and servant, and between teacher and student. Such a close connection, coupled with Tavi's unique commitment to Torah, justified Rabban Gamliel's departure from the norm (*Y. Berakhot* 5b).

What does Rabban Gamliel's course of action show us about his relationship to servitude and slavery? The language of the sources suggests that Rabban Gamliel saw his actions as an exception, and that Tavi was generally seen as an unusual slave. It is entirely likely that Tavi, and Rabban Gamliel's relationship towards him, deviated from the societal norm. But was Rabban Gamliel alone in his familial feelings for a slave?

The Talmud relates a contemporaneous episode which demonstrates the relationship of Rabbi Eliezer, Rabban Gamliel's brother-in-law, to his maidservant (*B. Berakhot* 16b; *Semaḥot* 1:9–10). When Rabbi Eliezer's gentile maidservant died, his students came to console their master, perhaps following the example set by Rabban Gamliel. Seeing the students enter and surmising their intent, Rabbi Eliezer ascended to the upper floor to avoid meeting them. Not to be rebuffed, the students followed their master. The chase continued with Rabbi Eliezer entering an anteroom and the students at his heels. With his students in hot pursuit, Rabbi Eliezer proceeded to the reception room. Cornered by his students and realising that the message he was trying to convey had not been comprehended, Rabbi Eliezer reproached his followers with a colourful metaphor: "I thought you would be scalded with warm water, but now I see that you are not scalded even with boiling hot water! Did I not already teach you that condolences are not offered for the demise of slaves? Just as when a person loses other chattel, all that should be said is: 'May the Omnipresent replace your loss.'"

Why did Rabbi Eliezer first hint at the law rather than spelling it out explicitly? As an educator, Rabbi Eliezer could have seized the moment when his students offered their condolences as a teaching instance to convey lucidly the law that comfort is not offered for departed gentile slaves. Moreover, Rabbi Eliezer did not even give his students an opportunity to talk; perhaps they would have recited the approved formula. Instead, Rabbi Eliezer fled from confrontation with his disciples, as if he preferred not to talk about the issue, and was uncomfortable with the law.

I would suggest that during the earlier discussion in the *beit midrash,* Rabbi Eliezer may have been able to relate the prohibition against offering condolences for slaves when it was purely theoretical. Faced with the loss of a member of his household, the sage may indeed have been grieving, unable to face his students who might relate to his bereavement as one relates to the death of an ox or donkey.

A third source supports this suggestion. Rabbi Yose qualified the rule that there is no eulogising of gentile servants and maidservants: "For a worthy slave, we say: 'Woe for the loss of a good and trustworthy person, who enjoyed the fruits of his hard work.'" Rabbi Yose's students were surprised by this statement, which sounded like a tribute to the deceased. They challenged him: "If this is what is said for a worthy slave, what have you left to be said for worthy Jews?" The passage ends at this point and we are left to ponder Rabbi Yose's response to the penetrating question of his disciples. Perhaps the venerable sage stood before the students with a broad grin, as if to say: "Indeed, I have left nothing, for a worthy person should be remembered and acclaimed, regardless of social standing."

Slavery in any form is a blot on history, past and present. It is worthy to note that the talmudic sages, despite owning slaves (as per contemporary social norms), did not relate to their servants as mere property. They looked beyond the balance sheet value of their bondsmen, seeing real people, having genuine feelings for them and grieving at their demise. Thus our tradition provides a paradigm for moving towards the eradication of class differences.

BERAKHOT 16B

Who knows four?

We know four! Four are the Mothers and three are the Fathers ...." Thus we sing towards the end of the traditional Pesaḥ *seder*. How serious are we about there being four Matriarchs and three Patriarchs? Our sages tell us that the official labels "Mother" and "Father" are reserved solely for our famous predecessors: the foremothers Sarah, Rebecca, Leah and Rachel, and the forefathers Abraham, Isaac and Jacob (*B. Berakhot* 16b). Even other ancestors of the Jewish people – such as Bilhah and Zilpah or the twelve tribes – do not merit this title.

Our sages ask why this honorific is limited to these forebears. The Talmud considers the possibility that Abraham, Isaac and Jacob are our Fathers since we know that we descend from them, whereas we do not know which of the tribes is our ancestor. This line of reasoning is rejected, however, since we call both Leah and Rachel "our Mother," even though we do not know whether either of them is our ancestor. If we belong to the tribe of Dan, Naftali, Gad or Asher we are the progeny of Bilhah or Zilpah, not Leah or Rachel. Thus our ancestral biological mother may not be one of our national Matriarchs. The Talmud concludes that the seven progenitors of the nation were of particular importance; beyond this closed circle, our ancestors do not carry the same weight. Though this concludes the talmudic discussion, we cannot avoid the question: what is the significance of the title granted to these forebears?

An early approach suggests that our sages are merely declaring who deserves the honour of these designations (*Hai Gaon*). Alternatively, these ancestors merited direct communion with God, therefore we wish to acknowledge them as our ancestors (*Rabbi Yehuda Arye of Modena*). However, these attitudes minimise the significance of the talmudic passage, leaving the words of the sages as mere labels of honour, either for conferring honour on our founding parents or claiming distinction for us, their descendants. Surely there must be more to the designation of Patriarchs and Matriarchs?

Another commentator proposes that the significance of the titles lies in the prayer service. Mentioning the Patriarchs is obligatory, whereas adding a supplication such as "He who answered Reuben, our father…" is permitted but not required (*Ra'avad*). But this approach falters when considering the Matriarchs, who are not mentioned in the traditional prayers (*Rashba*). What, then, is the significance of singling them out as our Mothers?

An alternative line of thought sees the founding parents of our nation as charged with setting the tone for the future. Thus the originators of the Jewish people set about refining their progeny in preparation for the formation of a new nation. Only one of Abraham's children, Isaac, was to continue on the path of his parents. Isaac and Rebecca also had one son, Jacob, who maintained the legacy he received. Jacob, with his wives, is the first of our forebears to have all his children follow in his footsteps. Indeed, while Jacob's children may have been righteous people, they cannot be considered founding Fathers, for they were born into the reality of a fledgling nation. The seven ancestors are recognised as the Patriarchs and Matriarchs of the Jewish people in recognition of their momentous achievement – forming a distinct people with a unique message for humanity (*Eitz Yosef*).

Continuing with this line of thought which focuses on actions, a further approach found in rabbinic thought sees the deeds of the founders of our nation as portentous (*Tanḥuma*). One biblical commentator explains the lengthy and detailed scriptural descriptions of the lives of our forefathers as a prediction for what will happen in future generations (*Ramban*). The actions of other progenitors of our nation, in contrast, do not carry the same predictive force. Indeed, the tribes are each known as a *shevet* or *mateh*, meaning boughs that branch off from a central trunk. They are not the source of growth; they are offshoots from it. Thus declaring who our forebears are foretells our destiny.

A variation on this approach can be derived from the words of another commentator. In a different context, Maharal of Prague (1512?–1609) deals with the ancestral merit available to community leaders. The sages state that those who toil for the community out of pure motives are assisted by the merit of our forefathers (*M. Avot* 2:2). These ancestors are forebears of the Jewish people as a unit, a congregation that exists with a changing constituency. Anyone who serves this assemblage merits the backing of the founders of this unit. Though Maharal does not cite our talmudic passage, we can suggest that revealing the identity of our Matriarchs and Patriarchs tells us whose merit accompanies us. The amazing power to make use of this merit is bequeathed to all members of our nation. The good deeds of our other ancestors lack this far-reaching impact. Thus it is not only that our forebears' deeds set a pattern which our lives tend to follow, but also that they provide us with lasting merit which helps deal with the vicissitudes of reality, particularly for all who undertake to serve the assembly.

Aside from the benefits bestowed upon us as descendants of these giants, there is a further implication in acknowledging our forebears. The conduct of the progenitors of the Jewish people is to be considered a guidepost for our own behaviour, as per the maxim: "The deeds of the ancestors are symbolic for their descendants." We delve into the vicissitudes of their lives, poring over every detail and focusing on every action, treating them as paradigms and seeking to learn from them.

On Pesaḥ, we sit with our family as the beloved *seder* ritual draws to a close, singing "Four are the Mothers and Three are the Fathers." We are telling ourselves, our children and all those around us that these founding personalities carry weighty significance for our people; their lives are worth exploring and emulating.

BERAKHOT 16B

Hand motions during prayer

OUR BODY IS an important medium of expression. We sit up when we are attentive and slouch if we are bored. Raised eyebrows indicate doubt; a scrunched nose shows distaste; a smile conveys joy. Hand gestures are also key in conveying a message; for some, tying their hands down would be akin to cutting out the tongue. To be sure, postures have varied meanings in different cultures, but all societies have norms with regard to the body as a vehicle of articulation. It is therefore to be expected that our sages relate to various aspects of our stance during prayer.

One aspect of appropriate posture during prayer that has undergone changes over the generations is the positioning of the hands during prayer.

The sages say that the verse *Thus I will bless You all my life; I will lift my hands for Your name* (Psalms 63:5) refers to different parts of the prayer service (*B. Berakhot* 16b). Since Torah study is referred to as *my life* (Deuteronomy 30:20), the beginning of the verse – *all my life* – may refer to reciting *Shema*, which is considered the minimum necessary to fulfil the daily obligation of Torah study (*B. Menaḥot* 99b). Thus the verse can be read: *I will bless You* with that which is *all my life*, namely Torah study (*Maharsha*).

Our sages continue: the remainder of the verse – *I will lift my hands for Your name* – refers to the *Amida*. Does this mean our hands should be raised while praying? Various biblical passages seem to indicate that this is indeed the appropriate gesture for prayer (Genesis 14:22; I Kings 8:22, 54; II Chronicles 6:13; Isaiah 1:15; Lamentations 3:41). For example, as the Jewish people fought Amalek, Moses stood atop a hill with outstretched arms, encouraging his warriors and beseeching God for assistance. The battle continued and Moses' hands began to tire. Aaron and Hur each supported one arm until Israel was victorious (Exodus 17:8–16). The people mimicked Moses and they too raised their hands to God (*Pirkei DeRabbi Eliezer*). Interestingly, this was not the first time Moses raised his hands in prayer. When Pharaoh begged Moses to request the end of the plague of hail, Moses declared that he would leave the city and stretch out his hands to God, and the plague would cease (Exodus 9:27–33).

In esoteric sources we see that it is dangerous – and hence forbidden – to stand with hands raised to the heavens. Following this line of thought, one authority opines that raising hands to the heavens is reserved for the holiest of people. Moses stood thus as he prayed before the Almighty, and those present even followed his lead. This, however, does not grant the general public licence to follow this practice, as is indicated by the silence of the talmudic authorities on this matter (*Rabbi Yaakov Emden*).

With the advent of Hasidism, extravagant gestures became widespread in the revived prayer ritual. Here the hands were not held in a beseeching manner, but were part of fierce movements during prayer. Rabbi Shneur Zalman of Lyady (1745–1812) is said to have banged his hands on the wall during his fervent prayers, such that he drew blood. Eventually carpets were hung opposite his place of prayer so the Hasidic master would not injure himself.

These practices were condemned by the opponents of Hasidism. In a work published soon after the rise of the nascent movement, the fiery scholar Rabbi Yaakov Emden (1697–1776) censured the practice of gesturing during prayers, one manifestation of which was clapping during the service. He lamented: "Ask yourself if they would dare do so in the presence of a king of flesh and blood. Why, he would have them thrown down so that their limbs would be shattered and their bones broken."

To be sure, these practices were denounced even by Hasidic masters when they were done for show and did not reflect true emotions. A creative reading of the verse *And when the people saw, they swayed, and stood far off* (Exodus 20:15) is attributed to the Baal Shem Tov (Besht, c. 1700–1760): "If a person sways in prayer in order that people see him and admire his piety, it is a sign that he is *far off*, remote from God."

Even sincere gestures were not considered essential to heartfelt Hasidic prayer. Some masters opined that immobile prayer reflected a higher level than prayer with bodily movement.

Despite advocating bodily movement, the Hasidic norm did not strictly follow the biblical paradigm or the talmudic dictum. Indeed, an eerie silence hovers over the issue of outstretched arms during prayer in much of the post-talmudic literature. One notable exception is Rabbi Avraham (1186–1237) the son of Maimonides. An advocate of a return to original prayer styles, he promoted raising the hands when petitioning God. However, no such gesture is prescribed when praising or thanking the Almighty. Rabbi Avraham's approach was echoed by some later authorities (*Rabbi Elazar Azikri*), but never became the accepted practice.

Some halakhists suggest that prayer with outstretched arms is the manner of gentile prayer, and therefore should be avoided (*Be'er Sheva*). Modern scholars have demonstrated that a serious issue is at stake here: Christians viewed Moses' outstretched arms as prefiguring the crucifixion. This would explain the reticence of Jewish artists to portray this biblical incident, while their Christian counterparts display no such hesitation.

It is therefore understandable that codifiers ignore this talmudic passage. They generally opt to follow a different talmudic passage and rule that during the *Amida* the hands should be clasped over the heart, the way a servant stands before his master with awe and respect (*B. Shabbat* 10a; *Maimonides*; *Shulḥan Arukh*). Other authorities hold that hand positioning is entirely dependent on societal norms; the posture during prayer should reflect how we would stand before a human sovereign (*Menorat HaMaor*). Thus we see that cultural environs have impacted on our prayer norms.

Various aspects of our prayer service have been influenced by the practices of our gentile neighbours. But should this be our focus as we explore prayer rituals? Jewish commentators and halakhists have rarely cited gentile norms as the motivation for prayer models, focusing instead on the contemporary import of the practised custom.

This provides us with a strong paradigm for our consideration. Much of our practice may not be organic to Jewish tradition. Nevertheless, as we adopt rituals we seek to give them relevant meaning, focusing not on the external impetus, but on the significance with which these practices invest our lives. There is a common thread that runs through the various suggestions over the generations about what to do with the hands during prayer: the goal of focusing the mind, improving concentration and assisting heartfelt communion with the Almighty. Thus one halakhist (*Arukh HaShulḥan*) contends that there is no prescribed gesture for prayer; hands should simply be positioned such that they facilitate quality prayer.

BERAKHOT 16B

Heralding the onset of a new month

THE TALMUD TELLS us that various sages would add personal supplications after finishing the formal prayer service. Some of these heartfelt prayers have made their way into our liturgy and become part of our fixed prayer service. Rav's prayer addendum has become a standard part of the text recited in the Ashkenazi prayer rite on the Shabbat that precedes Rosh Ḥodesh (the first day of the new lunar month). In this prayer we announce the beginning of the new month and pray for it to be a blessed one.

As we look to the onset of a new month, the words of Rav's prayer are most appropriate (*B. Berakhot* 16b): "May it be Your will, God our Lord, that You give us long life, a life of peace, a life of goodness, a life of blessing, a life of sustenance, a life of physical health, a life in which there is fear of sin, a life in which there is no shame or humiliation, a life of wealth and of honour, a life in which we have a love of Torah and a fear of heaven, a life in which You fulfil all our heart's desires for good."

Beyond the desire to ask for a month blessed with manifold goodness, the passage mentions the term "life" eleven times. This corresponds to the eleven times each year when we bless the new month. It is only before the month of Tishrei, the onset of the new year, that we do not pronounce the blessing.

When we examine this prayer, a number of questions arise. Let us examine three of the issues: the text of the prayer, the meaning of one of the phrases and the appropriateness of the prayer for Shabbat.

1. THE CARELESS TYPESETTER

The most obvious issue concerns the text. As with so many prayers, over the ages the wording of the prayer has evolved slightly. Thus what we find in some prayer books does not exactly match the original text recorded in the Talmud. Notably, in the Hasidic tradition, three words are appended at the end of the prayer: *bizkhut tefillat Rav,* in the merit of the prayer of Rav. What might be the reason for this addition?

One avenue to understand this addition is based on the talmudic passage which comments on a literal reading of the biblical verse: *O that I might dwell in Your tent of the worlds, take refuge under Your protective wings, selah* (Psalms 61:5). The sages note that the psalmist appears to be requesting to live in two worlds simultaneously. The Talmud explains that King David turned to the Almighty with a request that Torah should be cited in his name posthumously in this world. Indeed, we have a tradition that when Torah is cited in the name of a deceased scholar, it is as if the lips of the deceased in the grave move along with those of the living scholar . Thus the dead can be said to be alive in two worlds concurrently (*B. Yevamot* 96b–97a; *B. Bekhorot* 31b). Following this tradition, when we recite the prayer before Rosh Ḥodesh, the lips of Rav, the deceased author of the prayer, move. We ask God that our requests be granted – not in the merit of our own prayer, but in the merit of the prayer of Rav which he is reciting along with us.

Of course this begs the question: why do we not evoke the merit of other prayer authors, whose lips are also presumably reciting the prayers along with us? Perhaps we should conclude the silent *Amida* with the words "in the merit of the Men of the Great Assembly," the sages who established the text of this central prayer?

Another version records a slightly different textual addition: *bizkhut tefillat rabbim,* in the merit of the prayer of the masses. We do not generally mention individual prayer authors during the service, and this prayer should be no exception. We recall, however, the merit of the community as we ask for our requests to be granted. This approach too may be questioned: would we not want to evoke the merit of communal prayer for all our supplications, not just those recited before Rosh Ḥodesh?

Some authorities are against saying these three words altogether – not because of their content, but due to the suspect history of their inclusion. These authorities suggest that the inclusion of these words was a product of a series of mistakes. According to one explanation, the original text did not include these three words, as per the extant talmudic text. At some stage, the source of this prayer was annotated and below the text the words *tefillat Rav* were written, indicating that this was the prayer of Rav as it appears in the Talmud. An ignorant copyist or typesetter saw these words, thought they were part of the prayer, and appended them to the text. However, the words "*tefillat Rav*" have no meaning, and thus another word was added – *bizkhut,* "in the merit of." Unfortunately, the meaning of the phrase was still unclear. The merit of which "rav" was being evoked? Thus the words were altered to read *bizkhut tefillat rabbim,* and the merit of communal prayer was being called upon to justify a month filled with blessing (*Benei Yisaskhar*; *Arukh HaShulḥan*).

Another author offers a different account of the mistakes that led to the addition of the word *bizkhut.* The original annotation was *Berakhot tefillat Rav,* meaning that this was the prayer of Rav as found in the talmudic tractate *Berakhot.* Alas, a copyist saw the word *Berakhot,* mistook the Hebrew letter *reish* for the letter *zayin,* and miscopied the word *Berakhot* as *bizkhut* (*Torah Temima*).

The influence of the copyists, typesetters, printers – the so-called *boḥur-a-zetzer,* the lad whose vocation was to set the letters that were to be printed – is astounding, often perplexing and at times troubling. This is hardly the forum for an indictment of the *boḥur-a-zetzer,* or perhaps an indictment of those who entrusted him with this important task. Nevertheless this tale reminds us of the importance of meticulous transmission of our tradition, so that our children will not have to grapple with texts that we have negligently corrupted.

2. A MONTH OF EXERCISE

While the requests we recite when hailing the onset of a new month are generally standard, there is one request that is particularly cryptic and must be deciphered – our request for a life of *ḥilutz atzamot* (translated above as "a life of physical health"). What is a life of *ḥilutz atzamot*?

In Modern Hebrew the term *ḥilutz atzamot* is used for stretching the limbs or physical exercise. Thus people who are going for a walk after sitting at their computer all day might comment that they are going out *leḥaletz et ha'atzamot.* Was Rav asking for a life of stretching? Many of us acknowledge the importance of exercise, yet still find it challenging to find the time, the energy and the willpower to act. Are we asking the Almighty for assistance in this area – "Please grant us a life filled with physical exercise"? The proposition conjures up some entertaining images. Can you imagine proclaiming the new month while meditating about your treadmill, while thinking about your exercise bike, while bemoaning the fact that your gym membership has lapsed?

What was Rav thinking about when he asked for a life of *ḥilutz atzamot*? The phrase first appears in a prophecy of Isaiah: *God will guide you constantly, He will satisfy your soul with pure sustenance,* ve'atzmotekha yaḥalitz, *and you will be like a well-watered garden, like a water source whose waters do not disappoint* (Isaiah 58:11). What was the prophet Isaiah prophesying? Whenever we have a biblical word or phrase whose meaning is uncertain, the first recourse is to seek other biblical passages where the word or phrase appears.

The word *atzamot*, or *etzem* in the singular, appears throughout the Bible and undoubtedly means bones. We can see this from the very first biblical operation. The anaesthesiologist was the Almighty, who also performed the operation, and the patient was Adam. It was a delicate operation – a rib or maybe even an entire side had to be removed from Adam and reconstructed into another person, Eve. The operation was a success. When the patient awoke and saw the results, he exclaimed: *This one at last is* etzem me'atzamai (*a bone of my bones*) *and flesh of my flesh* (Genesis 2:21–23).

The meaning of the root made up of the three Hebrew letters *ḥ-l-tz* is more puzzling, for it appears to bear more than one meaning. In fact the Talmud also grapples with the meaning of this word in the context of release from levirate marriage, a procedure known as *ḥalitza* (*B. Yevamot* 102b).

The biblical verse says that part of the *ḥalitza* ceremony involves a widow doing something described by the verb *ḥ-l-tz* to the shoe of her deceased husband's brother (Deuteronomy 25:9). The Talmud questions whether she is removing the shoe from her brother-in-law's foot or putting it on his foot. From the biblical context, the Talmud concludes that the verb *ḥ-l-tz* here means "remove" – that is, the widow is to remove the shoe as part of the *ḥalitza* ceremony.

Our sages, however, acknowledge that the biblical root *ḥ-l-tz* also has other meanings, one of which is to ready or strengthen (*Vayikra Rabba* 34:15). Thus those soldiers who go first into battle are said to be the *ḥalutzim* who go before the army (see Numbers 31:5, 32:29–32; Deuteronomy 3:18). Based on this meaning of the root *ḥ-l-tz,* the pioneers who first came to the Land of Israel were called *ḥalutzim* because they readied the land for our people. In Modern Hebrew the striker in soccer is called a *ḥalutz.*

What does the verb *ḥ-l-tz* mean in the case of Rav's blessing? It would appear that Rav borrowed the phrase from Isaiah. Regarding the prophecy of Isaiah, one of the sages tells us that the promise *ve'atzmotekha yaḥalitz* is the ultimate blessing. What is so great about this blessing? Well, that may depend on the meaning of the verb in that context – does it mean to remove or does it mean to strengthen?

If *ḥ-l-tz* in the blessing means to remove, it is a promise that our bones will be removed, perhaps from the harsh judgment of hell. If it means to strengthen, then the blessing refers to the physical realm. In the list of blessings in the prophecy of Isaiah, only this blessing directly affects the body; the other blessings merely promise external benefits. This may be the reason that the blessing is so valuable (*Maharsha*). According to this approach, no bones are being removed; rather they are being strengthened.

So what did Rav mean when he requested a life of *ḥilutz atzamot*? Was he referring to removing the bones or strengthening them?

While we may not be able to resolve this with certainty, Rav's other requests appear to focus on physical well-being. Moreover, it is entirely unclear that the bones of even the worst sinners are sent to hell; it would appear that hell is a world of punishment for the *souls* of the wicked (*Riaf*).

Thus we can conclude that Rav would request – and we continue to request on the eve of each new month – that the Almighty fortify our bones and strengthen our physical bodies.

3. SHABBAT REQUESTS

Shabbat is a special time. We dress differently and we eat differently; we walk differently and try to talk differently. Everything about Shabbat is different when compared to the other days of the week. On Shabbat we even pray differently. The tempo, the tone, the tunes and the text are all Shabbat appropriate. One of the main changes to the Shabbat prayer texts is that we do not make personal requests. Thus the text of the Shabbat *Amida* is altered so that the many requests that we ask for thrice daily – health, wealth, knowledge and more – are excised.

In this light, it is surprising that Rav's personal prayer requesting manifold blessings for life has been canonised as a text recited on Shabbat. Indeed, this decision vexes some commentators. Since we generally do not voice requests on Shabbat, why do we recite this prayer asking for our well-being?

Among Karlin Hasidim, this prayer is part of the service as it is everywhere else, but they treat it differently from other prayers. Karlin Hasidim are renowned for their powerful vociferousness; one who enters a Karlin synagogue should be prepared for supplicants screaming their prayers with all their might. Strangely, Rav's prayer is recited silently without fanfare by Karlin Hasidim. Perhaps this aberration, this comparatively silent recital, is a recognition that all requests for physical needs are inappropriate for the holy day.

One codifier – the Lithuanian authority Rabbi Yeḥiel Mikhel HaLevi Epstein (1829–1908) – feels strongly about the unsuitability of this prayer to the Shabbat service. In his halakhic work, *Arukh HaShulḥan*, he wonders who permitted the introduction of this new prayer into the Shabbat rite. True, the talmudic sage Rav had recited this text, yet he had made these requests during his weekday prayer; how did this text infiltrate the Shabbat service? The *Arukh HaShulḥan*'s concerns are so strong that he concludes his discussion by declaring that if he had the power, he would excise the prayer from the Shabbat service! However, he acknowledges that the force of accepted custom is close to insurmountable and hence any change to the accepted text would be highly unlikely.

The Hasidic master and halakhic authority Rabbi Ḥayim Elazar Shapira of Munkács (1871–1937) was also troubled by this prayer. Acknowledging that at first blush it is hardly appropriate for Shabbat, the Munkatcher Rebbe explains that there is an exception to the rule banning requests on Shabbat: requests for spiritual well-being are permitted. Thus at the conclusion of the *Amida* prayer – on Shabbat, just as during the week – we turn to the Almighty and request assistance in watching what we say and in grappling with those who speak evil of us.

The Munkatcher Rebbe's approach may justify some of the

requests in the pre-Rosh Ḥodesh prayer, such as "a life in which there is fear of sin" and "a life in which we have a love of Torah and a fear of heaven." This approach, however, hardly explains all the requests. We can scarcely construe requests for "a life of sustenance" and "a life of physical health" as asking for matters of the spirit!

The Munkatcher Rebbe therefore creatively suggests a different approach based on the words *bizkhut tefillat Rav* which the Hasidic tradition appends at the end of the prayer. As noted, many commentators grapple with this strange addition. The Munkatcher Rebbe suggests that this addition may have been an attempt to come to terms with the personal nature of Rav's prayer. By adding these words we turn the prayer into a quote from the talmudic passage, making it an exercise in Torah study rather than a petitionary prayer, and thus we avoid the appearance of asking for individual needs on Shabbat.

Another halakhic authority, Rabbi Shimon Sofer (1850–1944) of Erlau (today Eger, Hungary), distinguishes between prayers and blessings. Personalised prayer requests are indeed inappropriate for Shabbat, yet blessings that have a fixed text and are an accepted part of the service are undoubtedly permitted, even if there is an apparent element of request in the prayer. Indeed a close examination of the service reveals numerous prayers that include requests. The prayer that heralds the coming of Rosh Ḥodesh should therefore pose no problem.

Perhaps we can suggest an additional approach. While Shabbat is not the time for individual requests, the community is permitted to ask for its needs. The pre-Rosh Ḥodesh prayer should not be viewed as the prayer of an individual asking for his or her own well-being. It is a communal prayer recited while all stand. In this sense, the congregation declares that the welfare of the community is dependent on the welfare of its constituents. Thus Rav's prayer – when said not as an addendum to personal prayer, but as a communal recitation – is a prayer for the well-being of the community and is therefore justifiably part of the Shabbat prayer rite.

BERAKHOT 17A

Dust in the wind

AT THE CONCLUSION of prayer, the talmudic scholar Rava would add a personal supplication: "My God, before I was formed I was unworthy, and now that I am formed it is as if I had not been formed" (*B. Berakhot* 17a). One commentator connects Rava's prayer to another talmudic passage, which reports a vote on the question as to whether, from the human perspective, it is better that we were created or whether it would have been better had we not been created (*B. Eruvin* 13b). The show of hands revealed a sombre view of life, as it was decided that it would have been better for humans not to have been born. Why? Because if one does not exist, one cannot transgress the numerous negative commandments. This is the theme of Rava's prayer as well. I may not have been worthy before I was created, for I had no merits, but now that I have been brought into the world I am certainly not worthy, for I must have sinned (*Maharsha*).

Rava continues his personal supplication: "I am dust in my life, and surely I am dust in my death. Behold, before You I am like a vessel filled with shame and disgrace." Then, having painted a picture of an existence of no value – unworthiness, dust, shame and disgrace – Rava turns to God with a request: "May it be Your will, Lord, my God, that I sin no more. And the sins which I have committed before You, erase them in Your abundant mercy, though not through suffering or serious illness."

Another talmudic sage, Rav Hamnuna Zuti, adopted this short prayer as his confessional supplication on the holiest day of the year, Yom Kippur. We follow his example, and at the end of the *Amida* at each service on Yom Kippur we recite Rava's prayer as part of the confession.

Let us focus on one aspect of Rava's prayer – "I am dust in my life, and surely I am dust in my death." What is the significance of being like dust?

The image is of biblical origin. Dust first appears as the raw material for the creation of humans (Genesis 2:7), but quickly becomes part of the curse of physicality decreed against humankind: *For you are dust and you will return to dust* (Genesis 3:19). Acknowledging our dusty beginning and end is a recognition of our nature as physical human beings in this finite world.

Further in our talmudic passage, however, we are told that another scholar, Mar bar Ravina, actually beseeched God to be like dust: "And may my soul be like dust to all." This prayer is not reserved for Yom Kippur, but is appended to the thrice-daily *Amida,* suggesting that it reflects a central theme in our tradition. Indeed, in the Bible being like dust is considered a national blessing. Amongst the first blessings God bestowed upon our ancestors was that their progeny would be *like the dust of the earth* (Genesis 13:16). In a similar vein, as Jacob fled from Beersheba after appropriating his brother's blessings, he stopped to rest at the end of the day. At this bivouac Jacob had a fantastic dream in which he perceived angels ascending and descending a ladder that was firmly planted in the ground, but that reached up to heaven. The Almighty appeared to him with a promise: *And your progeny will be like the dust of the earth* (Genesis 28:14).

How are we to understand the image of being like the dust of the earth? Is this a positive and desirable condition? Or are we asking to be downtrodden and inconsequential?

The first biblical dust-blessing was bestowed on Abraham, and God elucidated: *And I will make your offspring like the dust of the earth; if a person could count the specks of dust of the earth, then your offspring will also be countable* (Genesis 13:16). Our small nation will be so numerous that we will be uncountable. Being like dust is a quantitative blessing.

An alternative approach returns to the first biblical references to dust. As we have seen, dust evokes the physical condition of human existence, the finite and fleeting nature of life on earth. In this sense, references to our dusty character are sobering reminders that we are not gods. Perhaps the promise to our forefathers that we will be like dust is a blessing telling us that we can attain the elusive quality of humility (*Anaf Yosef*).

One commentator, focusing on the insignificance of dust, suggests that we pine for a reality in which our enemies pay no attention to us and do not bother to curse us, for we are nothing more than dust to them (*Maharsha*). Perhaps we can relate to this blessing in light of our reality. Our tiny country, Israel, draws so much global attention, a truly disproportionate amount; our every move is scrutinised on the front pages of newspapers around the world. We can certainly relate to the wish not to be the focus of so much interest.

A further explanation offered by the commentators highlights a different aspect of dust – its eternal nature. Dust is never destroyed, and we pray that the Jewish people too will be everlasting (*Tosafot*). In biblical ritual law, in cases where a house must be torn down because it is afflicted with the spiritual disease of *tzara'at*, the dust remains. Though the constituent parts must be moved outside the city limits, the dusty raw material need not be removed (Leviticus 14). So too, even when there are those who wish to wipe us out entirely, we carry on. Despite being forced to move from place to place, chased out of city and state, we survive just like the everlasting dust of the earth.

Our people strive to be like the dust of the earth. This ideal does not spring from masochistic desires to be trampled. Rather, we seek the blessings in being dust-like: being uncountable, being humble, not being noticed, and – perhaps most importantly – being eternal.

BERAKHOT 17A

Adding a personal prayer

THE COMMUNAL TENOR of our set prayers is clearly expressed by the shared endeavour of the prayer service and by the use of the plural in almost all passages. Coming to the synagogue may be as much about assembling with our fellow human beings as it is about communing with the Almighty. It is therefore surprising to find the concluding paragraph of the central *Amida* phrased in the singular: "My God, guard my tongue from evil and my lips from speaking falsehood. May my soul be silent towards those who insult me, and may my soul be lowly like dust before all. Open my heart to Your Torah, and may my soul pursue Your commandments. As for all who plot evil against me, may You hastily thwart their counsel and upset their design." This prayer is followed by a biblical verse, also in the first person singular: *May the words of my mouth and the meditation of my heart be acceptable before You, God, my Stronghold and my Redeemer* (Psalms 19:15).

The source of this final paragraph of the *Amida* sheds light on the language employed. The Talmud records individual supplications that various sages would add before concluding their prayers (*B. Berakhot* 16b–17a). In these passages, the sages gave voice to their personal wishes or challenges and hence used the singular instead of the more standard plural. Included in this list is the personal prayer of Mar bar Ravina, which forms the basis of the accepted concluding paragraph of the *Amida* cited above.

Drawing on other talmudic material, we can at times surmise what led the sages to intone these particular supplications. Thus Rabbi Zeira, who was known for trying to influence wayward sinners to forsake their evil ways, added a prayer for Divine assistance in resisting their enticements and not learning from their ways: "May it be Your will, Lord, our God, that we not sin, nor be ashamed or disgraced before our ancestors" (*Iyun Yaakov*).

This entreaty may have even greater significance in light of the fact that Rabbi Zeira sometimes acted in ways that his scholarly colleagues disapproved of (*B. Sanhedrin* 37a). The Talmud relates that there was a group of thugs in the neighbourhood of Rabbi Zeira. Contrary to the approach of the sages, Rabbi Zeira befriended these uncouth neighbours. Upon his demise, the hooligans said: "Up until now, the short man with singed legs" – referring to the diminutive Rabbi Zeira – "prayed for mercy on our behalf. Now who will entreat God for clemency on our behalf?" With that, the ruffians did some soul-searching and resolved to repent.

Another example in which the Talmud provides a window into the personal prayer of a sage is Rabbi Yoḥanan's additional prayer at the end of his *Amida*: "May it be Your will, Lord, our God, that You look upon our shame and behold our unfortunate plight, and consequently attire Yourself with Your mercy, cover Yourself with Your strength, wrap Yourself with Your kindness and gird Yourself with Your graciousness. May the attribute of Your goodness and humility come before You."

Knowing what we do about Rabbi Yoḥanan, we can understand why he beseeched the Almighty to look upon his ill-fated existence. Rabbi Yoḥanan's ten sons all predeceased him. Rabbi Yoḥanan was distraught by this loss and could not bear the finality of parting from his children. He carried the bone of his tenth son with him wherever he went, as a reminder of his bereavement (*B. Berakhot* 5b; *Rashi*). Even his health was unenviable, as he was plagued by serious illness such that only during the winter was he strong enough to wear *tefillin* properly. During the summer, when his head was not sufficiently strong, he donned *tefillin* on his arm but not on his head (*Y. Berakhot* 4c). Rabbi Yoḥanan suffered from the life-threatening disease *tzafidna*, a scurvy-like condition that involved bleeding from the gums and that spread from the mouth to the intestines (*B. Yoma* 84a; *B. Avoda Zara* 28a). Considering these hardships, we can understand Rabbi Yoḥanan's heartfelt plea that God look upon his miserable plight and mercifully put an end to his troubles.

It is perhaps ironic that some of the supplications recorded in the Talmud, albeit with minor changes in syntax, have become institutionalised as part of our set prayer service. As we noted, one passage serves as the final paragraph of the thrice-daily *Amida*. One personal prayer is recited daily in the morning service. One supplication forms part of the additional Shabbat blessing that precedes a new month. A fourth passage is added to the end of the *Amida* on Yom Kippur. What can be said about this incongruous situation, in which personal prayers giving voice to an individual's predicament become part of an established prayer service?

The inclusion of such prayers may reveal the insightful abilities of our sages to compose personal prayers that seem to express each person's individual experiences as well. Who today can say that a prayer asking God to guard our mouths from falsehood is no longer relevant? Can we claim that an entreaty for God to mercifully consider our troubles has no currency in our world? Clearly these prayers are still relevant.

Moreover, these personal prayers may remind us of the timeless nature of human experience. The challenges faced by our sages in days gone by are distant only in chronology, not in essence. We, too, hope that our hearts can be pried open so the gems of our tradition can enter and enrich our existence. We, too, wish for the Almighty to frustrate the evil designs of our adversaries. We, too, want to meet God when He is wrapped in mercy and kindness.

Perhaps the institutionalisation of these prayers in the first person singular has an operative lesson as well. They remind us that in addition to what appears in our prayer books, a personal element should be included in our supplications. This private, individual prayer should be an addendum akin to the additions of our sages, giving voice to our own needs, hopes and desires as reflected by our own unique personal journey.

BERAKHOT 17A

Nachas for God

AT THE END of studying the book of Job, Rabbi Yoḥanan would say: "A person's end is to die, an animal's end is for slaughter and all are poised for death." He would then temper his sombre words by adding: "Fortunate is the one who grew in Torah, whose toil is in Torah, who gives *naḥat ru'aḥ*" – meaning pleasure, joy and pride or *nachas* in Yiddish parlance – "to his Creator, who grew up with a good name and who departed from the world with a good name. Of such a person, Solomon said: *A good name is better than good oil, and the day of death* [*is better*] *than the day of his birth* (Ecclesiastes 7:1)" (*B. Berakhot* 17a).

The sobering tale of Job is part of the Bible, yet it is not read at any set time during the year. Indeed, Job is one of the texts that can be read at times when Torah study is generally prohibited, namely when a person is mourning or on the fast of *Tisha B'Av* (the Ninth of Av), the designated day of Jewish national mourning (*B. Ta'anit* 30a). But even then, Job is not read publicly. Why then did Rabbi Yoḥanan make a habit of reading this biblical book so frequently that he was known for what he would say when he concluded the book?

Responding to this question, one commentator recalls that Rabbi Yoḥanan suffered great misfortune during his life, burying many children and carrying the scar of the tragedy wherever he went (*B. Berakhot* 5b). Thus he had the unfortunate opportunity to regularly read Job (*Torah Temima*).

Commentators ask: what was it about the book of Job that prompted Rabbi Yoḥanan's sombre words? One commentator focuses on the end of the book, where Job dies with a good reputation. This ending prompted Rabbi Yoḥanan to meditate on the importance of a good name (*Rashi*). Another commentator notes that the majority of the book deals with death and human suffering. Rabbi Yoḥanan was therefore moved to comment on these themes (*Maharsha*).

A close reading of Rabbi Yoḥanan's words reveals something surprising in one of his comments: "Fortunate is the one who grew in Torah, whose toil is in Torah, who gives *naḥat ru'aḥ* to his Creator." From Rabbi Yoḥanan's words it would appear that growing and toiling in Torah are distinct from giving pleasure to the Almighty. Doesn't God get *nachas* from those who grow in Torah and who toil in Torah?

The commentators notice this slight anomaly, and offer a variety of approaches to resolve it. One references the talmudic adage: "If someone is greater than his fellow, his evil inclination is greater than his fellow's" (*B. Sukka* 52a). Thus those dedicated to the pursuit of Torah bear the burden of a powerful evil inclination. Despite the unrelenting temptation they must deal with, the Almighty still has *nachas* from their efforts (*Iyun Yaakov*).

Another commentator explains Rabbi Yoḥanan's words by addressing the issue of the motivation for Torah study. A person may learn the hallowed texts of our tradition for purposes other than the lofty goal of connecting to the Almighty. Alas, there are those who study Torah as a means to an end – to achieve recognition or status. Such Torah study does not provide the Almighty with *nachas*; the only ones who derive pleasure from such study are the learner and his evil inclination. Thus, Torah study does not perforce entail *nachas* for God, and hence Rabbi Yoḥanan noted it as a goal in and of itself (*Riaf*).

A variation on this theme appears in the writings of another commentator. A person may study Torah solely for his own enjoyment – the challenge of deciphering a difficult text, of unraveling perplexing sources, of mentally engaging an existential issue. While such a venture is considered Torah study, it hardly gives *nachas* to the Almighty (*Anaf Yosef*). To be sure, Torah study should be enjoyable, yet this should not be the central motivation to study.

The Hasidic master Rabbi Mordekhai Leifer of Nadvorna (d. 1895) – following the commentators cited – expounds on Torah study that does not give God *nachas*. He begins by quoting the mishnaic dictum that distinguishes between the students of Abraham who merit this world and the World to Come, and the students of Balaam who are destined for Gehenna (*M. Avot* 5:19). Rabbi Mordekhai of Nadvorna notes that apparently Balaam was also a teacher – a rabbi of sorts – and he too had students. Alas, not all teachers are cut of one cloth. Imagine a teacher sitting with students lecturing. Suddenly, in the middle of the class, someone rushes in and breathlessly relates that a certain person has been incarcerated and is in dire need of immediate assistance. "Redeeming captives!" shouts the news bearer and turns to the teacher: "Can you go and argue his case before the authorities?" Imagine that the teacher responds: "I am busy teaching Torah now. As we all know, Torah study is the equivalent of all the other *mitzvot* put together. I am sorry, but I am unavailable at this time." This – explains Rabbi Mordekhai of Nadvorna – is the classroom of Balaam, and from such Torah study God has no *nachas*.

In contrast, imagine that the teacher gallantly turns to the students and says: "Pass me my coat. Let's go and plead before the authorities on behalf of our imprisoned brother." This is the classroom of Abraham our forefather. Such Torah study, though it has been interrupted, gives the Almighty great pleasure.

These approaches point in a common direction. While learning Torah is a grand endeavour, it should be conducted in the appropriate manner; otherwise, we can hardly expect it will please the Almighty. Thus Torah studied for personal gain or for pleasure alone is sullied by the impure motive; Torah studied without regard for the surrounding society, for our fellow human beings, is also lacking. Learning Torah may be among the worthiest enterprises of our tradition, yet even noble pursuits should be approached in the appropriate manner so that their potential is fully realised. Then, and only then, will God *shep nachas* from us.

BERAKHOT 17A–B

See your world in your life

AT THE END of any undertaking it is natural to assess the quality and impact of the experience. On occasion, we share these thoughts and feelings with those around us or with loved ones. At other times, these emotions linger in our consciousness, perhaps guiding our future course of action. What sentiments accompany us at the conclusion of an encounter with the texts of our tradition? How do we leave the *beit midrash*?

At the conclusion of a study session, as the sages prepared to leave the *beit midrash*, they would offer each other a heartening parting blessing (*B. Berakhot* 17a): "May you see your world in your life, and may your end be life in the World to Come and your hope for many generations. May your heart deliberate with understanding, may your mouth speak wisdom and may your tongue bring forth song. May your eyelids look straight before you, may your eyes be enlightened with the light of Torah and may your face be radiant like heaven. May your lips express knowledge and your insides rejoice in uprightness, and may your steps hasten to hear the words of the Ancient of Days."

Thus the sages give voice to the lofty goal of employing various parts of the body in the pursuit of godliness outside the protective cocoon of the *beit midrash*. These parting words speak of hope for future interactions with our beloved texts. They express a desire that the study endeavour should not be limited to the confines of the *beit midrash*, but should radiate beyond the walls of the study hall. As we step into a reality laden with physicality, as we travel through a world fraught with mundane distractions, we pray that the Divine encounter with the texts of our tradition will accompany us on our journey and illuminate our existence.

The opening of the parting blessing, however, is cryptic: "May you see your world in your life." What is meant by "your world" which we aspire to experience during our own lifetime? We shall see two approaches to this question, one that relates the phrase to this world and one that relates it to the next.

1. MASTER CHEFS OF THE FUTURE

This parting blessing of the sages is juxtaposed in the Talmud with the parting words of the sages from another study centre (*B. Berakhot* 17a–b). The words of these sages may shed light on the aspiration of seeing "our world" during our lifetime.

The sages would quote a biblical verse: *Our leaders are laden; there is no breach and no going out and no outcry in our streets* (Psalms 144:14). They add a short commentary on each phrase of the verse, explaining that *our leaders* in Torah should be *laden* with good deeds and the fortified wall of the tradition should strengthen participants, preventing betrayal of the values of our heritage. Thus the parting words affirm the vigour of the *beit midrash* enterprise, recognising the champions of the study hall and the potency of the educational venture, and coupling this avowal with a prayer for fidelity to our heritage. A truly encouraging expression to sum up the learning session.

Here too, however, one phrase – the very next request – is puzzling: "May we not have a child or a student who burns his food in public." Surely, we cannot be so concerned about the culinary skills of our protégés. It would indeed be bizarre if after a meaningful experience we parted ways with the words: "Be careful to turn off the oven!"

Elsewhere in rabbinic literature, we hear of the seriousness of burning food, when the sages discuss legitimate grounds for divorce (*M. Gittin* 9:10). According to one opinion, a husband may not divorce his wife unless he has found her immodest or unchaste. A dissenting opinion suggests that even if she ruins a dish it is valid grounds for divorce. The commentators attempt to mitigate this seemingly harsh opinion, offering a variety of explanations for how her culinary misconduct could justify the initiation of divorce proceedings. Some explain that burning the food is only the tip of an iceberg of acrimony that holds sway in the house. Others suggest that the wife consistently and spitefully burns the food in an attempt to annoy her husband. However we understand the wife's culinary practices, it seems we are not suggesting that a mere inability to cook is grounds for divorce.

Let us return to the blessing that asks that a child or student not burn the food. Here too, we are not simply pining for talented cooks in the future. Hopeless cooking should be understood metaphorically as referring to being careless about the task at hand. Sitting in the *beit midrash* is akin to preparing a meal: we pore over the text with care, cutting it into choice bite-size pieces and letting it stew until it is ready to be digested. An exquisitely prepared dinner is starkly different from a dish carelessly thrown together, and a Torah passage studied with care and grace cannot be compared to a sloppy reading. As we depart from the *beit midrash*, we pray that we have produced master chefs with refined tastes and not a generation that sees fast-food as the crowning achievement of the food industry. We hope that our offspring and disciples have been trained in patience and precision, and that they appreciate the fruits of toiling over the texts of our tradition with the goal of producing a dish of the finest calibre.

Returning to the first passage and bearing in mind the juxtaposition of the two parting formulae, we can now suggest a new understanding of the goodbye well-wish: "May you see your world in your life." What could be more "your world" than children and students? We dedicate so much time and effort to rearing the next generation, and it is in this future that we invest so much energy. Our personal encounters in the *beit midrash* may be spiritually satisfying on a personal level. Yet as we conclude, we express the hope that we will see a generation filled with diligence, devotion and patience. We look towards a future which will provide the necessary ingredients for an uncharred culinary masterpiece, the pinnacle of the *beit midrash* encounter.

2. A TASTE OF THE WORLD TO COME

Some commentators suggest that the blessing to "see your world in your life" refers to a life in which all physical needs are satisfied. Thus the parting blessing refers first to life in this world – "May you see your world in your life," and then continues with good wishes for the future – "and may your end be life in the World to Come, and your hope for many generations" (*Rashi*; *Maharsha*).

One of the Spanish commentators offers a different approach (*Ritva*). He understands both parts of the sentence to be referring to a reality that goes beyond our temporal existence: "When a person attains ultimate wisdom, it is akin to reaching the world of souls, for they are pure intellect. In this state the person attains a measure of the world of souls within his lifetime." The blessing should therefore be understood thus: may you see a portion of your World to Come during your physical, earthly lifetime.

The mystically minded halakhist and Hasidic master Rabbi Ḥayim Elazar Shapira of Munkács (1871–1937) seems to follow this second reading of the blessing. There is a halakha which states that if you have made the blessing on wine, and then a superior vintage is placed in front of you, you make an additional blessing (*Shulḥan Arukh, Oraḥ Ḥayim* 175). The Munkatcher Rebbe reports that his ancestors usually avoided reciting this blessing. However, his father and predecessor in Munkács, Rabbi Zvi Hirsch (1850–1913), would organise an annual gathering where he would make sure to meet even the most stringent halakhic requirements in order to make this blessing over a superior glass of wine. This special gathering was held in his *sukka* late on the second night of Sukkot. Each year at this assembly, Rabbi Zvi Hirsch would retell the story of Rabbi Ḥayim Yeḥiel Meir Shapira (c. 1789–1848), the Hasidic master known as the Seraph of Mogielnica.

The Seraph once drank a cup of wine at the festive meal on Shemini Atzeret – the eighth day appended to the festival of Sukkot – and announced that in the future we will have unparalleled spiritual enjoyment. All the prophecies will be fulfilled and we will even drink the wine of the Creator. Alas, what will be the importance of any beverage, even the wine of the Almighty, at the end of days?

"Therefore," continued the Seraph, turning to the Almighty, "Let us sample now the taste of the Creator's wine while we are still in bitter exile in this world." After these words, the Seraph sipped from the cup of wine he held in his hand.

The Munkatcher Rebbe returned to his father's practice: "Thus my father acted for a number of years before his passing. Each year on the second night of Sukkot at the appointed hour he would recount the words of the Seraph. In the year 1913, on the second night of Sukkot around that very time, my father passed away."

The Munkatcher Rebbe continued, reporting about the final

hours of the rabbinic pietist, Rabbi Amram Ḥasida (d. 1830), who in 1816 moved from Hungary to the Land of Israel. "Moments before the passing of Rabbi Amram Ḥasida, he recited a blessing with the Almighty's name stating that he had savoured the taste of the World to Come." Other sources record the text of Rabbi Amram's unique benediction: "Blessed are you God, our Lord, King of the universe, Who enlightens His servants with the light that has been hidden since the six days of creation."

The Munkatcher Rebbe concluded these tales with a cryptic mention of our talmudic passage: "This reflects the idea of 'You will see your world in your life,' and those with understanding will understand." The Munkatcher Rebbe thereby alluded to the fact that the Seraph of Mogielnica, Rabbi Amram Ḥasida and his father Rabbi Zvi Hirsch had in some way tasted the sweetness of the World to Come while still in this world.

A taste of the World to Come may be beyond the grasp of many of us; when we drink wine what we taste is the essence of the grapes, the meticulous caring of the vintner. The Munkatcher Rebbe may be suggesting that experiences of this world have a further dimension – the Divine spiritual plane that we seek. Thus when we enjoy *kiddush* wine every Friday night and on festivals, we hope to taste not only wine; we also aspire to savour the spiritual flavour of a Divine existence, even as we remain in this world.

Berakhot
Chapter Three

BERAKHOT 18A–B

Tiresome review

WHY DO WE need to review? Reviewing material already studied is such a laborious task. It lacks the excitement of uncharted waters, and once we have encountered an idea we are often loath to hear it again. Review is one of the more tiresome tasks that teachers set for their pupils, who often whine: "We have already done this." Adults, too, have a kneejerk negative reaction to a lesson already studied. Undeniably, the thrill of encountering new ideas makes learning a stimulating and thought-provoking venture. What then is the importance of review?

The Talmud reports a conversation between two sages, Rabbi Ḥiyya and Rabbi Yonatan, as they walked through a cemetery (*B. Berakhot* 18a–b). Rabbi Yonatan's *tzitzit* were hanging out, perhaps dragging over the graves as he walked (*Tur*). Rabbi Ḥiyya, who believed that the dead in their graves were cognizant of their surroundings, berated his colleague: "Lift up your garment, lest the deceased say, 'Tomorrow they will be joining us and now they mock us!'" Proudly displaying *tzitzit* taunts the dead, who no longer have the ability to wear the fringed four-cornered garment, or for that matter fulfil any of the commandments.

Rabbi Yonatan, however, was of the opinion that the deceased are unaware of their surroundings and therefore would not feel such an affront. He retorted: "Do the departed know so much? Doesn't Scripture say *For the living know that they will die, but the dead know nothing at all* (Ecclesiastes 9:5)!"

Rabbi Ḥiyya responded: "If you have read this verse once, you must not have reviewed it a second time. If you did review it a second time, you must not have reviewed it a third time. And if you did review it a third time, you must not have had it explained to you properly! For in truth, the biblical verse should be understood differently. *For the living* – referring to the righteous, who even after they have departed are called living – *know that they will die*, and hence consciously and purposefully direct their actions. The verse continues: *but the deceased* – referring to the wicked, who even in their lifetime are called dead – *know nothing at all*, for they do not consider the final reckoning of their misconduct, and continue to sin."

Rabbi Ḥiyya's spirited response points to an educational programme that requires encountering a text more than once in order to truly fathom its meaning. According to Rabbi Ḥiyya, had Rabbi Yonatan meticulously revisited the biblical passage, he most certainly would have understood the verse differently. As if to buttress this point, Rabbi Yonatan retracted his position after hearing Rabbi Ḥiyya's interpretation. Thus review is paramount to gaining full understanding.

Another talmudic passage describing the post-Sinai learning programme seems to offer a different reason for multiple encounters with the same text (*B. Eruvin* 54b). Having received the Torah from the Almighty, Moses set about transmitting the tradition to the nation. First, Moses gave the same lesson three times in a row: first to Aaron, then to Aaron together with his sons Elazar and Itamar and then to the three of them together with the seventy Elders. After the three classes, all those who sought the Divine word were welcome to come to the fourth lesson. Aaron, having been present for all four lessons, then assumed the role of teacher. Similarly, Elazar and Itamar and the Elders shouldered the responsibility for spreading the tradition once they had studied the tradition four times. Thus mastery of the material that conferred the right to serve as a teacher of the tradition was conditioned on encountering the tradition more than once.

The passage does not relate to Moses' education. One commentator understands that Moses too reviewed the tradition he received from the Almighty numerous times before teaching Aaron (*Maharsha*). Another source goes further. Citing the verses *Then He saw it and He declared it; He established it and also searched it out. And to humans He said…* (Job 28:27–28), the sages note that four verbs are used before any communication with humans. They conclude that the Almighty privately pored over the Torah four times before conveying it to the Children of Israel (*Shemot Rabba* 40:1).

In connection with this biblical verse, it is reported that Rabbi Akiva was once invited to read the Torah, yet he balked, saying that he had not properly reviewed the passage. For this, Rabbi Akiva was duly praised by his peers. Thus mastery of the tradition is dependent on multiple encounters with the text.

A third approach, offered by one commentator, explains that the first three encounters with a text are necessary to understand it. The fourth reading reflects a desire to study the material for no purpose other than for the sake of the Almighty (*Maharsha*). Elsewhere in rabbinic tradition we are told that even the 100th reading does not compare to the 101st; for while one who studies one hundred times is truly a righteous person, the extra encounter that goes beyond reflects even greater devotion to the Almighty (*B. Ḥagiga* 9b). Following this line of thought we can understand that review of Torah material may have a spiritual purpose that goes beyond mere understanding and mastery. Revisiting the tradition reflects a relationship of love. Just as we return time and again to people and places that are dear to us, so too we return to the beloved texts of our tradition.

Perhaps a fourth approach to review is expressed in the maxim of the sages that encourages us to revisit the Torah, considering it over and over again, each time analysing the text from a different perspective (*M. Avot* 5:22). We examine it and re-examine it because each time we see it from a different angle, the light is refracted slightly differently, and the colours are combined uniquely.

Reviewing a text assists understanding and may even lead to mastery. Studying it more than the prescribed number of times also reflects pure motives of devotion and fidelity. Moreover, each new encounter with the tradition sheds fresh light on it, illuminating further aspects embedded within the text. The timeless texts of our tradition can be explored time and again, with each new encounter consolidating what we have studied and revealing new understandings and innovative paths.

BERAKHOT 18A–19A

What do the dead know?

WHEN WE VISIT a cemetery or remember a lost loved one, we may find ourselves wondering whether the deceased are aware of us. Do they know what we are thinking about, what we are feeling? Do they empathise with our travails? Do they see our actions? Our talmudic sages are divided over the question of what the dead know. They offer three approaches (*B. Berakhot* 18a–19a).

The first approach, which – as mentioned above – is ascribed to Rabbi Ḥiyya, holds that the deceased know everything that is going on in this world and even discuss their surroundings. Thus Rabbi Ḥiyya berated his colleague Rabbi Yonatan for walking in the cemetery with his *tzitzit* dragging over the graves: "Lift up your garment, lest the deceased say, 'Tomorrow they will be joining us and now they mock us!'" In this vein, we are instructed not to enter a cemetery wearing *tefillin* or reading from a Torah scroll. According to some codifiers, it is not permitted to enter a graveyard carrying a Torah scroll, even if it is totally covered (*Shulḥan Arukh, Yoreh De'ah* 242:4). Elsewhere, a similar restriction is cited regarding the reading of *Shema* in a cemetery (*B. Sota* 43b). Likewise, we are enjoined that in the presence of the dead we should speak solely of matters that pertain to the deceased and avoid Torah discourse (*B. Berakhot* 3b).

These restrictions fall under the rubric of the verse: *One who mocks the poor affronts his Maker* (Proverbs 17:5). Brazenly displaying the opportunities we have for fulfilling God's commandments mocks the enforced inaction imposed by death. Thus the deceased are cognizant of their surroundings and may feel insulted, envious and perhaps even spiteful.

Rabbi Yonatan, traipsing through the cemetery with his *tzitzit* flowing behind him, was of a different opinion. He felt that the finality of death precluded any knowledge of worldly matters. Adducing scriptural support, Rabbi Yonatan was of the opinion that the deceased would not feel any affront – or for that matter, anything at all – on account of his blatant *tzitzit* wearing. The dead, he held, are unaware of the living. Later in the passage we are told that Rabbi Yonatan retracted his original position and accepted the view that the dead are cognizant of this world. Nevertheless, Rabbi Yonatan's initial approach may be behind the colourful declaration of another sage: "Disparaging the deceased is akin to disparaging a stone." This implies that the dead know nothing of our deeds, although it may possibly indicate that they merely do not care.

A middle position emerges from an episode with the sons of Rabbi Ḥiyya, Yehuda and Ḥizkiya, who travelled to their estates in distant villages. They stayed so long that they forgot the Torah they had studied, and subsequently went to great and painful lengths to recall it. Bemoaning their unfortunate plight, one brother turned to his sibling and asked: "Does our deceased father, Rabbi Ḥiyya, know about our anguish?"

Despite having forgotten his learning, the other brother replied: "It is written *His sons may attain honour and he*" – referring to the deceased – "*will not know it* (Job 14:21)." So our father is unaware of our distress.

The first brother countered: "Yet it is written *But his flesh will pain him and his spirit will mourn for him* (Job 14:22), and the sages have noted that a worm is as painful to the dead as a needle is to living flesh." The dead, it seems, do sense the decomposition of their bodies. Surely, our father must perceive our predicament.

The Talmud reconciles these texts: the deceased know of their own suffering, but are unaware of the pain of others. Further in the passage other exceptions are offered. Though the dead are not fully informed of worldly goings-on, they may be updated by the recently deceased. Alternatively, Duma, the angel appointed over the souls of the departed, can announce to the deceased who will be joining them. Our passage seems to conclude that indeed the deceased are aware of at least some worldly events.

On the basis of our passage, one of the commentaries elsewhere reaches the diametrically opposite conclusion, namely that the dead know nothing of this earthly world (*Tosafot*). Considering a further passage, this commentary is willing to acknowledge one exception: the dead can be made aware of our troubles through our prayer.

Alas, until our dying day we may never know the resolution of this conundrum. Yet the great rabbinic leader, mystic and legalist, Rabbi Yehonatan Eybeschütz (1690–1764), offers an appealing solution to the problem. He begins by citing the classic talmudic maxim "These and those are the words of the living God" (*B. Eruvin* 13b; *B. Gittin* 6b), which refers to conflicting normative opinions and implies that in an argument all positions reflect the Divine in some way. Building on this premise, Rabbi Eybeschütz suggests that in our passage, both opinions are true in that they are referring to two different kinds of people – some of the deceased are aware of what is occurring in this world, while others are not.

Rabbi Eybeschütz illustrates these two types. There are righteous people who live their lives caring for others, looking out for their neighbours and generally being interested in the public good and the society around them. Such people continue to be aware of the physical world even after their deaths, just as they were during their lifetime.

There are also people who may be extremely righteous in private, but they distance themselves from others during their lifetime. Such people find no time to consider the plight of those around them and the welfare of others, nor are they involved in communal ventures. In death, they continue to be unaware of their physical surroundings, as disconnected from this earthly world as they always were.

Rabbi Eybeschütz tries to avoid any value judgment of these two personalities; both may be righteous people with altruistic goals. Their worldly demeanour, however, continues to have impact even after their death.

As we go about our daily lives, it may be worth considering the proposition that our earthly conduct and interaction with our environs may one day define our post-death existence.

BERAKHOT 18B

Last-minute preparations

WHILE WE ARE judged on Rosh HaShana for our conduct over the entire year, we often seek to garner last-minute merits as the year draws to a close. How effective are these last-minute spiritual preparations?

The Talmud relates a tale of a pious person who, during a period of drought, gave a dinar to a pauper on the eve of Rosh HaShanah (*B. Berakhot* 18b). According to one commentator, the pious man may have been Rabbi Yehuda bar Ilai, who himself was extremely poor (*Maharsha*). It may very well have been the last coin left in the house, and his wife was not happy with his generosity. Feeling uncomfortable in the face of his wife's jibes and perhaps seeking solitude at this holy juncture in the Jewish calendar, the pious man went to the cemetery to spend the night there.

While in the graveyard he heard two spirits conversing with each other. One said: "My friend, let us roam the world and hear what is being said behind the curtain that partitions off the Divine Presence. We will hear of the misfortune that will come to the world this year."

"I cannot join you," responded the other spirit, "For I am buried in a matting of reeds." Apparently, when disembodied spirits roam the world, they appear dressed in their burial shrouds. The deceased spirit was embarrassed that her family had been too poor to purchase linen shrouds, and had been compelled to bury her in reed matting (*Ritva*).

Yet the trapped spirit did not begrudge her friend's roaming. She suggested: "You go, and tell me whatever you hear."

The spirit headed out, drifted around and returned to the cemetery. "My friend, what did you hear from behind the curtain?" asked the captive spirit.

"I heard that the crops of anyone who sows this winter at the time of the first rain will be destroyed by hail." Agriculture in the Land of

Israel is dependent on the winter rains. Generally there are three periods of rain: the first begins on the seventeenth of Ḥeshvan, the second on the twenty-third of the same month and the third on the first of Kislev. Crops planted at the first rainfall grow stiff by the second rainfall. If hail comes in the second period it may destroy the rigid plants. Seeds sown at the second rainfall are not harmed by hail then, for the fledgling plants are still pliable (*Rashi*; see Exodus 9:31–32).

Hearing the prognosis, the pious man avoided sowing his grain after the first rains, instead waiting for the second rain. When the hail came, the crops of many were destroyed, while the pious man's grain was unaffected.

Having benefited from a night in the cemetery, the pious person returned there the following year. Once again he heard the same two spirits scheming. The first one proposed: "My friend, let us roam the world and hear what is being said behind the curtain about the misfortunes that will come to the world this year."

"Did I not already tell you," replied the second spirit, "I cannot come with you for I am buried in a matting of reeds. You go, and tell me what you hear."

One commentator explains that the spirit declined to roam not because of embarrassment, as we suggested above, but because she was not free to wander until her body had decomposed. For this reason we bury the deceased in linen shrouds that decompose quickly, thus allowing a spirit to disengage from its body. In this case, the reed matting was slowing down the process and the spirit was therefore not free to roam. Her fellow spirit returned the next year with the same proposal, anticipating that the shroud would have decomposed over the year and set her friend free. Alas, this eventuality had yet to transpire (*Tzlaḥ*).

The free spirit went on her merry way. When she returned she reported: "I heard that crops sowed around the second rains will be destroyed by a dry wind." Such a blustery airstream would affect only crops recently planted. Crops planted during the first rains would have already taken root and would be able to withstand the wind (*Rashi*).

Once again the pious person acted upon the Divine decree to which he had been privy, and he reaped the rewards. His wife became suspicious and challenged him: "Last year everyone's crops were destroyed by hail except yours. And this year everyone's crops were destroyed by a dry wind except yours!" The pious person shared the entire story with his wife.

Within a short time, a quarrel broke out between the pious man's wife and the mother of the deceased girl whose spirit was trapped by the reed matting. As the two traded verbal blows, the wife scorned the mother, saying: "Come and I will show you your daughter buried dishonourably in a matting of reeds!"

When the next Rosh HaShana rolled around and the pious person camped out in the graveyard as had become his wont, he heard the free spirit urge the trapped spirit to roam and eavesdrop on what was being decreed behind the partition. The trapped spirit declined, this time for a different reason: "My friend, leave me be. The words that we have spoken between ourselves have already been heard by the living." And with that, the lifeline of the pious person to Divine decrees was severed.

What was the initial deed that brought about the change in fortune for the pious man? Perhaps it was his charitable act of helping out a pauper in times of trouble. This could be why the poor spirit buried in the reed matting was the appropriate medium for helping this pious man. Perhaps it was that the pious man had silently accepted his wife's taunts, preferring to avoid conflict rather than respond in kind. This would appear to be true in light of the subsequent squabble that precipitated the severing of his direct line to the Divine rulings. Or perhaps the pious person's deeds were merely reflective of his conduct over the entire year. We can never know with certainty, but the passage certainly seems to suggest that spontaneous acts of kindness may change one's fortune, and that prosperity can come from unexpected quarters.

BERAKHOT 18B

Public funds

Leaders at all levels of society bear responsibility for dispensing public funds. Charities need to consider carefully how they will distribute the monies so kindly entrusted to them. Which individuals are most worthy? Which individuals are most needy? Governments agonise over how to allocate scarce resources, with budget debates often the most protracted issue in a parliament and its committees. Even householders need to weigh their options wisely as they set aside a portion of their income for worthwhile philanthropic causes. While it is a privilege to make such decisions, the decision-maker is held responsible for his choices, and those entrusted to make such important determinations must be dependable, trustworthy and reliable.

The Talmud relates a tale dealing with the accountability of someone entrusted with public money (*B. Berakhot* 18b). The father of the talmudic scholar Shmuel was entrusted with orphans' money. When Shmuel's father passed away, his son was not by his side, and his father had told no one where he kept the orphans' money.

Suspecting the worst, people began to taunt Shmuel, calling him "the son of the one who consumed the orphans' money." Troubled by this snide heckling and hurt by the affront to his father's honour, Shmuel made his way to the courtyard of the cemetery. As a *kohen*, Shmuel could not enter the cemetery grounds, and remained outside the burial area (*B. Megilla* 22a). Shmuel faced the graves and addressed the deceased: "I seek Abba."

Abba was a popular name, and the dead spirits retorted: "There are many Abbas here."

Seeking to provide more detailed information, Shmuel responded: "I seek Abba the son of Abba."

This, too, was insufficient: "There are many Abbas the son of Abba here."

"I seek Abba the son of Abba, the father of Shmuel. Where is he?"

"He has ascended to the heavenly academy."

In the meantime, Shmuel spied the spirit of a former colleague, Levi, who was sitting at a distance from the other spirits. They appeared to be sitting in a circle, while Levi had positioned himself outside that ring.

"Why are you sitting outside the circle?" inquired Shmuel.

Levi responded: "I have not been admitted to the heavenly academy on account of the distress I caused Rabbi Afeis when I declined to go to his academy. I have been barred entry for the equivalent number of years that I did not accord Rabbi Afeis the respect due to him" (see *B. Ketubot* 103b). Despite being worthy of joining the heavenly academy, Levi was not granted entrance. Nevertheless, he did not belong in the circle of the undeserving spirits either. Thus he sat alone (*Gra*).

It is unclear why the Levi episode is a necessary part of this tale. Perhaps recounting Levi's punishment for paining Rabbi Afeis is an indication of the retribution that awaited those who maliciously insinuated a misappropriation of the orphans' money by Shmuel's father.

While Levi and Shmuel were talking, Shmuel's deceased father arrived. Shmuel noticed that his father was both crying and laughing. Shmuel asked: "Why are you crying?"

The father replied: "For you will soon be coming here to join me," implying that Shmuel's death was approaching.

Hearing news of his impending demise, Shmuel quickly asked: "Why then are you laughing?"

"For you are highly regarded in this world," answered the deceased father. He may have been referring either to the world of the living or to the heavenly realm.

Seizing the opportunity to help his peer, Shmuel promptly responded: "If I am so highly regarded, then let them admit Levi to the heavenly academy on my account." The strategy worked and Levi was given leave to enter.

Now Shmuel turned to his father with the purpose of his visit: "Where is the orphans' money?"

"Go take the monies from inside the place of the millstones. The money on the top and the money on the bottom are ours, while the money in the middle belongs to the orphans."

Surprised by this method of storage, Shmuel inquired: "Why did you leave the money this way?"

"So that if robbers were to steal any of the money, they would take ours first, since our money was on top. And if the dirt was to cause some of the money to rot, our money at the bottom would be destroyed before the orphans' funds were affected." Not only had Shmuel's father not pilfered the orphans' money, he had gone to great lengths to protect their interests, putting his own funds in danger in favour of the safety of the money of his charges.

Despite being a learned and pious person (*B. Beitza* 16b; *Rashi, Ḥullin* 111b), Shmuel's father appears as a nondescript character. Throughout rabbinic literature, he is known simply as his famed son's father. In this passage, where we are privy to his name – Abba – we learn that it is the most common of names. Even when his spirit is called from the dead, it is raised by the name of his illustrious son: "I seek Abba the son of Abba, the father of Shmuel."

Yet Shmuel's father is a paragon of virtue. Custodians of public funds must be extremely concerned with the well-being of their constituents, perhaps even at the expense of their own personal financial security. How we would laud contemporary leaders were they to improve the lot of their constituents at their own expense!

The seemingly characterless name of Shmuel's father – Abba, meaning father – reveals his essence as a father figure to the unfortunate orphans. Just as it would be incongruous for a parent to steal from a child, it is inconceivable that Shmuel's father would embezzle the orphans' money.

Being in charge of the money of others is a privilege, but as with so many honours and opportunities, this privilege entails responsibility. A leader is more than a ruler; a leader is a civil servant, and the public interest should be paramount in any reckoning he makes. True, this sets a high moral standard, but it is a worthy benchmark to which we should aspire as we debate the best use of public funds.

BERAKHOT 19A

Reading far-fetched tales

AT TIMES WE read tales in the writing of our sages that hardly seem realistic: fantastic accounts of magical creatures, feats foreign to human experience, stories that defy rational thought. As readers of our tradition, we choose whether to accept these accounts as historical records, whether to seek a hidden message in these extraordinary tales, or whether to summarily dismiss these passages as fantasy.

There exist talmudic passages that are challenging in a different way: accounts that require no belief in the occult, but are still hard to swallow. In these cases, we need not contend with seven-headed monsters whose heads are lopped off when a sagacious assailant bows in prayer (*B. Kiddushin* 29b). All we have is people – often sages – who act in ways that while not impossible, are certainly improbable. What makes such passages challenging is that even though these accounts require no special belief in unnatural phenomena or supernatural forces, what they present is difficult to accept as fact. They seem unlikely, but they could have happened. How do we relate to such passages?

Before we suggest a possible approach, let us look at an example. We are generally enjoined to judge others favourably (*M. Avot* 1:6; *Derekh Eretz* 1:31), and our assessment of a sage's actions should be charitable. Thus we assume that a scholar caught transgressing at night has repented by morning (*B. Berakhot* 19a). Our sages buttress this rule with a number of examples (*B. Shabbat* 127b; *Eliyahu Zuta* 16). Let us recount one tale.

Once there was a person who travelled from the Upper Galilee to find work. He found employment in the south, where he toiled for three years. At the end of his service, just before Yom Kippur, he turned to his employer and requested: "Give me my wages, so that I may go and support my wife and children."

The employer responded: "I have no cash."

According to one version of the tale, the employee saw grain in the fields and hence asked: "Then give me produce."

"I have none."

Trying another tack, the worker proposed: "Give me land."

"I have none."

Perhaps seeing animals in their pens, the employee suggested: "Give me livestock."

"I have none."

"Give me pillows and bedding."

"I have none."

Crestfallen, but without protesting, the worker picked up his belongings. Empty-handed, he journeyed home.

Following the Sukkot holiday, the employer took his employee's wages and loaded three donkeys – one with food, one with drink and one with delicacies – and made his way to his worker's home. After the employer arrived and they had finished eating and drinking, he handed the employee his wages, saying: "Please tell me – when you asked for your wages, seeing that I had money on hand, and I said that I had no cash, of what did you suspect me?"

"I said – perhaps you have chanced upon cheap merchandise and purchased it with the cash."

"And when you requested livestock, seeing animals on my property, and I said that I had none, what did you think?"

"I said – perhaps you have leased your animals to others."

"And when you asked for land and I said that I had none, what did you think?"

"I said – perhaps you have rented it to others."

"And when I told you that I had no produce, what did you think?"

"I said – perhaps the produce has not been tithed."

"And when I told you I have no pillows and bedding, what did you think?"

"I said – perhaps you have consecrated all your belongings to heaven."

Surprisingly, the employer responded: "Indeed this was the case. I forswore benefit from all my belongings on account of my son Hyrkanus, as a ploy to urge him to study Torah. Later, when I came to my colleagues in the south, they annulled my vows." Concluding with a blessing for the patient worker, the employer said: "And as for you – just as you judged me favourably, so may the Omnipresent judge you favourably."

This tale sounds unconvincing to a critical ear, as do so many others like it. A sceptic would certainly claim that many of the stories preserved in rabbinic literature are self-serving: lauding the bearers of our tradition, painting them as superhuman, and granting them immunity from any criticism and – more significantly – any challenge to their authority. Such scepticism is difficult to allay since it is based in the realm of personal belief. Nevertheless, such passages can and should still be read – if not for their historical value, then for their didactic worth.

Our sages are interested in leaving us a record of preferred ethical conduct, not a history textbook. The idea that talmudic stories may not be meant as history may find support in our tale of the unpaid worker. While later authorities identify the protagonists as well-known sages, the passage itself provides scant information about their pedigree. According to one version, the employee had never studied the Written Law or the Oral Law. Only towards the end of the passage is there a somewhat more personal touch. We hear that the employer sought to encourage his child – a lad with a Hellenistic name – to study Torah, and later approached his peers, the sages, to rescind his vow. The actors' names remain a mystery and the storyteller does not use any honorific; the heroes remain anonymous, not linked to any historical time or place. The message may be that the historical credibility of these accounts is less significant than their thrust.

Rereading the above tale in light of this approach, the passage resonates differently. The seeming nebulousness and lack of credibility may be the exact point that the sages are trying to highlight. When attempting to judge everybody favourably no matter what the circumstances, even distant possibilities should be taken into account, rather than assuming the worst.

Thus we have a model for reading passages that appear to be historically dubious, and we have an impetus to preserve them, cherish them and to plumb their depths. Our sages bequeath us unconvincing tales, not to convince us of their historicity, but rather to provide us with guidance on our life journeys.

BERAKHOT 19B

Human dignity as a legal consideration

OUR SAGES RULE that a person who realises that he is wearing a garment made of *sha'atnez* – the forbidden admixture of wool and linen (Leviticus 19:19; Deuteronomy 22:11) – must promptly remove the clothing. This applies even if he finds himself in a public area, and undressing will cause him considerable humiliation (*B. Berakhot* 19b). Explaining the reason for this seemingly callous ruling with its apparent disregard for the wearer's dignity, the Talmud offers a biblical verse: *There is no wisdom and there is no understanding and there is no counsel against God* (Proverbs 21:30). The law is the law, and human embarrassment does not abrogate Divine regulations.

The talmudic passage continues, providing us with other examples in which God's honour takes precedence over people's. Normally we are enjoined to accord respect to our teachers. However, where there is a danger of the Almighty's name being desecrated (due to a mistake on their part), this principle no longer holds sway, and we are permitted to speak our minds.

Considerations of human dignity are overridden if taking them into account would lead to transgressing a commandment, thus desecrating the Almighty's name. This law is discussed in an episode that appears elsewhere in the Talmud (*B. Menaḥot* 37b–38a). The sage Ravina was once walking behind Mar bar Rav Ashi on Shabbat. From his vantage point, Ravina noticed that unbeknownst to Mar bar Rav Ashi the *tzitzit* from one corner of his garment were torn, rendering it unacceptable for fulfilling the *mitzva* of *tzitzit*. Wearing such a garment in public constitutes a transgression of the prohibition of carrying on Shabbat, since clothing with non-kosher *tzitzit* cannot be considered a true garment (*Mordekhai*).

Mar bar Rav Ashi continued on his way, unaware of his error. We might have expected Ravina to yell after his friend, for there are no excuses when one needs to fulfil the commandments of God. Mar bar Rav Ashi would have undressed right there in the marketplace with no regard for any accompanying embarrassment. Strangely, Ravina kept silent, saying nothing and following the sage home. When they reached the home of Mar bar Rav Ashi, Ravina told him about the torn *tzitzit*. Mar bar Rav Ashi responded: "Had you told me, I would have thrown off my garment right there!" Indeed human dignity is no consideration when faced with a transgression of a Divine command.

Unhappy with the implications of Mar bar Rav Ashi's exclamation, the Talmud asks: do we not have a principle that human dignity is so great a concern that it supersedes even negative commandments of the Torah? Mar bar Rav Ashi need not have humiliated himself by publicly undressing even had he known that his *tzitzit* were invalid, since human dignity would have superseded the biblical prohibition against carrying on Shabbat. The Talmud responds that human dignity does not override all biblical proscriptions; it takes priority over only one – the prohibition against flouting rabbinic authority. We are instructed: *You shall not deviate from the word that they will tell you* (Deuteronomy 17:11). This verse empowers halakhic authorities to legislate and makes rabbinic enactments binding under Torah law. These enactments, however, are not followed when doing so would result in someone being humiliated.

Let us return to our two scholars making their way through the streets on Shabbat, one carrying a garment and the other following wordlessly. At his home, Mar bar Rav Ashi was actually chastising his colleague. Carrying on Shabbat is not a rabbinic enactment but a biblical one; you should have told me, and I would have cast off my garment in public without regard for any feelings of shame!

The Talmud offers an alternative version of the entire incident. Ravina did indeed call his colleague's attention to the ripped garment, notifying Mar bar Rav Ashi that he must remove the clothing rather than carry it through the streets on Shabbat. Mar bar Rav Ashi, however, balked and retorted: "Do you think that I need to cast off my garment? Doesn't human dignity supersede negative commandments of the Torah? I need not embarrass myself."

The Talmud questions Mar bar Rav Ashi's shying away from undressing. As we have noted, the rule positing the superiority of human dignity applies only to rabbinic legislation, while carrying in the streets is a biblical prohibition. The Talmud explains that carrying in a public domain is indeed prohibited by Torah law. Mar bar Rav Ashi was walking, however, in a thoroughfare that was defined as "public" only according to rabbinic legislation. According to Torah law this area would have been considered private, either because it was narrow or because it did not have the requisite number of people traversing it. In an attempt to bring the law in line with contemporary realities, the sages redefined the area as "public" and extended the carrying prohibition to it. However, when applying this new rabbinic categorisation would result in a disregard for human dignity, the area reverts to its original status. Thus Mar bar Rav Ashi was permitted to remain clothed.

The common thread to both versions of the story is that concern for human dignity trumps rabbinic legislation.

This is also the thrust of another law (*B. Shabbat* 81a–b). Handling stones on Shabbat is generally forbidden under the rabbinic legislation of *muktzeh* – the prohibition against handling objects that have no use or a forbidden use on Shabbat. Stones are a classic example of an item with no use. Nevertheless, in the days before toilet paper, the sages ruled that one may take three sharp-sided stones into the latrine on Shabbat. In this case, the abrogation of the rabbinic ban on *muktzeh* is rooted in a concern for human dignity. Similarly, these stones can be taken to a rooftop outhouse even though this involves physical exertion, which is rabbinically proscribed. Again, the licence is granted for the sake of human dignity.

Here lies the key to understanding rabbinic legislative power. The sages are charged with the task of developing Jewish law, innovating and generally ensuring that it does not become petrified. While fulfilling this role, halakhic authorities must take an entire range of considerations into account. The written word is central, but it is only one of the pieces in the puzzle. Other factors, such as discomfort and pain, financial consequences and, of course, human dignity are not disregarded. While the Divine origins of the written code make it relatively unmalleable in human hands, the developed and developing rabbinic additions to the code strive to make Jewish law a living, relevant and vibrant tradition.

BERAKHOT 20A

Extraordinary first steps

THE RABBI OF Pezinok, today in Slovakia, once guided a prospective convert through the process of becoming a Jew. This was in contravention of local laws that forbade conversion without governmental licence. The prospective convert had completed the process, requiring only circumcision to finalise his new Jewish status.

Alas, following the circumcision the flow of blood could not be stemmed and the unfortunate convert found himself in tremendous pain. Because the conversion was illegal, a qualified doctor could not be called, lest the authorities hear of the crime. A great fear settled on the Jewish community and no one knew what to do.

The rabbi decided that he and the convert would quickly travel to the great Rabbi Moshe Sofer (1762–1839) – known by the title of his work *Ḥatam Sofer* – to seek his counsel. Upon their arrival in Pressburg, they told their tale to the Ḥatam Sofer. He sadly told them: "I have no advice for you. The only course is for the two of you to travel to the Duna River and drown yourselves for the sanctification of God's name." The poor convert and the rabbi heard the suggestion of the Ḥatam Sofer and decided that they had no choice but to follow it.

On the way to their impending death, after they had covered a considerable portion of the distance, they met an elderly man. He asked them: "Where are you going?" and warned them, "It is dangerous here! The river is wild and may sweep you to your death!" After repeated inquiries by the elderly man, the duo eventually told him why they had come to the area.

"You need not act upon that advice, for I am an expert circumciser and I have a powder that slows the bleeding of the wound and prevents the pain." Immediately the old man used the powder and the convert's haemorrhaging and pain subsided.

Naturally the rabbi and the convert wanted to thank their kind helper and offer to take him to his destination. Yet, when they turned, they realised that he had disappeared. Their conclusion was obvious – it must have been Elijah the prophet, who attends every circumcision! They hurried back to the Ḥatam Sofer's house to tell him of their miraculous salvation. They reported the entire episode, and then the rabbi asked the Ḥatam Sofer: "Why did you need to command us to go and throw ourselves in the river; couldn't you have sent Elijah directly to our town?"

The Ḥatam Sofer responded: "Do you think that without your self-sacrifice Elijah would have appeared to you? Only once you demonstrated your willingness to go beyond your human limits and sanctify the name of God could you hope for a miraculous appearance by Elijah." The Ḥatam Sofer's admonition would seem to be reflected in the following talmudic exchange (*B. Berakhot* 20a).

Rav Pappa asked Abbaye: "Why do we not merit miracles as did earlier generations?" Rav Pappa continued, elaborating on the question: "We afflict ourselves and cry out in prayer asking for rain, and no one pays any attention. In previous generations, when there was a drought Rav Yehuda would merely remove his shoe as a sign of discomfort, and the heavens would open."

Abbaye responded: "Earlier generations made tremendous sacrifices in order to sanctify God's name. Having gone beyond what was required of them, they could ask the Almighty to transcend the boundaries of nature and perform miracles for them."

The idea that we need to show a willingness to extend ourselves before we can expect Divine assistance is a theme that runs through much of our literature. The Mishna details ten wonders that occurred in the Temple (*M. Avot* 5:5). In this list we find that during the thrice-yearly pilgrimage to Jerusalem, when the Temple courtyard was packed, people stood tightly pressed together. Yet when they bowed down, miraculously they prostrated themselves with ease. We can ask: why not miraculously let them stand with ease as well? The answer is that only once the throngs of people were willing to stretch their own comfort boundaries for the opportunity to stand in the courtyard of the Temple did the borders of that physical space expand to grant them more room.

In a similar vein, when the recently freed Jewish people stood at the edge of the Reed Sea with the Egyptian soldiers charging behind them, they cried out to God for assistance in their dire predicament. The Almighty responded to Moses' entreaties: *Why are you crying out to Me? Speak to the Children of Israel – they should travel!* The raging sea, however, did not split until Nahshon courageously entered the waters and was nearly engulfed by them (Exodus 14:15; *B. Sota* 37a). In order to set the stage for Divine assistance, we need to take that first extraordinary step.

Let us conclude with a final tale (*Kohelet Rabba* 1:1). Rabbi Ḥanina ben Dosa saw his fellow townspeople taking various offerings to Jerusalem. He thought to himself: "Everyone is taking offerings up to Jerusalem, but I take nothing?"

With this in mind, he went to the empty land outside the city and found a sizeable rock. He chipped it, chiselled it, polished it and proclaimed: "Behold I take upon myself to take it up to Jerusalem!" Rabbi Ḥanina ben Dosa then sought to hire workers to transport the stone and five men chanced to come his way. The workers agreed to lug the boulder for a significant fee to be paid immediately. The sage, however, did not have such a sum on him and the workers moved on.

Hiding their identity, five angels appeared and made a similar offer. Though they did not demand immediate payment, they added a stipulation: "on condition that you bear some of the weight." Undoubtedly, the angels could have carried the stone without assistance. Rabbi Ḥanina ben Dosa accepted their offer, placing his hand beneath the rock. When they reached Jerusalem, Rabbi Ḥanina ben Dosa looked for the workers to pay their wages but they were nowhere to be found. His repeated inquiries led the sages to the conclusion that angels had carried his stone.

We often wish for supernatural intervention, magical salvation that defies the course of nature. Yet we might ask ourselves: are we willing to go beyond our own comfort zone, to act in ways that defy how we define ourselves? Are we willing to transcend the contours of our self-image for the sake of the One from Whom we are requesting assistance? People who are unwilling to extend their preconceived boundaries cannot expect God to stray from the natural boundaries of this physical world.

BERAKHOT 20B

Rules and exceptions

It is a commonplace that exceptions prove rules, which in any case are made to be broken. Is this really so? Certainly the authors of the rules had no intention that their rules should be violated. Moreover, in what way does an exception "prove" a rule? On the contrary, an exception brings the all-encompassing nature of a rule into question. How should we view the rules that are stated throughout the Talmud?

Broadly, the term "rule" can be used in at least two contexts. First, there are specific rules, that is, precepts that demand performance or proscribe actions. Second, there are general rules that seek to organise and summarise a class of precepts.

In the first sense of the term, the Mishna tells us that women are not obligated to read *Shema* nor don *tefillin*, yet they do have to pray, affix a *mezuza* to their doorposts and recite Grace After Meals (*M. Berakhot* 3:3). These precepts can be restated in the second sense of the term "rule," encapsulating them in summarising statements: "Women are exempt from all time-bound commandments" and "Women are obligated in all commandments that are not time-bound" (*M. Kiddushin* 1:7).

The Talmud asks why the specific examples were stated rather than the general rule (*B. Berakhot* 20b). While it is possible that specific examples give rise to a general rule, the Talmud offers a different explanation. In each specifically mentioned case, we might have reached the opposite conclusion – that the observances are indeed mandated for women. For example, reciting *Shema* each morning and each evening is mandated, to give voice to the Almighty's sovereignty. Due to the profound significance of this declaration, we might think that women are obligated to read *Shema* despite its time-bound nature. Similarly, while *tefillin* is a daytime obligation, its biblical juxtaposition with the obligation of *mezuza* might lead us to the conclusion that women are obligated to don *tefillin* just as they are obligated to affix *mezuzot* (Deuteronomy 6:8–9).

Conversely, the last three items mentioned in the Mishna – prayer, *mezuza* and Grace After Meals – are not time-bound, yet in each case we might conclude that women are nevertheless exempt. The biblical verse *Evening and morning and noon I pray and I cry out, and He hears my voice* (Psalms 55:18) might lead to the conclusion that prayer is time-specific and therefore women are exempt. The biblical juxtaposition of *mezuza* and Torah study might indicate that women are not obligated to affix *mezuzot*, just as they do not have an independent obligation to study Torah (Deuteronomy 11:19–20). Lastly, Grace After Meals is similar to a time-bound precept inasmuch as we eat at set times, as the verse says: *When God gives you meat to eat in the evening and bread to satiate [you] in the morning* (Exodus 16:8).

Thus in each case the Mishna makes explicit the particular application, thereby indicating that the specific rules do conform to the general principle, and negating the possibility that these items are exceptions.

This talmudic explanation may appear strange. If there are general rules regarding women's obligations, why might we consider deviating from them?

To answer this question it is necessary to understand the nature of the Talmud's general rules. Elsewhere in the Talmud, the sages question the validity of the general rules governing women's obligations by listing exceptions to the rules (*B. Kiddushin* 33b–34a). The sages explain that general rules are not sources of law, they are organising principles and hence prone to exceptions.

Furthermore, even if a rule is qualified by a list of exceptions, there is no guarantee that all the exceptions have been detailed. For instance, in performing the ritual of *eruv* we set aside food so that an enclosed area is considered to be jointly owned. This is a necessary requirement to permit carrying on Shabbat in a rabbinically defined public domain. The sages tell us that any type of food may be used except for water and salt (*M. Eruvin* 3:1; *Rashi*). Even though this rule ("any type of food may be used") is qualified ("except for salt and water"), nevertheless the qualification is not exhaustive. Truffles and mushrooms, which are not mentioned here, are nevertheless not acceptable choices for the *eruv* because they are not considered nourishing food (*B. Eruvin* 27a).

Thus another aspect of the reason for stating specific examples becomes apparent. General rules are not all-encompassing, and exceptions are likely. By stating specific examples of a general rule, we eliminate the possibility that those examples might be classified as exceptions to the rule.

In sum, though rules are not made to be broken, they are not as all-encompassing as they might appear; general rules are indeed subject to exceptions. Even a qualified general rule is not hermetically sealed and the possibility of further exceptions still exists.

From here we turn to another qualified rule mentioned in our tractate: "Everything is in the hands of heaven, except for fear of heaven" (*B. Berakhot* 33b). While this statement is not a legal maxim requiring a specific action, it is nevertheless phrased like a rule that is qualified. As we have seen, however, even qualified general rules are not exhaustive. In fact, elsewhere in the Talmud the rule is restated with a different exception: "Everything is in the hands of heaven, except for sickness brought on by exposure to cold and heat" (*B. Ketubot* 30a–b).

What then is the use of a general rule, and why bother qualifying it? If rules are subject to exemptions, and qualifications are not exhaustive, then what is a rule's utility? A rule serves as a starting point, an organising principle from which discussion can begin, while the exceptions exhibit the fallibility of the rule. More importantly, exceptions demonstrate that any departure from the general rule must be on justifiable grounds. Rules are not made to be broken, yet they are not made without exception. Exceptions do not prove rules, though they demonstrate the boundaries of the rules and the cases when departures from the rule may be valid.

BERAKHOT 20B

For pity's sake

THE BIBLE PROUDLY tells us that God *does not show favour*; the rich and famous are not given preferential treatment in judgment before the Almighty. In fact, Scripture intimates that this attribute is what makes God *great, mighty and awesome* (Deuteronomy 10:17). Yet in seemingly open contradiction of this principle, the priestly blessing explicitly exhorts God to show favour to those being blessed (Numbers 6:26).

This glaring paradox has perplexed many. Bloriya the convert asked Rabban Gamliel about this incongruity (*B. Rosh HaShana* 17b–18a). Before Rabban Gamliel could respond, Rabbi Yose HaKohen jumped in with a parable: "Imagine a person who owes his friend money. While standing before the king, they agreed upon a due date for the debt, and the debtor swore by the life of the king to repay. The date arrived, but the debtor was unable to repay the money. The debtor made his way to the king to appease him, for the debtor realised he could not keep his word. The king graciously agreed to waive his honour, but added: 'Go and appease your creditor.'" Rabbi Yose HaKohen unpacked the parable, explaining that displays of favour are allowable when it comes to our relationship with the Almighty. God can munificently bestow favour and suppress anger and umbrage, in the case of an affront to Divine honour. When it comes to interpersonal relationships, however, God refuses to put aside claims. In such a case, the parties must come to terms with one another.

This was the accepted explanation for the biblical contradiction until Rabbi Akiva offered a different one: God shows special consideration before passing judgment. Once a Divine verdict has been reached there is no room for favouritism, and the ruling must be carried out. This explanation is offered anonymously elsewhere in the Talmud (*B. Nidda* 70b).

These two approaches do not really explain how God can bestow favour in light of the declaration that the Almighty does not act in this way. The explanations rely on limiting the applications of one of the verses, even though no such limits appear to arise from the biblical texts.

The Talmud records God's own answer to this question (*B. Berakhot* 20b). In this passage, it is the ministering angels who accuse God of not keeping the Divine avowal against favouring: "You are partial to the Children of Israel, as is evident from the priestly blessing!" God responds: "What do you expect?! Should I not favour Israel? In my Torah I told them that after they are satiated they should bless Me. They are so scrupulous that they recite Grace After Meals even after eating an amount as small as an olive or an egg!"

Biblical law mandates the recitation of a blessing after eating to the point of satiation. The verse commands: *When you eat and are satisfied, then you must bless God your Lord* (Deuteronomy 8:10). The sages discuss whether Grace After Meals should be recited after eating the equivalent of the mass of an olive or an egg (*M. Berakhot* 7:2). Whatever the minimum volume requiring Grace After Meals, this amount is more like a snack than a feast, and we would hardly expect to be sated after such a nibble.

Another source that follows a similar line of thought has the Divine attribute of judgment accusing the Almighty of being too lenient towards His people and favouring His subjects (*Eliyahu Zuta* 23). God replies: "How can I not be compassionate? When the Jewish people left Egypt they were willing to accept all the commandments. Moreover, they are willing to teach the tradition, gather in groups to study and even pay from their own pockets to hire teachers!"

These two Divine responses barely hold water. The perplexing contradiction remains, as the Almighty appears to flout the biblical declaration against showing partiality. Perhaps God is saying: "How can I not show them favour? They may not always deserve it – and perhaps I should not grant it – but I cannot help Myself." Parents are generally partial to their own children. Which parent doesn't think that his or her children are the brightest or cutest of all children? God – as our Parent – sees only the good in us. It is as if the Almighty says: "They are My children; they are loyal to Me, doing My bidding, even going beyond the letter of the law. How can I not favour them?"

Elsewhere in the Talmud, a tale is told of a drought in the Land of Israel (*B. Ta'anit* 23a). The spring was near; most of Adar, the last winter month, had passed. The rains had not arrived and the situation was bleak. A message was sent to the Second Temple sage Ḥoni: "Pray that rain should fall." Ḥoni acquiesced, but despite his prayers the rains did not come. He drew a circle on the ground. Standing inside it, he adamantly addressed the Almighty: "Master of the universe, Your children have turned to me, for I am like a family member of Yours. I swear that I will not move from here until You show mercy to Your children."

Miraculously it began to drizzle, whereupon Ḥoni's disciples turned to him and remarked: "It appears that the rains are falling only enough to release you from your oath!" Once again Ḥoni turned heavenward and declared: "This is not what I asked for! I requested rains that fill wells, cisterns and caverns." Torrential rains began to fall. The students hurriedly came to Ḥoni, saying: "It looks like the rains are intent on destroying the world." Ḥoni turned to the Almighty a third time and complained: "This is not what I asked for! I expected rains that bring blessing and express goodwill."

The rains began to fall steadily, continuing until all the inhabitants of Jerusalem were forced to high ground on the Temple Mount. "Master," implored the students, "Just as you prayed for the rains to come, pray that they should cease." Ḥoni, however, was reluctant and replied: "I have a tradition that we do not pray for the cessation of an abundance of good."

Nevertheless, in light of the dire circumstances, Ḥoni ordered: "Bring me a thanksgiving sacrifice." A bull was brought, and Ḥoni placed his two hands on the animal saying: "Master of the universe, Your people cannot withstand either an excess of good or an excess of punishment. If You are angry with them, they cannot survive; if You are too good to them, they cannot survive. May it be Your will that the rains cease and that there be relief in the world." A gust of wind blew, the clouds dissipated and the sun shone. The people went out into the fields and collected truffles and mushrooms.

The leading rabbinic figure of the day, Shimon ben Shetaḥ, sent a stern message to Ḥoni: "If you were not Ḥoni, I would have you excommunicated! You have taken the heavenly keys for rain into your own hands and thus have desecrated the name of God with your capricious requests."

Shimon ben Shetaḥ continued: "But what can I do to you, for you misbehave and the Almighty fulfils your requests! You are just like a child who is naughty, yet the parents do the child's bidding."

In the liturgy of the High Holy Days we often recall the duality of our relationship with the Almighty. God is at once a master over us and a parent to us. We play the dual role of servants and of children. Yet we would undoubtedly prefer the parent-child bond over the master-serf relationship. For that way, when sitting in judgment God will feel compelled to be partial towards us, just as parents favour their children.

BERAKHOT 21A

Learning never ends

THE TALMUD SEEKS a biblical source for the benediction recited before studying Torah. It suggests a verse from the *Ha'azinu* poem recited by Moses just before his death (Deuteronomy 32:3): *When I proclaim the name of God, acknowledge the greatness of God* (*B. Berakhot* 21a). As we have seen, the sages discuss the most appropriate wording for this blessing, and the codifiers accept all the suggested texts (*B. Berakhot* 11b; *Shulḥan Arukh, Oraḥ Ḥayim* 47:5). Today, these benedictions are part of the daily morning liturgy.

The Talmud continues with a discussion of the possibility that a blessing should be recited at the completion of Torah study. Though there appears to be no explicit source for such a blessing, one sage suggests that it is derived from the requirement to recite a benediction after eating. The required Grace After Meals has its source in the biblical verse: *When you eat and are satisfied, then you must bless God your Lord* (Deuteronomy 8:10). The Talmud suggests that one might derive the requirement of a blessing after Torah study using *a fortiori* reasoning.

Since, biblically speaking, food does not require a blessing before it is consumed, yet does require an after-blessing – then surely Torah, which requires a blessing before the act, should require a blessing afterwards as well! The Talmud rejects this legal manoeuvre, claiming that food and Torah are inherently different and hence not subject to comparisons. Food provides physical sustenance, but Torah provides everlasting life. The two are unrelated and cannot be compared. The accepted practice is, in fact, that no after-blessing is recited when an individual studies Torah.

Nevertheless, there is still room for an afterword of sorts. The Mishna relates that Rabbi Neḥunya ben Hakkana would offer a short prayer when he entered and exited the *beit midrash* (*M. Berakhot* 4:2). Those present inquired about the nature of this prayer. "When I enter, I pray that no mishap should be caused by me; and when I depart, I give thanks for my portion," explained the sage. The Talmud offers the full text of the prayer (*B. Berakhot* 28b). Upon departure, Rabbi Neḥunya ben Hakkana would say: "I give thanks before You, God my Lord, that You have placed my portion amongst those who sit in the *beit midrash* and You have not placed my portion amongst those who sit on the street corners. I arise early and they arise early. I arise for words of Torah, and they arise for words of futility. I toil and they toil. I toil and receive reward, while they toil and do not receive reward. I hasten and they hasten. I hasten to the World to Come, and they hasten to the depths of hell."

Rabbi Neḥunya ben Hakkana's prayer – though private and personal in origin – is recommended for all who enter and exit the *beit midrash* (*Shulḥan Arukh, Oraḥ Ḥayim* 110:8). This prayer also forms part of the special thanksgiving passage recited at the completion of study of an entire tractate of Talmud.

It is important to note that Rabbi Neḥunya ben Hakkana did not recite a benediction; rather he offered a prayer that gave thanks for the opportunity afforded him and expressed hope for future opportunities. This was not a blessing praising God; it was a supplication beseeching the Almighty.

Let us return to our talmudic passage. Is the rejection of a blessing at the conclusion of a Torah study session merely the result of an unsuitable use of the *a fortiori* legal mechanism, or may there be a deeper reason for the rejection?

The scholarly leader of Lithuanian Jewry in Israel, Rabbi Elazar Menaḥem Man Shach (1898–2001), once met a group of advanced students and told them: "I have long been bothered by a certain question posed by the classic talmudic commentator *Penei Yehoshua*" – Rabbi Yaakov Yehoshua Falk (1680–1756). He quickly added: "But I doubt whether this question would bother you."

Urged by the students to reveal the question, Rabbi Shach repeated: "I doubt whether you would even find the question difficult, and there is really no point in sharing it with you."

The students were not discouraged and continued to pester their teacher. Perhaps they secretly hoped that they would be able to answer the question posed by the *Penei Yehoshua,* as they often tried to do with other such quandaries encountered during their studies.

Once Rabbi Shach realised that they were not to be dismissed, and they truly desired to be privy to the question that was bothering him so, he decided to share it with them. "The *Penei Yehoshua,* relating to our passage, asks the following question: how can there be a blessing at the conclusion of learning Torah? Is there ever really a time that can be considered 'the conclusion of learning Torah'? We are commanded to study Torah constantly!"

Rabbi Shach continued caustically: "This question certainly does not bother you, since at the end of your study sessions you close your books. You clearly do have a concept of 'the conclusion of learning Torah.'"

Rabbi Shach concluded: "A true student of Torah must feel that the Torah is unlike any other discipline. Students of Torah must realise that the tradition is our life; it is all we desire. Only through this awareness can we ascend to great heights of Torah."

Now let us travel to the other side of the world. In a summer camp in Victoria, Australia, the mornings were dedicated to Torah study while the afternoons and evenings were filled with assorted camp activities. Every morning after breakfast and clean-up, campers would gather with their counsellors to learn Torah. At the conclusion of the study session, the camp microphone would boom: "Learning never ends! Learning never ends! Learning classes are now over. Please proceed to…"

At first blush, this announcement sounds ridiculous and contradictory. Yet it contains a deep truth about Torah study. A particular

Torah class or learning session may be finite, but the enterprise of Torah study is an ongoing venture. For this reason, there is no blessing after Torah study: learning never ends.

BERAKHOT 21B

Holy congregations

IF YOU ARE one of those people who occasionally arrives late to services, you are familiar with the dilemma of how best to catch up to the congregation. Should I omit passages? Should I race through the prayers? The sages are aware of human nature and discuss the rules of prayer for latecomers (*B. Berakhot* 21b).

There are two opinions as to what stragglers should do if they arrive after the congregation has begun the central *Amida* prayer. According to both approaches, latecomers must quickly assess their ability to catch up. One opinion suggests that if they can catch up with the congregation before the leader begins the responsive *Modim* prayer towards the end of the *Amida* repetition, they should hurriedly pray. If not, they should wait to start praying, so that they can first recite *Modim* with those present.

A second opinion places the catch-up point far earlier. Latecomers may begin their prayers only if they will catch up with the congregation in time to join in for *Kedusha* towards the beginning of the *Amida* repetition. Otherwise they are instructed to wait, join the congregation for *Kedusha* and only then offer their own prayers.

The Talmud clarifies the root of this argument. The question at hand is whether an individual may recite *Kedusha* alone or whether it can be said only in a congregational setting. The short *Kedusha* passage relates to the transcendent sanctity of the Almighty. Hence its name *Kedusha,* meaning holiness. The first opinion suggests that an individual may say *Kedusha* alone; hence the catch-up point is *Modim*. The second opinion holds that *Kedusha* is a responsive communal prayer, and therefore latecomers must catch up with the congregation by this prayer. Normative opinion adopts the latter approach. *Kedusha,* and for that matter all prayers that have an element of sanctity, must be recited in a *minyan,* a quorum of ten.

The quorum requirement for holy matters goes beyond the prayer ritual. When faced with threats to our religious practice, we are enjoined – in the worst-case scenario – to sacrifice our lives rather than transgress the Almighty's commandments (*B. Sanhedrin* 74a–b). The sages tell us that if we are ordered to disobey halakha in public or forfeit our lives, we must sacrifice our lives in order to sanctify the name of God. This is the case even if the violation is a minor infraction, if the intent of the order is to wipe out religious observance. The Talmud asks: what is the definition of "public" for this rule? Our sages explain that "public" is no fewer than ten Jews.

We see that there is a quorum requirement for the sanctification of God's name as well as for prayers that have an element of sanctity. What is the source for these quorum requirements? In both cases the sages quote the biblical verse: *And I will be sanctified among the Children of Israel* (Leviticus 22:32). Sanctity is mentioned in this verse, but where do we see the number ten? Rabbinic sources deal with this question in a number of places. When relating to *Kedusha,* the sages offer a *gezeira shava,* a kind of syllogism, based on the word *tokh* (among) which appears both in the verse dealing with sanctity and in the context of the rebellious Korah episode: *Separate yourselves from among this congregation* (Numbers 16:21). Just as in the case of Korah there were ten, here too we require ten. Alas, nowhere do we have evidence that Korah's faction comprised ten people. On the contrary, the biblical account seems to describe a large rabble. Different suggestions – all based on the *gezeira shava* mechanism – are offered in our rabbinic texts (*Bereshit Rabba* 91:2; *Y. Berakhot* 11c; *Y. Megilla* 75b).

The most interesting approach retains the original *gezeira shava* but adds an extra link. The sages list the rituals that require a quorum of ten: the opening blessing before reading *Shema,* the *Amida* repetition, the priestly benediction, the public reading of the Torah, the supplementary reading from the Prophets, certain funeral and mourning practices, the seven blessings recited for a bride and groom and the use of God's name in the group invitation (*Zimmun*) to the Grace After Meals (*M. Megilla* 4:3). In reference to this list, the Talmud seeks the source for the magical number of ten, and proceeds with a double *gezeira shava*. The reappearing word *tokh* connects sanctity to an *eida*, a congregation, in the Korah episode, and the word *eida* is also used elsewhere to describe the reconnaissance team that surveyed the Land of Israel. Although this team had a dozen members, two of the party did not present a negative report and were excluded from Divine rebuke (Numbers 14:27). Thus matters of sanctity require a quorum of ten (*B. Megilla* 23b).

At least one commentator does not appreciate this explanation. How can we derive the rule that matters of sanctity require a quorum of ten from the slanderous spies who spoke badly of the Land of Israel? It is far more appropriate to prefer a different *gezeira shava* that derives requirements regarding holy matters from the conduct of righteous people. The commentator felt that it is so distasteful to arrive at the quorum requirement in this manner, that the original talmudic text may have been corrupted (*Rabbeinu Baḥya*).

Despite this objection, we might suggest that the sages deliberately choose to derive the number ten for a holy quorum from the far-from-holy spies. The sanctity of a quorum is not defined by the calibre of the individuals who form the group. A prayer group is permitted to recite hallowed prayers because it has come together to commune with God, not because the members of that group are necessarily pious or godly. Similarly, sanctifying the Divine name in public is not dependent on the identity of those present. According to this line of reasoning, the shameful spies provide the perfect paradigm for a holy quorum.

We come to pray as individuals, each of us with our own merits and, unfortunately, with our own embarrassing baggage. Yet when we stand together, we are suddenly viewed differently and permitted to recite special prayers, as we are considered a holy congregation.

BERAKHOT 22A–B

Power of the people

WHERE IS THE locus of power in the Jewish legal system? Who ultimately decides questions of halakha? Instinctively, we might suggest that the rabbinic authorities have sole jurisdiction in the halakhic process. They decide questions of law and have the mandate to legislate new laws or abrogate old ones. Indeed, halakhic authorities are invested with much power, and their influence over Jewish norms is immeasurable. Nevertheless, the halakhic system recognises another institution that plays a significant role in the development of halakha: the people.

A person who experiences a seminal discharge – known in talmudic literature as a *ba'al keri* – is prohibited by biblical law from partaking of sanctified products, such as *teruma* (the "heave" offering given to *kohanim*) and Temple sacrifices (Leviticus 15:16). During the Second Temple period, Ezra the Scribe expanded the restrictions placed on a *ba'al keri*. He decreed that a *ba'al keri* must not recite words of Torah before immersion in a *mikveh* (*B. Bava Kamma* 82a–b). In this light, we can understand the Mishna's ruling that a *ba'al keri* should contemplate the words of *Shema* rather than recite the prayer aloud (*M. Berakhot* 3:4). Almost all sages cited in the Mishna and parallel sources accepted the contemporary applicability of Ezra's decree. All, that is, except for one sage – Rabbi Yehuda ben Beteira (*B. Berakhot* 22a–b).

Rabbi Yehuda ben Beteira taught that words of Torah cannot contract ritual impurity, and hence a *ba'al keri* need not immerse in a *mikveh* before studying Torah. To illustrate his stance, the Talmud relates an episode with the sage and one of his students. The disciple was a *ba'al keri* and had not immersed in a *mikveh*, when he was asked to recite teachings before his master. Nervously, he began to stammer. Rabbi Yehuda ben Beteira calmed his student: "My son, open your mouth and let your words shine forth, for the words of Torah do not contract ritual impurity." The sage continued, citing scriptural support for this notion: "It is written *Behold, My words are like fire, says God* (Jeremiah 23:29). Just as fire is not susceptible to ritual impurity, so too Torah – the word of God – is not prone to ritual impurity."

In permitting a *ba'al keri* to recite words of Torah, it appears that Rabbi Yehuda ben Beteira disregarded the ancient decree of Ezra requiring *mikveh* immersion. This scenario is problematic, for generally speaking rabbinic decrees can be rescinded only by a later court of greater size and wisdom than the original legislating body (*M. Eduyot* 1:5). It would be presumptuous for Rabbi Yehuda ben Beteira to ascribe to himself greater wisdom than the famous Ezra the Scribe. How, then, could the sage discount Ezra's ban?

This very question bothers one of the medieval commentators, who proceeds to offer three solutions (*Tosafot*). The first approach suggests that Rabbi Yehuda ben Beteira denied the historicity of the decree. Ezra never issued a ban on Torah study by a *ba'al keri*, and hence Rabbi Yehuda ben Beteira was not bound by any earlier legislation. This is a problematic approach, given that all other talmudic sages accepted Ezra's decree as historical fact.

The second solution acknowledges the historical authenticity of Ezra's decree, but suggests that the decree was enacted with a release clause whereby any later generation could rescind the earlier decree, even if the later authority did not have the required pedigree. While there is no evidence of such a stipulation, such a mechanism was known to the sages and its application is suggested elsewhere in the Talmud in an entirely different context (*B. Mo'ed Katan* 3b).

A third and most fascinating approach also accepts the historicity of Ezra's ban, but sees the licence for Rabbi Yehuda ben Beteira's stance in subsequent events. Even though Ezra enacted the prohibition, the people rejected the ban, effectively nullifying Ezra's legislation and ensuring that it never achieved binding legal status.

It should be noted that we have no evidence of such a mass rejection of Ezra's decree. Nevertheless, such legal power invested in the people is reported in another instance as well. The Mishna considers oil produced by gentiles to be a forbidden product, and the ensuing talmudic discussion explores the history of the prohibition (*M. Avoda Zara* 2:6; *B. Avoda Zara* 35b–36b). According to one opinion, Daniel instituted the ban, and centuries later it was repealed by the court of Rabbi Yehuda the Prince. Here too, the Talmud asks how the later court could audaciously rescind the decree of the earlier authority. The sages explain that indeed we have here an ancient decree, yet this ban never took hold among the people. Thus the later court merely investigated the history of the prohibition. Once they realised that the ban on gentile oil never enjoyed widespread acceptance, they declared Daniel's decree null and void.

Even though we may sometimes feel that halakhic authority rests solely in the hands of the rabbis, the Jewish legal system actually recognises the power of the people. They can act as an upper chamber of parliament that has the right to reject rabbinic legislation. The licence given to the people is not only for rejecting rabbinically initiated legislation. A full discussion of the legal mechanism of *minhag*, custom, is beyond our scope. Nevertheless, we can broadly say that *minhag* is the mandate granted to the people to initiate legislation.

The legal power of the people is a unique feature of the halakhic system. Other legal systems grant the people the right to remove legislators at the end of their term of office. However, while they may be subject to public pressure as long as they are in office, at the end of the day the lawmakers can choose to ignore dissent, disregard protests and legislate as they please. Eventually they may be taken to task for this and pay the price for it at the voting booths, but until such time they have relative legislative freedom. Not so in the Jewish legal system, where the people constantly vet the legislation of rabbinic authorities. The Jewish legal system does not grant this inimitable prerogative to any one individual or identifiable group. It is, however, a salient right which reflects the fact that the venerable Jewish legal system is communally owned.

BERAKHOT 24B

Worth paying the price

THE SAGE RABBI Abba decided to make the journey from his native Babylonia to the Land of Israel (*B. Berakhot* 24b). Rabbi Abba, however, faced one serious problem. His teacher, Rav Yehuda, held that it was halakhically prohibited to move to the Holy Land before the messianic era.

Rav Yehuda's opinion was rooted in the prophetic verse: *They shall be brought to Babylon and there they shall remain, until the day when I remember them – says the Lord – and bring them up and restore them to this place* (Jeremiah 27:22). In context, this verse refers to the Babylonian exile following the destruction of the First Temple, an exile that ended with the return to Zion and the rebuilding of the Temple. The prophecy and its fulfilment belonged to a bygone era, but Rav Yehuda understood the biblical passage to be applicable to all exiles. Thus he proscribed leaving anywhere in the Diaspora without the Almighty's approval.

Fearing that his master would forbid the journey (*Rashi, Shabbat* 41a), or perhaps having already been told by him not to travel (*Rashi, Ketubot* 110b), Rabbi Abba prudently avoided Rav Yehuda as he prepared for the momentous journey.

On the eve of his departure Rabbi Abba was torn. Should he totally avoid Rav Yehuda? Perhaps he should properly take leave of his master? Eventually he decided: "I will go and stand outside the study hall, learn something from him, and then I will leave."

When he arrived, Rabbi Abba found a *tanna* (someone who memorised and recited vast amounts of rabbinic material) repeating an ancient teaching before Rav Yehuda: "If someone was standing in prayer and he passed wind, he must wait until the odour has dissipated and then he may continue praying." The Talmud offers a second version of the teaching that Rabbi Abba heard: "If someone was standing in prayer and needed to pass wind, he must first step back four cubits. Once the odour has dissipated, he may return to his prayer, by opening up with the following supplication: 'Master of the universe, You formed us with many openings and many cavities. The shame and humiliation which we endure during our lives is revealed and known before You, and at our end maggots and worms await us.' Having completed this supplication acknowledging human frailty, one then continues from the place where he interrupted his prayer."

Without having spoken directly to his teacher, Rabbi Abba ceremoniously declared: "If I had come to hear only this thing, it would have been sufficient for me!" And with that, he departed for the Holy Land.

How could Rabbi Abba flout his teacher's stance on relocating to the Land of Israel? Moreover, if Jeremiah's prophecy truly prohibits such a move, how could he act contrary to the prophetic directive?

Rabbi Eliyahu of Vilna (1720–1797), known as the Gaon of Vilna or simply as the Gra (an acronym for Gaon Rabbi Eliyahu), explains that Rabbi Abba understood Jeremiah's prophecy to be referring to the Temple vessels which are the subject of the preceding biblical verses. Thus he saw no prohibition in returning to the Land of Israel before the advent of the messianic era, and decided to act on his understanding.

While this suggestion explains Rabbi Abba's willingness to act contrary to his teacher's position, there is no evidence that he disagreed with Rav Yehuda's interpretation. Furthermore, we are left wondering about Rabbi Abba's parting declaration. On the eve of such a meaningful voyage, why was he so moved by a teaching about passing wind during prayer?

The Baghdadi scholar Rabbi Yosef Ḥayim (1834–1909) explains Rabbi Abba's conduct by recounting a tale he heard of a learned person who had tremendous enthusiasm for Torah study. This scholar was careful not to waste a moment, and five minutes would never pass without his learning Torah. Once a close relative of this scholar passed away and he observed the prescribed seven-day mourning period. During mourning, the joyful study of Torah is forbidden, but this scholar was so attached to Torah study that he hid in an inner room and opened the holy books. While he was clandestinely holed-up and studying Torah, suddenly his peers entered. They were stunned to find him with an open book in his hands. "What are you doing?" they demanded. "A mourner is forbidden to study Torah!"

Sheepishly the scholar replied: "I know that I am transgressing the words of the sages. And I know that I will certainly be called to task for this on the Day of Judgment. I am, however, willing to suffer the punishment that will be meted out, whatever that may be. You see, I cannot restrain myself in the face of the anguish I feel from not studying Torah; it is as painful for me as death!"

Rabbi Yosef Ḥayim uses this story to shed light on the motivations of Rabbi Abba. Even though he acknowledged the prohibition against leaving the Diaspora for the Land of Israel, his pining for the Holy Land was so great that he was willing to incur any heavenly penalties imposed provided that he could immigrate to the Promised Land.

Rabbi Yosef Ḥayim goes on to explain Rabbi Abba's parting pronouncement. Rabbi Abba heard a law about someone whose bodily functions necessitated an interruption in prayer, but what piqued his interest was the additional supplication to be offered before returning to prayer. The first interruption was unpreventable, but once the smell had dissipated, an immediate return to prayer was called for. Interjecting other business during a canonised prayer is not normally sanctioned. Rabbi Abba saw that for the higher purpose of offering a small but sincere apology, the offender was permitted to tarry.

Having heard this teaching, he knew that he had made the right decision. Indeed, returning to the Land of Israel was, perhaps, prohibited so long as the exile endured. Yet for the sake of living in the Promised Land, it was permitted to ignore the prohibition. This seemingly mundane teaching, about bodily functions during prayer, strengthened Rabbi Abba's resolve to fulfil his dream.

A student may blurt out an inappropriate but funny quip during class, and the teacher – barely suppressing a laugh – is obliged to punish the cheeky student. "That was a good one," I remember a teacher of mine saying, "But you will have to pay for it!"

There may be occasions in our tradition when misconduct is worthwhile despite the penalty it carries. While it is undeniably difficult to identify which values justify such a course, two examples present themselves here: Torah and the Land of Israel.

Berakhot
Chapter Four

BERAKHOT 26B

Sacrifices of the heart

WHERE DO OUR prayers originate? And why do we pray three times a day? The Talmud discusses the source of our thrice-daily prayer service, offering two opinions as to the inspiration for this practice (*B. Berakhot* 26b). The first approach suggests that the three forefathers each instituted one service. Abraham inaugurated the morning *Shaḥarit* prayer; Isaac introduced the afternoon *Minḥa* service; while Jacob was the first to pray the evening *Ma'ariv*.

A biblical source is adduced for each of these attributions. First, *And Abraham rose early in the morning and* [*went*] *to the place where he stood before God* (Genesis 19:27). The Hebrew term for "stood," *amad*, is used to describe prayer in the Bible. Thus we have Abraham's early morning *Shaḥarit* (see Psalms 106:30). Second, *And Isaac went out to meditate in the field towards evening* (Genesis 24:63). The Hebrew term translated here as "meditate," *lasu'aḥ*, may refer to prayer. Thus we have a reference to Isaac instituting the afternoon *Minḥa* prayer (see Psalms 102:1). Third, speaking of Jacob, *And he came upon a certain place and rested there for the night, for the sun had set* (Genesis 28:11). The Hebrew word for "and he came upon," *vayifga*, is an expression used to refer to prayer. Hence Jacob's evening *Ma'ariv* (see Jeremiah 7:16). One Hasidic commentator puns on the Yiddish word for prayer, *davenen*, saying that it comes from the Aramaic *de'avinan*, "of our Fathers" (*Benei Yisaskhar*).

A second approach in the Talmud holds that the prayers were established to correspond to the daily Temple sacrifices. Each morning in the Temple, the *tamid* sacrifice was offered. *Shaḥarit* corresponds to this sacrifice. *Minḥa* corresponds to the daily afternoon *tamid* sacrifice.

Ma'ariv corresponds to the burning of leftovers on the altar performed in the evening. The sages go further, explaining that according to this line of thought, the prescribed times for the prayer services are derived from the stipulated times for the sacrifices. For example, the disagreement as to whether the morning *tamid* could be offered until midday or only until the fourth hour after sunrise is reflected in an argument as to the required time for *Shaḥarit*.

Comparing the two opinions presented in the Talmud, a difference is apparent. While the first approach clearly identifies those *who* instituted the prayers – our forefathers – the second approach merely tells us *why* the prayers were designated. The Talmud does not identify the legislating body which instituted the prayers corresponding to the Temple sacrifices. Rashi explains that it was the Men of the Great Assembly who established the three prayer services to correspond to the Temple service.

Who were these Men of the Great Assembly? The Great Assembly was a body of sages that, according to tradition, convened at the beginning of the Second Temple period.

Rabbi Yaakov ibn Ḥabib (c.1450–1516) points out that identifying the Great Assembly as the legislating body is noteworthy, for this institution existed while the Temple was still standing. Thus the Men of the Great Assembly could not have instituted the prayer services as a replacement for the sacrificial service. Perforce, the newly instituted prayers were to complement – not supplant – the Temple sacrifices.

Elsewhere in his commentary, Rabbi Yaakov ibn Ḥabib reports that one of his congregants approached him on Yom Kippur after reading the *avoda*, the passages that describe the Yom Kippur Temple service. He asked the rabbi: "How can this be considered the holiest day of the year nowadays? The focus of this day was the Temple service, the sacrificial offerings and the incense, yet regrettably we lack all of this today."

Rabbi Yaakov ibn Ḥabib records his response: "I encouraged the questioner with the following answer. I reminded him that apart from the priestly sacrifices, we have another type of service that is even more wonderful and more valuable, namely the Levite service. Many Levites would sing and play instruments to thank and praise the Almighty. And one could argue that this service was greater than the sacrifices, since the sacrificial service was performed with the hands, while the songs were sung using the mouth and focusing the mind."

Rabbi Yaakov ibn Ḥabib identifies our prayers with the Levite songs as opposed to the animal sacrifices, suggesting that the Levite accompaniment was a superior mode of worship. To buttress this innovative contention, he continues: "Isn't this obvious? Sacrifices were legally limited to the physical confines of the Temple, while prayer in any pure place transforms that location into a microcosm of the Temple." The thrust of his argument is clear. The ultimate worship of the Almighty is not through burning animals. Heartfelt prayer, mirroring the Levite song, is the true path to God. That is why sacrifices were accompanied by prayer, even when those sacrifices were the centre of daily ritual.

In truth, the secondary nature of the sacrifices is an idea expressed by the prophet Micah (Micah 6:6–8): *With what shall I approach the Almighty, bow before the God on high? Should I come before Him with burnt offerings, with year-old calves? Would the Almighty be pleased with thousands of rams? Myriads of streams of oil? Should I give my first-born for my transgression, the fruit of my womb for the sin of my soul?* Micah roundly rejects the sacrifices as the ultimate Divine service, seeing the Temple offerings as peripheral to the true path of worship. Instead, Micah advocates a path which is deeply personal: *It has been told to you, O man, what is good and what the Almighty demands of you – only to do justice, to love kindness, and to walk humbly with your God.*

BERAKHOT 26B

Paths in prayer

As explained previously, the Talmud presents two opinions as to the origins of the *Shaḥarit, Minḥa* and *Ma'ariv* prayer services. According to one opinion, our prayers were instituted by the forefathers, and as such they are ancient rites that date back to the beginning of the history of our people. The second approach suggests a later date – the prayers correspond to the daily Temple sacrifices (*B. Berakhot* 26b).

How are we to understand this ostensibly historical disagreement? Who really established our prayer rites? One possible approach is to suggest that the forefathers instituted the prayers and that, years later, the sages linked the prayers to the Temple sacrifices. There were, therefore, two stages to the process of instituting the prayers. First, the forefathers mandated the prayers, and then the sages established the detailed frameworks of the prayers based on the Temple rites.

Alternatively, it could be suggested that the forefathers innovated the concept of the three daily prayers. Yet prayer services did not become widespread practice until Temple times.

Using the tools of legal analysis we can suggest a variation on this approach. The Talmud may be describing two types of sources for the prayers – the historical source and the legal source. In legal theory, historical sources are the factual background for legislation. Historical sources themselves do not create normative law, they merely tell the story of why the law was enacted, how the law was inspired, and what issue the law comes to address. A law becomes normative only when it has a legal source, that is, an act recognised by the system as being able to create binding law.

In our case, the historical source of our prayers may indeed date back to Abraham, Isaac and Jacob. The binding obligation to pray, however, is not due to the prayers of our forefathers. The three daily prayers became normative law only when our sages enacted the requirement to pray, parallel to the concurrent obligation of Temple sacrifices. While over the generations many may have followed in the footsteps of our forefathers and prayed daily, prayer as a halakhic obligation was not instituted until the Second Temple period.

There are numerous examples of laws that have a source rooted in history and a later legal source that turns the practice into mandated law. Thus, for instance, the prohibition of eating the sciatic nerve of a kosher animal is traced back to the blow Jacob received during his struggle with a mystery assailant: *Therefore the children of Israel eat not the thigh muscle that is on the socket of the hip to this day* (Genesis 32:33). Nevertheless, the prohibition did not become normative law until it was enacted years later at Sinai. Similarly ritual circumcision is traced back to Abraham, yet it is incumbent upon us because it was legislated in the Torah, not because Abraham circumcised himself (see *M. Ḥullin* 7:6 and *Commentary of Maimonides*).

Beyond the legal analysis of historical and legal sources of halakha, the dual sources of our prayer services suggest two paradigms for the prayer endeavour. We do not all pray in the same manner. There are those of us who stand in prayer like a lone Isaac in a field, hoping that when we lift our eyes our beloved will magically be approaching. We pray as individuals, almost alone in a hostile world. Our travails are personal and our heartfelt prayers reflect this solitude. Even when we stand with a congregation, our prayers are essentially lone ventures, journeys we undertake with just our prayer book for company. The pace of the congregation seldom matches the beat of our supplications. While we acknowledge the value of the community, we often find it limiting or even suffocating. All we want is a quiet corner in the synagogue to offer our sincere prayers to the Almighty. Such supplicants follow the path of the forefathers, who ventured to forge their own prayers.

There are others of us who come to synagogue primarily to pray with the community. For us, the only true prayer service is one undertaken together with peers. We thrive on the communal singing, on saying passages aloud and together. If we are left alone without a community, our prayers are empty shells bereft of verve; they go nowhere and in a flit they are thankfully over. We are honest enough with ourselves to realise that our prayers cannot reach the heights we desire, but we sincerely hope that our supplications will be accepted on the coattails of our peers. Such supplicants reflect the sacrifices in the Temple, where the service was essentially communal.

Of course life is rarely – if ever – cut of one cloth. Most of us oscillate between these two paradigms. One day we crave a private corner, the next day we feel as though we have nothing to say without the community. We have two paradigms of prayer – our forefathers' prayers and the Temple sacrifice service – so that we all can find a path, regardless of the mood in which we find ourselves.

BERAKHOT 27B

Power to create obligations

CONSIDERING THE CONTEMPORARY lack of a binding central halakhic authority, the possibility of enacting or abrogating halakha seems remote. The halakhic system, however, contains certain alternative legislative mechanisms. While the authority and the responsibility to create law must lie first with the authorised legislative body, "the people" as an anonymous, unsystematic, unreflective entity also wield considerable halakhic power. One mechanism entrusted in the hands of the people can be seen at work in the development of the obligation to pray the evening *Ma'ariv* service.

The sages tell us that *Ma'ariv* "is not fixed." The Talmud then discusses the meaning of this assertion. It dismisses the possibility that the statement indicates that there is no mandated time for the evening service (*M. Berakhot* 4:1; *B. Berakhot* 27b). Rather, it concludes that the phrase refers to a dispute as to the status of *Ma'ariv*. According to one opinion, *Ma'ariv* – like the other prayer services – is obligatory. A dissenting opinion holds that it is an elective prayer service, that is, it is "not fixed." The logic behind this position is that *Ma'ariv* was instituted to correspond to the evening burning of the sacrificial leftovers on the Temple altar. This procedure was not essential to the validity of the sacrifices that had been offered during the day, and hence *Ma'ariv* is not essential either (*Rashi*).

The Talmud records a later Babylonian dispute as to which opinion should be adopted. Following the rules for arriving at normative law, the accepted position is that *Ma'ariv* is an optional service. The implication of the optional nature of *Ma'ariv* is that we are less stringent regarding the time of the prayer and there is no repetition of *Amida* by the prayer leader.

Nevertheless, when people began consistently praying *Ma'ariv*, its status changed, reflecting the people's desire to accept *Ma'ariv* as an obligatory prayer. While it was originally an optional service, when the people accepted upon themselves to pray it, *Ma'ariv* became obligatory (*Bahag*). This unofficial decision of the people carries implications for the laws of *Ma'ariv*. One who mistakenly recites the weekday *Ma'ariv* on Shabbat or on one of the festivals must repeat the prayer. Despite its original optional nature, it is now considered obligatory and hence if it is not recited properly it must be repeated.

While *Ma'ariv* is a well-documented and accepted example of the legal power of the people, we do have other instances of this mechanism. For example, women are exempt from fulfilling the obligation to count the *omer* between Pesaḥ and Shavuot (*Maimonides*). This exemption is due to the rule that women are excused from time-bound positive commandments (*B. Kiddushin* 29b; *B. Berakhot* 20b). The seventeenth-century Polish halakhist Rabbi Avraham Abele Gombiner (c. 1633–c. 1683) – known by the title of his commentary *Magen Avraham* – writes that even though women are exempt from counting the *omer*, "they have already accepted it upon themselves as an obligation." While the position of the Magen Avraham is not widely accepted and is certainly difficult to source, the development he is referring to reflects the power of an anonymous body of women to create a halakhic obligation.

A third example of this legal mechanism comes once again from the arena of women's obligation to fulfil time-bound commandments. The great talmudic mind, influential halakhist and humble rabbinic figure Rabbi Akiva Eiger (1761–1837) opens his compendium of responsa with a discussion of women's obligations in various rituals. He quotes the accepted position that women are exempt from time-bound commandments, but adds: "Most of our women are stringent and are careful and diligent to fulfil most time-bound commandments, such as *shofar*, *sukka*, *lulav* and making *kiddush* on festivals. It is as if they have accepted these upon themselves as obligatory." Rabbi Akiva Eiger is intimating that the women have chosen to waive their exemption and treat these time-bound commandments as binding.

A final example emerges from the laws of Ḥanukka. Let us examine the talmudic description of how the festival is to be celebrated (*B. Shabbat* 21b). The essential commandment of Ḥanukka is for one light to be kindled every night of the holiday in every household. Those who wish to enhance their performance of the directive kindle one light for each and every household member each night. A third level of observance is prescribed for those who wish to fulfil the commandment in the optimal way: kindling the number of lights corresponding to the day of the festival. There is a dispute as to how to go about doing this. The School of Shammai feels that on the first night, eight lights should be kindled, and that on each night thereafter the lights should be decreased by one. Thus the number of lights corresponds to the number of days left until the end of the festival. The School of Hillel holds that that the lights should correspond to the days already celebrated. One light should be kindled on the first night, and each night an additional light should be kindled so that on the last night eight lights are lit. Thus our sages present a unique tiered system for fulfilling the obligation of kindling lights.

Curiously, however, when Rabbi Yosef Karo (1488–1575) codifies the laws of Ḥanukka, he omits any reference to the multiple levels of the commandment, citing only the third option (*Shulḥan Arukh, Oraḥ Ḥayim* 671:2). Indeed, commentators on the code wonder what happened to the other tiers (*Peri Megadim*).

We may suggest that here too the people have taken an elective practice and elevated it to an obligatory level. This has been achieved through the widespread acceptance of kindling the eight-branched *ḥanukkiya*. Indeed, nowadays we would be hard-pressed to locate a household that opts for the lower tiers. Moreover, there are legal implications of this change in status. Even though only the first light kindled is a fulfilment of the original obligation, it is forbidden to use any of the lights kindled for mundane purposes (*Shulḥan Arukh, Oraḥ Ḥayim* 674:1). The holy status accorded to all the lights is the result of the people's actions.

Our unique legal system accompanied us into exile. Since our legal institutions were destroyed and we were faced with the formidable task of preserving our tradition, we employed various mechanisms to deal with our exilic reality. Yet one halakhic institution remained strong – the people. No one person or any identifiable group can be credited with exerting sovereignty and control over this body. This anonymous entity, expressing its opinion unconsciously and unsystematically, has continued to articulate its view through action, shaping and reshaping the contours of Jewish practice. One option exercised by the people has been the granting of obligatory status to certain practices which were originally elective. This mechanism highlights the halakhic power invested in the people.

BERAKHOT 27B–28A

Preservation and innovation

THE TENSION BETWEEN guarding sanctified traditions and innovating along uncharted routes is part of the fabric of contemporary Judaic discourse. Each avenue is concurrently attractive and hazardous. The preservation of time-honoured traditions carries the danger of a fossilised world-view. Yet as we open the doors to change we run the risk of forsaking the path of our ancestors. This tension may be at the root of one of the most famous rabbinic compromises (*B. Berakhot* 27b–28a).

Rabban Gamliel, the head of rabbinic Judaism in his day, conducted the academy with a strict elitism, allowing only the finest students to participate in the conversation of the *beit midrash*. To enforce this restriction, a guard was posted at the doorway to prevent the entry of students whose outward behaviour did not reflect their inner selves. Rabbinic literature records three incidents in which Rabban Gamliel sought to impose the authority of his office on others (*M. Rosh HaShana* 2:8–9; *B. Berakhot* 27b; *B. Bekhorot* 36a). This iron-fisted approach led to a disregard – and even trampling – of his esteemed rabbinic colleagues. Rabban Gamliel's repeated mistreatment of the respected Rabbi Yehoshua distressed the other rabbis, who resolved to depose the authoritarian leader.

Alas, identifying an appropriate replacement was no simple task. Rabbi Yehoshua was immediately ruled out, since appointing Rabban Gamliel's adversary would unnecessarily hurt the ousted leader. Rabbi Akiva was the obvious choice to head the academy, but his candidacy was rejected in light of the concern that he would be unable to invoke ancestral merit should the unseated Rabban Gamliel – a descendant of the Davidic line – curse him. Finally it was decided to appoint the wise Rabbi Elazar ben Azarya, a tenth generation descendant of Ezra the Scribe and hence of royal descent. He was also sufficiently wealthy to be able to travel to Rome on official business.

Presented with this opportunity, Rabbi Elazar ben Azarya was hesitant. He returned home to deliberate before making a decision. His wife was not in favour of his taking the position, ominously warning: "They will appoint you today and cast you out tomorrow!"

Rabbi Elazar ben Azarya countered: "Better to use precious glassware today, though it will shatter tomorrow."

The only remaining obstacle to accepting the appointment was the scholar's youth. Divine intervention removed this barrier; a miracle occurred and the beard of the then-eighteen-year-old Rabbi Elazar ben Azarya turned white, giving him the appearance of a venerable seventy-year-old sage.

Taking office, Rabbi Elazar ben Azarya unassumingly changed some *beit midrash* procedures. The doorman was removed and entry was granted to all those who wished to plumb the depths of the tradition. Everyone participated in the discussions, from great scholars to weavers from the Dung Gate in Jerusalem (*M. Eduyot* 1:3). Even the overthrown Rabban Gamliel was a welcome participant. Hundreds of benches were brought in to accommodate the increased enrolment.

This inclusive atmosphere extended to halakhic decisions of that day, as Yehuda the Ammonite was permitted to marry within the Jewish community. Despite his Ammonite origins, it was determined that contemporary Ammon did not parallel biblical Ammon, and hence the scriptural prohibition against accepting Ammonite converts did not apply. The creative ambiance left its mark, and that very day was celebrated as the beginning of the mishnaic enterprise, as people recounted ancient traditions that were then duly recorded for posterity.

Seeing how the *beit midrash* was flourishing under its new management, Rabban Gamliel began to question his own exclusionary style of leadership. In a dream, the deposed leader was assured – perhaps merely to comfort him – that he had not erred.

In a heroic act of regret, Rabban Gamliel chose to approach his adversary, Rabbi Yehoshua, in a bid for reconciliation. Initially, Rabbi Yehoshua rejected the entreaties of his counterpart. He acceded to the request only when Rabban Gamliel pleaded: "Forgive me for the sake of my father's house." Thus Rabban Gamliel invoked his position as the vestige of the Davidic line, which Rabban Yoḥanan ben Zakkai had requested that Vespasian spare on the eve of the destruction of Jerusalem (*B. Gittin* 56a–b). It seems that Rabban Gamliel perceived his task to be that of the bearer of the sacred heritage.

A new predicament arose. Who should now head the academy? The regal Rabban Gamliel remained the most fitting leader, certainly following his conciliation with Rabbi Yehoshua. But removing Rabbi Elazar ben Azarya without due cause would hardly be fair. For the scholar it would constitute a decrease in holiness, a vector foreign to the tradition.

At the root of this quandary may have been a greater issue that transcended the individual scholars. The dilemma may have focused on the ideal leadership style and the ultimate aspirations of the *beit midrash*. Should we seek to preserve the tradition in its purest form, even at the cost of excluding certain voices from the discussion? Or should the doors to the *beit midrash* be thrown wide open with no opinion silenced, thus running the risk of adulteration, in the name of innovation?

A fifty-fifty power-sharing arrangement was dismissed because of the need for an undisputed leader who would set the tone and convey the direction and purpose of the academy. Furthermore, the sages may have felt that preservation and innovation need not be granted equal time. Once a modification has been made, the safeguarded structure is irrevocably changed. True, the tradition should accommodate changes in our environs, yet such transformations need to be weighed very carefully, in order to prevent the corruption of or even the tarnishing of our hallowed heritage. With this tension in mind, the solution arrived at is fascinating. Rabban Gamliel was to serve as the head of the institution for three weeks out of every month, while the remaining week would fall under the purview of Rabbi Elazar ben Azarya.

The balance between the worthy endeavours of safeguarding sacred conventions and allowing room for altering the established order is a precarious one. We aspire for an unpetrified law, though it should not be so malleable that it has no backbone; we seek to guard our heritage from alien influences, though we desire a tradition that is pliable enough to allow for change. To this day we continue to grapple with the challenge of identifying the elusive equilibrium between preservation and innovation.

BERAKHOT 28A

Adding benches to the *beit midrash*

As mentioned above, when Rabbi Elazar ben Azarya replaced Rabban Gamliel as the head of the academy, he immediately instituted a number of changes (*B. Berakhot* 28a). Under Rabban Gamliel's regime, entry to the *beit midrash* was limited to those students whose outward actions accurately reflected their inner selves. A guard was stationed at the door, and the admission of many a prospective student of the tradition was barred. The guard's job was an impossible one. How was he supposed to test the inner nature of each student applying for admission?

Some commentators assert that this guard could not have been human. He must have been a Divine messenger, otherwise he would have had no chance of fulfilling his appointed task (*Rabbi Menaḥem Mendel of Rymanów*). Others suggest that the task was so difficult that the doors were simply locked; only those who desperately wanted to learn found an alternate way to enter the *beit midrash* (*Rabbi Avraham Yaakov Friedman of Sadigora*).

Be the nature of the sentry what it may, his services were no longer employed by the newly appointed Rabbi Elazar ben Azarya. Inviting everyone to enter the *beit midrash*, the new administration removed the mysterious guard from his post and the doors were thrown open. As people poured in, new benches were quickly added. The Talmud presents two views as to how many seats were added. According to one opinion, four hundred benches were added, while another view suggests it was seven hundred.

This is a curious disagreement. How could there be such a discrepancy? This question could summarily be dismissed by pointing out that the Talmud has no ambitions of writing history. Our sages are imaginatively painting a vivid picture of an expanded *beit midrash*, as all those who were previously denied entry suddenly gained admission.

While the Talmud may not attempt to present a historic record of events, it does strive to be an educational tool on both a normative and an ethical plane. Thus we have the licence – and maybe even the responsibility – to seek greater significance and pertinent meaning in the new benches.

One commentator offers an innovative explanation of this bench disagreement. Everyone agrees that four hundred benches were physically added to the *beit midrash* on that day. Those who propose the number seven hundred are not describing the seating capacity, but rather the atmosphere of learning. Four hundred benches may have been added, but it felt as if seven hundred benches were filled with students, all experiencing a surge in Torah study and an educational renaissance. Even the learning of old-time students was spurred to new heights, as new perspectives, fresh insights and enthusiasm revitalised the entire *beit midrash* (*Ketav Sofer*).

A collective study endeavour with an open-door policy results in not just a quantitative increase in the number of students, but also a qualitative upgrade in the learning experience. Appropriately, the day that the doors were opened was remembered as an unparalleled day of Torah study. No question was left unanswered, no person was left outside. Even the ousted Rabban Gamliel participated in the discussion and was moved to question his own management style.

This spirit of inclusiveness extended not only to the top echelons of the learning pyramid; the entire spectrum of Jewish society was present in the *beit midrash* on that day. This mood affected the halakhic decisions of the day, as people who were previously not considered Jewish were permitted to marry within the Jewish community.

In this light, it is surprising that some commentators offer a different and more negative explanation of the additional seats. They begin by questioning why the sages cite the number of additional places rather than the number of additional students. Surely we are more interested in the people than in the furniture. The Talmud may be stressing that the introduction of benches was in itself a noteworthy novelty. In the past, when only the purest students were permitted to enter, there was no need for seating. Each person gaining entry was happy to stand attentively and learn. The spiritual focus on the pursuit of Torah and the burning desire to study forestalled the need for a place to sit and rest. The new students – even with their excitement and aspirations – still needed to sit, hence the new benches. The benches tell us not only about the number of students, but also of their calibre. The new benches therefore represent a hidden critique of the new policy allowing everyone to enter the *beit midrash* (*Ahavat Yisrael*).

The benches may have been an innovation, but decrying their introduction seems to go against the flow of the Talmud passage. As we have mentioned, the sages laud that matchless day, declaring it the beginning of the enterprise to record the Oral Law. Perhaps we can view the innovative additional seating in another light.

Indeed, Rabbi Elazar ben Azarya removed the guard, opening the gates to the *beit midrash* and inviting all to participate. But at times opening the doors is insufficient. What happens once the invitee enters? Does the guest feel welcome? Our sages are suggesting that not only did Rabbi Elazar invite people to enter, he also made them feel welcome by offering each of them a place to sit. Without that seat, new students may not have felt at ease and would have been hesitant to contribute. They would have felt like spectators, not participants. By bringing in new benches, Rabbi Elazar ben Azarya was saying: "You are all welcome here. You are part of this communal endeavour. Let us learn together."

Thus the new head of the academy encouraged and empowered students to take part in the discussion. It is only in such a welcome and accepting atmosphere that the *beit midrash* can fulfil its potential and be a place of creative thought, lively discussion and growth.

BERAKHOT 28B

Minding other people's business

IF A PERSON misses a class or doesn't turn up for prayer services, what is the appropriate response? Should we inquire about the person's well-being? Or should we pay no attention to the absence, respecting the individual's autonomy and privacy by not mentioning it? Certainly modern sensibilities urge us to avoid minding other people's business.

Once Rav Avya fell ill and was unable to attend the weekly lecture of Rav Yosef, which was delivered on Shabbat before the additional *Musaf* prayer (*B. Berakhot* 28b; *Rashi*). The following day, when Rav Avya was feeling better, he came to the study hall. Abbaye wished to make sure that their teacher Rav Yosef would not feel slighted by absence. Using the respectful third person, Abbaye asked Rav Avya: "What is the reason that master did not come to the lecture?"

Rav Avya answered: "I felt faint and was unable."

Understanding that Rav Avya meant that he had felt faint from hunger, Abbaye continued: "Why didn't you eat something light and then come?" Rav Avya explained that his course was rooted in the opinion that forbids eating before the *Musaf* prayer. Normative halakha does not follow this opinion; while it is forbidden to eat a meal before *Musaf*, snacking is permitted (*Shulḥan Arukh, Oraḥ Ḥayim* 286:3).

Abbaye accepted Rav Avya's halakhic position. However, he was still not placated, and persisted: "You should have prayed *Musaf* privately, eaten something light and then come!"

Once again Rav Avya's path was guided by law. He retorted: "Don't you accept the opinion that it is forbidden for a person to recite the prayers before the congregation does?" Abbaye did accept this rule, but explained that it applies only to one who is present with a congregation. Outside the synagogue, one may privately pray before the congregation, and this is what Rav Avya should have done.

Why was Abbaye sticking his nose into Rav Avya's business?

Before we turn to a possible answer, the Talmud records a similar incident, only this time it is a student inquiring about a teacher's absence (*B. Berakhot* 7b–8a).

In a seemingly intrusive probe, Rabbi Yitzḥak asked Rav Naḥman: "Why have you not been coming to the synagogue to pray with the congregation?"

Rav Naḥman answered simply "I am unable," referring to his frail state of health (*Rashi*).

Rabbi Yitzḥak was not to be deterred. He suggested: "Let them assemble ten people for the master so that he can pray with a quorum."

Rav Naḥman balked at the offer. "It is too much trouble," he said, as he did not want to burden others (*Magen Avraham*).

Rabbi Yitzḥak persisted with a new suggestion: "Why don't you ask a messenger to inform you when the congregation is worshipping so that you can pray at the same time?" In this way Rav Naḥman would at least be able to pray at the same time as the congregation, if not at the same place.

Wondering about the significance of private prayers that coincide with communal prayers in a different location, Rav Naḥman asked: "Why are you being so adamant?" Rabbi Yitzḥak responded with a rabbinic exposition of the verse: *But as for me, my prayer is to You, God, at a favourable time* (Psalms 69:14). When is a *favourable time*? At the time that the congregation prays. Thus those who pray alone should ensure that their supplications are timed to coincide with the prayers of the congregation.

Let us return to the beginning of the passage. How did Rabbi Yitzḥak have the gall to question Rav Naḥman? Surely, if the master did not attend services, he had good reason, and it is hardly the place of the pupil to inquire about the master's absence.

The key to understanding both these passages may be found in another talmudic passage earlier in our tractate (*B. Berakhot* 6b). Our sages tell us that if there is a regular attendee at the synagogue who – for whatever reason – fails to attend one day, the Almighty inquires about this missing person, seeking to understand the reason for the absence (*Rashi*).

A biblical source is offered for the assertion that God inquires after a God-fearing person: *Who is there among you that fears God and listens to the voice of His servant? One who walked in darkness and does not have light* (Isaiah 50:10). Expounding this verse, the passage continues: "Not having light" depends on the reason for the absence; only if the missing person has skipped the service for a non-*mitzva* objective do we say that he does not have light. Indeed, our sages rule (*B. Berakhot* 11a) that one who is involved in a *mitzva* is released from the obligation to perform other *mitzvot*, including prayer.

Thus we see that the practice of inquiring after a missing person is traced back to the Almighty, who expectantly awaits the arrival of regular attendees. Should the regulars not turn up, God inquires as to their whereabouts.

Interestingly, the printed editions of the Talmud use the causative (*hif'il*) form of *mash'il* to describe God's inquiry, rather than the usual simple (*kal*) form of *sho'el*. When we shift from biblical Hebrew to rabbinic Hebrew, there is a general move away from the simple form. In this case, however, the use of the causative may indicate that the Divine paradigm is encouraging imitation. God inquires, but is also trying to show us that we should ask about our absent peers. God is trying to make us into the type of people who care about the well-being of others.

With this model in mind, we can understand the two passages quoted above. Rabbi Yitzḥak inquired about Rav Naḥman's absence from prayer and Abbaye asked Rav Avya why he had missed class.

Why are we encouraged to ask about our colleagues' whereabouts? It is certainly not just a fact-finding mission, for in both talmudic tales the inquirer followed up with practical suggestions aimed at finding a way for the absent sage to be part of the collective enterprise in some way.

It seems that such inquiry reflects an interest in the other and makes the absent person feel like an essential contributor in a shared undertaking. Indeed, the line between showing an interest and intruding may not be clearly defined. Nevertheless, a *laissez-faire* attitude is not the solution; such an attitude indicates indifference and coldness.

If people know that they will be missed, that they play a part in a joint venture – whether it is prayer, study or any worthy endeavour – they are more likely to realise that every person in the community makes a contribution that is irreplaceable.

BERAKHOT 28B

Prayers for learning

JEWISH TRADITION PRESCRIBES how we should start the day. Immediately after waking up in the morning, the *Shaḥarit* prayers are to be said. Following the service, before going out to pursue a livelihood, we are enjoined to repair to the *beit midrash* for Torah study. The sages emphasise the benefit that accrues to someone who juxtaposes Torah study with prayer: "One who leaves the synagogue, enters the *beit midrash* and engages in Torah study will be privileged to greet the countenance of the Divine Presence" (*B. Berakhot* 64a; *B. Mo'ed Katan* 29a). A biblical proof text is cited to buttress this idea: *Go from strength to strength, appear before the Almighty in Zion* (Psalms 84:8). This means if you go from the stronghold of the synagogue to the stronghold of the *beit midrash*, then you will be privileged to appear before God.

According to one commentator, the possibility of being privileged "to greet the countenance of the Divine Presence" indicates that going from the synagogue to the *beit midrash* is akin to fulfilling the commandment regarding the thrice-yearly pilgrimage to Jerusalem for the festivals. The Bible repeatedly describes the pilgrims as appearing before the presence of the Almighty (see Exodus 23:17 and 34:23; Deuteronomy 16:16). In a Temple-less world, we can still fulfil this *mitzva* in a manner of sorts, by going from the synagogue to the *beit midrash* (*Maharsha*).

This talmudic advice was codified as Jewish law. The codes further mandate that delving into the texts of our tradition each morning should take place at a fixed and sacrosanct time; even great business opportunities should not encroach on it. Moreover, even those who are not proficient in analysing Torah texts should still make their way to the *beit midrash* and take part in the Torah endeavour in some capacity (*Shulḥan Arukh, Oraḥ Ḥayim* 155:1).

This idea is reflected in the order of the laws which are presented at the beginning of our tractate. After detailing the times for daily prayers, the Mishna immediately proceeds to the topic of prayers to be recited upon entering the *beit midrash*. As we discussed, Rabbi Neḥunya ben Hakkana would recite a short prayer before entering the *beit midrash* and upon leaving (*M. Berakhot* 4:2; *Tiferet Yisrael*). Seeing him offering this brief prayer, onlookers inquired: "What is the nature of this prayer?"

The sage replied: "When I enter, I pray that no mishap should be caused by me; and when I depart, I give thanks for my portion." A fuller text of these supplications is presented in the Talmud. The full prayer against mishaps, to be recited upon entry into the *beit midrash*, is: "May it be Your will, God my Lord, that no mishap should be caused by me. May I not stumble in a matter of law; may my peers rejoice over me. May I not declare pure that which is impure, and not declare impure that which is pure. May my colleagues not stumble in a matter of law; may I rejoice over them" (*B. Berakhot* 28b).

The tone of this personal prayer makes it sound like the person about to enter the *beit midrash* does so with trepidation or at least some apprehension. He evidently wonders: will my colleagues rejoice in what I have to contribute? Or will they jeer at me when I stumble? The Babylonian *beit midrash* environment hardly sounds inviting. This is all the more apparent when one compares this prayer with the text of the prayer recited before entering the *beit midrash* in the Land of Israel: "May it be Your will, God my Lord and the Lord of my ancestors, that I take not offence at the words of my colleagues, and that my colleagues not take offence at my words; that we do not declare impure that which is pure, and that we do not declare pure that which is impure; that we do not declare forbidden that which is permitted, and that we do not declare permitted that which is forbidden. [If this were to occur] I would find myself embarrassed in this world and in the next world" (*Y. Berakhot* 7d).

There are two significant differences between the Babylonian prayer and the supplication recited in the Land of Israel. First, the Babylonian version is recited solely in the singular, whereas the prayer from the Land of Israel uses both singular and plural. The learning endeavour in the Land of Israel evidently was a communal pursuit in which decisions were made in concert; in Babylonia, it was evidently each scholar for himself. All one could do was pray that his peers would rejoice in what he had to say.

A second difference is that in the Land of Israel there appears to have been a greater concern for emotions. The supplicant prays that he not offend others, nor be offended by them. In the Babylonian version there is no parallel concern; indeed, heated exchanges were integral to the Babylonian *beit midrash* (*B. Kiddushin* 30b). The Israeli *beit midrash* appears to have been gentler than its Babylonian counterpart.

Each *beit midrash* is different; each learner is different; and we each enter the *beit midrash* with different aspirations. Each learning situation calls for a different type of prayer appropriate to the challenges of that particular *beit midrash*. Hence our prayers before entering will understandably differ.

Reading the two passages together, we can suggest that perhaps the most important aspect of saying a prayer before entering the *beit midrash* is not the content of the prayer, but its very existence. It matters less what we say and more that we turn to God before we begin to study. In this way, the *beit midrash* experience is more than an intellectual exercise; it becomes an opportunity to forge a relationship with the Almighty. Probing our sacred texts in the *beit midrash* is another avenue to connect to God. Accordingly, the *beit midrash* venture naturally follows and complements the morning encounter with God in the synagogue.

We could therefore argue that the most important aspect of the passages is the question that is posed in both Talmuds: when entering the *beit midrash*, what prayer do we offer?

BERAKHOT 28B

Set texts for prayer

In a number of cases, Jewish law orders an individual to act in a manner most suitable to the masses, even when the individual would personally be better served by following a different course. The law has little choice but to address the needs of the majority, even at the expense of those of an individual. Nevertheless, when it comes to spiritual pursuits this attitude can frustrate personal growth.

A primary example is set prayer. The Talmud tells us that Shimon HaPekuli, the cotton merchant, arranged the eighteen blessings of the *Amida* before Rabban Gamliel in Yavne (*B. Berakhot* 28b). Another tradition attributes the order of the blessings to Ezra the Scribe and the Men of the Great Assembly, a legislative body that existed during the end of the Babylonian Exile and the early Second Temple period (*B. Megilla* 17b, 18a). The two conflicting accounts are reconciled by the Talmud's suggestion that the original sequence was forgotten, and Shimon HaPekuli subsequently reinstated it. Either way, we can ask: why do we need an order at all? Indeed, why are standard prayer texts necessary?

Let us explore three aspects of the set texts of the *Amida*. First, we will contemplate the utility of standard prayer texts. Second, we will address the connection between the mandated texts and their long gone authors. Finally, we will consider the significance of the order of the blessings of the *Amida*.

1. FOR THE BENEFIT OF THE PEOPLE

A clearly defined prayer formula provides a framework accessible to all. Such set prayers present a scaffold for people unable to author their own prayers, a structure through which they can connect to their heritage and commune with God. Moreover a standardised text unites supplicants under one banner and helps to create community.

Regularised prayer has advantages. Yet the moment the prayers are given a defined, bounded form they are also limited. This can lead to a perplexing situation that challenges many a supplicant: if we feel inspired to stand before the Almighty and pour out our hearts, set prayer can be suffocating.

A number of explanations are offered to explain why set prayer is necessary. The first Chief Rabbi of the Land of Israel, Rabbi Avraham Yitzḥak HaKohen Kook (1865–1935), offers a particularly satisfying approach. Rabbi Kook's explanation appears in a context seemingly divorced from that of set prayer: a discussion about *bikkurim*, the first fruits that were brought to Jerusalem and presented to the *kohanim*.

The Torah instructs that bringing *bikkurim* be done with pomp and pageantry, and institutes a prescribed text for the rite (Exodus 23:19; Deuteronomy 26:1–11). The Mishna tells us that originally all those who knew how to read the set text would do so on their own (*M. Bikkurim* 3:7). Those who were unable to read the required verses would repeat the words after the priest. Alas, this practice resulted in some people refraining from bringing *bikkurim* because they were ashamed that they could not read the prescribed text. As a result, a new procedure was instituted. Henceforth everybody would repeat the text after the priest, whether or not he was able to read it on his own.

While the new arrangement solved one problem, it may have resulted in another. Those who were able to read the prescribed text were denied the opportunity to fulfil the rite optimally. Rabbi Kook points out that normally, where a deviation from the general practice does not harm the public, it should be allowed so that each individual can reach personal spiritual heights. In the case of *bikkurim*, however, this was clearly not the case. If individuals were to depart from the norm, this would entirely defeat the point of the new rule. Furthermore, once a practice has been officially adopted, an individual may no longer choose to act differently from the community.

At this point Rabbi Kook turns to the case of set prayer. Those who are deeply spiritual would undoubtedly benefit from an unregulated prayer rite, a system in which the inner soul could roam freely in search of the Almighty. For the sake of the masses, however, a fixed rite was instituted so that the majority of individuals would be afforded the opportunity to pray. As with *bikkurim*, once a set text has been legislated, none may stray from it any longer, even if they perceive that for them personally, a different way would be better.

Rabbi Kook is quick to dispel the notion that the set text denies personal spiritual growth. Doing something for the benefit of the community always involves relinquishing some individual return. Rabbi Kook's explanation of this state of affairs is uplifting: the ultimate benefit for an individual is when the collective grows. Any personal growth that would have resulted from choosing a route different from that of the group is dwarfed by the gain amassed via being part of the collective. Rabbi Kook adds that the individual should actually feel tremendous joy at the opportunity to contribute to the collective by forgoing a personal spiritual experience.

Rabbi Kook sees the development of the *bikkurim* rite as an archetype for understanding the individual's sacrifice to assure the well-being of the group, and he adds the institution of set prayers as a second example. I would like to propose a third example taken from our customs under the wedding canopy.

Before a groom betroths his bride, a blessing on the holy act is said. What great joy for a groom to sanctify the union by reciting a blessing before placing the ring on his bride's finger. This was indeed the custom in many locales. However, it is not the general practice today. Nowadays, the rabbi usually recites the blessing on behalf of the groom. Why is this? One commentator explains the prevalent custom by suggesting that it offers an opportunity for the rabbi to bless the couple (*Gra*). Other authorities offer an explanation similar to what we have seen regarding *bikkurim*. Since some grooms do not know how to recite the blessings and we do not want to embarrass them, the blessings are always recited by a third party (*Taz*). Thus the groom is compelled to forgo the opportunity of proudly reciting the blessing over the betrothal of his bride, for the sake of the lofty value of not embarrassing another.

Leaders and people capable of soaring piously – concludes Rabbi Kook – must at times be prepared to curtail their own spiritual journey, giving up experiences they might savour. They must instead remain true to the accepted norm. This is all for the sake of the spiritual growth of the collective. This knowledge in itself should prove spiritually satisfying and fulfilling.

2. PRAYER AS STRONGBOX

Do the identities of the authors of our supplications and their intentions have any significance when we stand in prayer before the Almighty? Or is the substance of our prayers solely a function of the meaning we impart to the words we say? The Talmud appears to deem authorship important, faithfully attributing the prayers to their original authors. Why?

As noted, it was Shimon HaPekuli who arranged the *Amida*. The leader of rabbinic Jewry, Rabban Gamliel of Yavne, then turned to his colleagues and queried: "Is there anyone here who is able to write *Birkat HaMinim*, a benediction against heretics?" These dissenters whom Rabban Gamliel wished to censure were Jews who had been enticed by early Christianity and strayed from the path of tradition. Their presence within the Jewish community, coupled with their belief in Jesus, was seen as a threat to the fabric of Judaism. Rabbinic leadership decided that there was no place in Jewish society for such heretics and hence sought to denounce them in the *Amida*. The Talmud relates that Shmuel HaKatan arose and authored such a blessing.

What was the challenge in composing this portion of the *Amida*, and what expertise was needed to author the benediction?

If we contrast the new addition with the rest of the *Amida*, we see that the entire *Amida* is filled with kindness and love. The benediction censuring the heretics is the only section of the *Amida* that contains negative sentiments. Indeed, it is entirely natural that one who tries to uproot or destroy the faith of others will incur the wrath of those who hold the beliefs to be essential and sacred. A benediction against heretics, therefore, should have been the easiest section to compose, as many people would have passionately despised these agitators.

Though an angry reaction to heretics is understandable, Rabbi Kook opines that a benediction reverberating with negativity must be composed only by one who is pure of heart. We can be certain that such a person would not introduce personal feelings of hatred into the canonised texts of the liturgy. This untainted person could author the benediction with wholesome motives and the purest of intentions. By referencing another talmudic passage, Rabbi Kook further explains why Shmuel HaKatan was truly suited to compose this portion of the *Amida* decrying heretics.

The Talmud relates that Rabban Gamliel invited a rabbinic quorum of seven sages in order to officially declare a leap year (*B. Sanhedrin* 11a). When the quorum assembled, they found that one had come uninvited. "Who has come uninvited? Let him leave!" bellowed Rabban Gamliel. Without hesitation, Shmuel HaKatan stepped forward and said: "It is I who have come uninvited. But I did not come to participate as a member of the quorum; I came to learn practical halakha." Rabban Gamliel responded with kind praise: "Be seated, my son, be seated. All the years are worthy of being made into leap years by you." The Talmud concludes the account by telling us that in fact, Shmuel HaKatan was not really the guilty party, yet he owned up in order to save the interloper from embarrassment.

Elsewhere in talmudic literature, the sages offer some insight into Shmuel HaKatan's name (*Y. Sota* 24b). According to one approach, Shmuel would minimise his own status and hence was known as *HaKatan*, the lesser. Another approach suggests that Shmuel HaKatan was only slightly less holy than the biblical prophet Samuel. Either way, Shmuel HaKatan was clearly no small player.

A telltale saying of Shmuel HaKatan is found in the Mishna (*M. Avot* 4:19): "Shmuel HaKatan says, *When your enemy falls, do not exult, and when he trips, your heart should not rejoice. Lest the Lord see it and be displeased, and avert His wrath from upon him* (Proverbs 24:17–18)." Shmuel HaKatan's aphorism, recorded alongside other rabbinic adages in *Tractate Avot*, is indeed strange. He merely quotes a verse without adding any insight! Herein lies the key to understanding the many aphorisms in *Avot*. The dicta quoted are clearly not the only words of a given sage. We already know that Shmuel HaKatan's contribution to Jewish tradition goes far beyond this verse. Rather, the maxims represent favourite sayings of each sage; these are sayings that they would repeat regularly, urging the community to consider them carefully.

In the case of Shmuel HaKatan, he would exhort his followers to focus on this verse and its implications. Though the other might be your adversary, the enemy's downfall is not a cause for celebration. It is this recognition that made Shmuel HaKatan uniquely qualified to compose *Birkat HaMinim*.

Why is the intent of the author important? When we pray, we invest the words with meaning from our own meditative thoughts. This idea might lead us to wonder whether those of us who are not pure of heart should even be reciting this portion of the *Amida*. The pure focus of the author – in this case Shmuel HaKatan – does not appear to be connected to the words of the liturgy.

Here too, Rabbi Kook provides us with direction. He writes that we recite the words of the liturgy by the rights granted to us by their exalted authors. Though we may be distant from these people of exceptional spirit, we rely on them and their lofty intent when we recite their prayers. The words of our prayers are umbilically connected to the intentions of the sages who authored them.

The founder of the rabbinic institute where Rabbi Kook studied in his youth, Rabbi Ḥayim of Volozhin (1749–1821), goes even further. Even if we can gain insight into the meanings of the words of prayer, what we understand is still no more than a drop in the ocean when we realise the depth imparted to them by the sages who composed them.

Interestingly, the Hebrew word for "word" in talmudic parlance is *teiva* (pl. *teivot*). *Teiva* is also a box or container of sorts. The words of our prayers can be seen as *teivot*, strongboxes containing the thoughts of the authors.

It is our aspiration to open the vaults of prayer and access the intentions of the authors. Even if we do not succeed in retrieving all the original connotations and we find ourselves simply mumbling words, these words are nevertheless invested with meaning by the great authors who bequeathed them to us.

3. UNDERMINING THE DREAM

As noted, the Talmud grapples with conflicting reports as to who put together the sequence of the *Amida* blessings. The different traditions are reconciled with the following account of historical events. The order was first set by the Men of the Great Assembly during the early Second Temple period. It was later forgotten, and Shimon HaPekuli reinstated the original arrangement at the end of the Second Temple period.

One commentator suggests that the order of so central a prayer as the *Amida* could not possibly have been forgotten. The talmudic passage must mean that the reasoning for the order was forgotten. Thus Shimon HaPekuli's contribution was to recover the reasons behind the sequence (*Ben Ish Ḥai*).

The historical account of the sequence of the blessings refers to the original eighteen blessings of the *Amida*. The nineteenth benediction condemning heretics was not part of the original liturgy of the Men of the Great Assembly; rather, as we saw, it was authored by Shmuel HaKatan at the end of the Second Temple period. The question must have arisen: where in the *Amida* should the added passage be inserted?

The most obvious option would be to append this later addition to the end. Such a proposal, however, could not be entertained, since the *Amida* has a conscious tripartite structure. The first three blessings are one unit, and touch on the themes of the Almighty and the Divine relationship with our forebears. The final three blessings are also viewed as one unit and are composed of praise and thanksgiving. The bulk of the *Amida* sets out various requests. Appending the nineteenth blessing – a request for the demise of those who seek to undermine Judaism – to the end of the *Amida* would disturb this configuration. The most likely possibility, then, would have been to add the blessing as the last of the benedictions of the middle section. However, this was not the route chosen. Instead, the new passage was inserted between the eleventh blessing, which pines for the restoration of the judicial system, and the twelfth blessing, which seeks support for the righteous.

The Talmud recounts that the order of the middle blessings was based on a prophetic sequence described in Scripture. The ingathering of the exiles will follow a blessing of prosperity. Once the exiles return home, the justice system will be restored. With the Divinely sanctioned judicial system in place, judgment will be visited on the wicked. When the sabotaging heretics cease to exist, the place of the righteous will be exalted (*B. Megilla* 17b–18a). Accordingly, in the *Amida* the request for prosperity is followed by the call for the ingathering of exiles, followed by the appeal for a restoration of Divine justice, followed by the petition against the heretics, followed by the prayer for God to support the righteous.

An alternative explanation of the sequence can be derived from a tale of two Hasidic masters. In 1865, Rabbi Aharon of Chernobyl (1787–1871) travelled to the Russian town of Makarov for the wedding of his grandson. Soon after his arrival, his younger brother – Rabbi Yitzḥak of Skver (1812–1885), known as Reb Itzikl – arrived and immediately paid a visit to Rabbi Aharon. At that time the Russian rulers, responding to reports from informers, had decreed that the leaders of the Chernobyl Hasidic dynasty needed permission from the authorities to leave their homes. It was with great difficulty that Rabbi Aharon had procured authorisation to travel to the wedding.

With an air of despair, Rabbi Aharon asked his brother: "What do these evil people want from us? Do they despise us because they think we are righteous? We know the truth that we are really nothing!"

Reb Itzikl replied: "The nineteenth blessing against informers was a later addition and should have been appended to the end of the *Amida*. Why is it followed by the blessing regarding the righteous? Our sages understood that in each generation there would be those who would undermine the pious." Reb Itzikl was suggesting that the existence of the righteous is perforce coupled with the presence of troublemakers. Thus a prayer for the protection of the pious is the mirror image of the prayer for the downfall of agitators.

We can expand on this idea. Not only is the benediction decrying heretics strategically placed before the blessing for support of the pious, it is also well placed after the blessing that expresses our hope for a Divinely guided legal system.

The operation of a just legal system is no small feat. Tough decisions have to be made. There is almost always at least one party who is unhappy with the result. While constructive criticism may be a necessary check on the judiciary, such critiques can easily descend to acts that undermine the viability and the stability of the system. The blessing against the heretics should be read not only as an affirmation of the true principles of faith; the blessing also relates to the *malshinim*, the informers, who would undercut central authority, thus destabilising the tradition and chipping away at the pillars of the system of justice.

In this light we can understand the placement of the benediction against agitators. We pine for a legal system that reflects our glorious past, that is Divinely piloted, that manifests justice and fairness. Yet we know that with that dream come the inevitable hecklers who seek to spoil all that is good, and knock over any sturdy structure we attempt to construct. It is these enemies whom we must avoid. It is from these enemies that we request Divine protection.

BERAKHOT 29B–30A

If you can be good, do not be called bad

OUR PRAYERS HAVE various sources; some date back to our forefathers, others to the Second Temple period. The Talmud tells us that *Tefillat HaDerekh,* the wayfarer's prayer recited when embarking upon a journey, is based on an instruction given by Elijah to one of the talmudic sages. He said: "Do not become angry and you will not sin; do not become intoxicated and you will not sin; and when you depart on a journey, beg leave of your Creator and then set out." Our sages explain that begging leave of God refers to the wayfarer's prayer (*B. Berakhot* 29b–30a).

The Talmud then explores the prayer in detail. First, the text is presented: "May it be Your will, God my Lord, that You lead me towards peace, that You direct my steps towards peace and that You maintain me in peace. May You rescue me from the hand of every foe and ambush on the road. May You bless my handiwork, and grant me grace, kindness and mercy in Your eyes and in the eyes of all who see me. Blessed are You, God, who hears prayer." Based on the rule that prayers should be recited as communal requests, an emendation is suggested in which the plural is used rather than the singular: "that You lead *us* towards peace."

Having established the text itself, the Talmud considers the appropriate time for reciting it. We are told that travellers should say the prayer as soon as they embark upon their journey. Codifiers explain that this means as soon as they have left the city limits (*Mishna Berura* 110:29). Among later scholars there is some discussion as to whether the prayer must be said within a certain distance of the city so that it fulfils the requirement of "begging leave" from the Almighty.

Finally, the appropriate posture for the recitation of this supplication is discussed. The Talmud offers two views. Rav Ḥisda maintains that the prayer must be said while stationary, while his colleague Rav Sheshet feels that it could be recited even while in motion.

The passage continues, relating an incident that occurred while these two scholars were on the road together. Rav Ḥisda – as per his own opinion – stopped walking and began to pray the wayfarer's prayer. Rav Sheshet, who was blind but could obviously sense that something was amiss, turned to his attendant and enquired: "What is Rav Ḥisda doing?"

"He is standing still and praying," replied the attendant.

Rav Sheshet then said to his attendant: "Help me stand up too, and I will pray." And then, as if to explain his behaviour which contradicted his own ruling regarding the required posture for the wayfarer's prayer, he added: "If you can be good, do not be called bad." He meant that when you can go along with others or do them a kindness without cost, there is no need to incur resentment by refusing to do so. While Rav Sheshet's concluding epigram has a biblical ring to it, the Talmud tells us elsewhere (*B. Bava Kamma* 81b) that it is in fact distilled from the biblical verse: *Withhold not good from those to whom it is due, when it is in the power of your hand to do it* (Proverbs 3:27).

As we have seen, Rav Sheshet was of the opinion that there was no requirement to stand still for the wayfarer's prayer. Since the party with whom he was travelling had halted anyway – as per Rav Ḥisda's view – he felt that there was no need for a blatant and demonstrative insistence on his opinion. Rav Sheshet wanted to avoid a confrontation, since standing still did not involve any additional inconvenience and was not contrary to his own ruling; he merely deemed it unnecessary.

We should recall that these particular scholarly travellers were no strangers to disagreement. Elsewhere the Talmud describes the awesome trepidation they felt in each other's presence when they came together to study. Rav Ḥisda's lips would tremble on account of Rav Sheshet's comprehensive knowledge of the sages' dicta; he feared that Rav Sheshet would challenge him to resolve apparent contradictions between various statements of the sages. At the same time, Rav Sheshet's entire body would shudder when he considered his colleague's analytical skills that could give rise to complex questions (*B. Eruvin* 67a; *Rashi*). Lively discussion was likely a central part of their daily study routine, and their disagreements are often recorded in the Talmud.

In light of this passage, Rav Sheshet's conduct while journeying with Rav Ḥisda is fascinating. Rav Sheshet chose to sidestep an opportunity to express his opinion, and publicly acted in accordance with Rav Ḥisda's view.

Did the fear of Rav Ḥisda's razor-sharp mind lead Rav Sheshet to dodge a clash? This is unlikely; despite the report that Rav Ḥisda's keen intellect made him tremble with fear, Rav Sheshet nevertheless did not hesitate to argue with his colleague on countless occasions. If Rav Sheshet's dread of Rav Ḥisda was so obsessive that he subverted his own opinion, we most likely would encounter other occasions where he refrained from disagreeing with him. Yet this passage stands out on the talmudic landscape.

Perhaps we can explain that Rav Sheshet was driven by an entirely different feeling: a sense of confidence that permeated his actions such that he did not feel a need to wave the flag of his opinion at every opportunity. Since his opinion was known, momentarily halting his journey for the wayfarer's prayer would not constitute a violation of his principles.

In this light, we can reread Rav Sheshet's final words of explanation: "If you can be good, do not be called bad." Avoiding confrontation is laudable. When it can be done without conceding beliefs or standards, it is most certainly the preferred course of action, and reflects a healthy relationship.

The challenge, therefore, is to identify those situations where avoiding a dispute would constitute compromising one's own principles. When must we stand strong and not yield an inch despite shaking in apprehension at possible responses or objections? And when should we give ground, or at least adopt a flexible stance, under the banner of "If you can be good, do not be called bad"? This is indeed a point to ponder.

BERAKHOT 30B

A conscious approach to prayer

RABBI ZEIRA ONCE saw his colleague Rabbi Ḥiyya bar Abba finish his prayer and then immediately pray again (*B. Berakhot* 30b). Rabbi Zeira sought the reason for this strange behaviour. He analysed the possibilities: "If you tell me that you repeated the prayers because you did not have the proper mindset the first time, we have a tradition from Rabbi Eliezer that a person should always assess himself before embarking on prayer. If he is able to concentrate, he should pray; if he is unable to concentrate, he should not pray!"

The commentators explain that lack of concentration during the first part of the *Amida* invalidates the entire *Amida* (*Tosafot*). Other authorities add that *Modim*, the prayer of thanksgiving, also requires full attentiveness, though there is a question as to whether a lack of focus invalidates that prayer (*Semak*). Rabbi Zeira was suggesting that if the issue was one of concentration during prayers, it should have been resolved before Rabbi Ḥiyya bar Abba began praying. Thus that could not be the reason for his repeating the *Amida*.

Having dismissed that first possibility, Rabbi Zeira moved on to a second scenario: "Perhaps you omitted the special addition for Rosh Ḥodesh, and therefore repeated the *Amida*." Rabbi Zeira quickly rejected this reason as well, citing a teaching dating back to the Second Temple period. If one mistakenly omits mention of Rosh Ḥodesh in the *Ma'ariv* evening prayer, there is no need to repeat the *Amida*, for he can recite the addition in the *Shaḥarit* prayer the following morning. If he forgot in *Shaḥarit*, he need not repeat the prayer. This is because he will mention Rosh Ḥodesh in the additional *Musaf* prayer, which is said only on Rosh Ḥodesh. If instead of the Rosh Ḥodesh text for the *Musaf* prayer, he recited the regular *Amida* and neglected to mention the auspicious day, he need not recite *Musaf* again, for he still has the opportunity to mention Rosh Ḥodesh in the afternoon *Minḥa* prayer. Relying on this teaching, Rabbi Zeira concluded that there was no reason for Rabbi Ḥiyya bar Abba to repeat the *Amida* (unless he was praying *Minḥa,* a possibility not entertained by Rabbi Zeira).

It was now Rabbi Ḥiyya bar Abba's turn to explain his actions: "Indeed I forgot the Rosh Ḥodesh addition, and this precipitated my repetition of the *Amida.* With regard to the teaching you cited – this tradition was said only in regard to a congregation. I, praying alone, was required to repeat the *Amida.*"

Under what circumstances is a repetition following an omission not required? Commentators offer two possibilities. According to one approach, when one prays with a congregation the special Rosh Ḥodesh addition is recited by the leader of the service in the *Amida* repetition. Hence the individual is not required to repeat the silent *Amida* since he will hear the addition during the public repetition. When praying alone, however, even though there will be other opportunities to recite the Rosh Ḥodesh addition, the *Amida* must be repeated because for that particular prayer it was omitted entirely (*Rashi*).

A second approach suggests that the tradition is not referring to individual congregants but to the prayer leader. The leader need not repeat the silent *Amida* if the Rosh Ḥodesh addition was omitted, for such a requirement would place an unnecessary burden on the congregation. Hence we rely on the leader mentioning Rosh Ḥodesh in the repetition. Someone praying alone, however, must always repeat the *Amida* if the Rosh Ḥodesh addition was omitted. This was the case of Rabbi Ḥiyya bar Abba (*Bahag*).

The Talmud presents a second discussion about someone who omits any mention of Rosh Ḥodesh. According to this passage, forgetting the Rosh Ḥodesh addition in the *Ma'ariv* prayer never obligates a repetition. A slip-up at *Shaḥarit* or *Minḥa,* however, requires a repetition of the prayer. The basis of this distinction is that in Temple times, before the calendar was fixed, the court would publicly declare a new month based on the testimony of witnesses who saw the new moon. This judicial act never occurred at night, and hence a *Ma'ariv* omission does not necessitate an *Amida* repetition.

A difference between the two passages is apparent. The concerns of the first passage are the opportunity to mention Rosh Ḥodesh in subsequent prayers, and the difference between an individual and a congregation. The second passage spotlights the time for declaring the new month as the determining factor in questions of repetition. The different foci give rise to different normative possibilities. Jewish law follows the second passage and differentiates between an omission in *Ma'ariv* and an omission in *Shaḥarit* or *Minḥa* (*Shulḥan Arukh, Oraḥ Ḥayim* 422).

Let us return to Rabbi Zeira's first assumption and the tradition he quoted: before praying, a person should always assess whether he is sufficiently focused. One of the Hasidic masters of our generation, the Gerrer Rebbe – Rabbi Pinḥas Menaḥem Alter (1926–1996), known as the Penei Menaḥem – related the following. A *rosh yeshiva*, a head of a talmudic academy, once complained that the students' learning smacked of superficiality. When he wished to explain how serious the problem was, he used the term *daven* – the Yiddish word for prayer. He grumbled: "They *daven* up a few pages of Talmud!"

The Penei Menaḥem was dismayed at this description. Should we conclude that praying is to be done cursorily and that only Torah learning needs to be a conscious endeavour? The opposite seems to be true, for the Talmud permits superficial study: "A person should always recite Talmud, even if he quickly forgets what he has learned and even if he does not understand what he is saying" (*B. Avoda Zara* 19a). In contrast, with regard to prayer – as Rabbi Zeira indicated – one who cannot concentrate is instructed to wait until he is able to focus. Thus the Penei Menaḥem concluded that prayer, more than anything else, requires a conscious approach and an attentive heart.

Berakhot
Chapter Five

BERAKHOT 30B

A heavy head in prayer

OUR SAGES INSTRUCT us to pray the *Amida* prayer with *koved rosh* (*M. Berakhot* 5:1). Literally, the phrase *koved rosh* means heaviness of head, and one commentator suggests that the instruction is referring to the correct posture for prayer. People should bow their heads in prayerful concentration, just as a person experiencing pain is forced to hunch over (*Arukh*).

Elsewhere in the Talmud we find a discussion regarding the appropriate stance during prayer (*B. Yevamot* 105b). Two sages were sitting together when one suggested that "One who prays must look down, as it says: *My eyes and My heart shall be there* – referring to the earth – *all the days* (1 Kings 9:3)."

His colleague retorted: "The worshippers' eyes should be raised, as it says: *Let us lift our hearts with our hands to God in heaven* (Lamentations 3:41)."

A third sage chanced upon the duo and asked: "What are you talking about?"

"We are discussing prayer."

The third sage, quoting his father, suggested a teaching that found a middle ground: "One who prays must look down, while the heart should be directed heavenward, in order to fulfil the meaning of both verses." The instruction in our tractate to pray with *koved rosh,* meaning that we should bow our heads in prayer, fits with this talmudic exchange.

Other commentators, however, see the *koved rosh* directive as reflecting more than posture. One commentator innovatively suggests focusing on another meaning of the Hebrew root of *k-v-d,* namely sweeping clean. People are enjoined to sweep out their minds, getting rid of foreign thoughts and trivial concerns before the onset of prayer. The mind should be clear and pure for the prayer experience (*Tzemaḥ Tzedek*).

In the talmudic discussion regarding *koved rosh*, the sages seek a source for this requirement (*B. Berakhot* 30b). As we shall see, different biblical prayer paradigms are considered, and from the thrust of the passage a third meaning of *koved rosh* emerges. According to this approach, *koved rosh* should be contrasted with *kalut rosh*, light-headedness. Prayer should be undertaken with *koved rosh* – reverence and awe (*Rashi*).

Hannah was childless, and when she came to the Tabernacle she offered a heartfelt prayer asking that she be blessed with a child. The verse depicts the scene in which, "bitter of spirit," she prayed to God (1 Samuel 1:10). Our sages understand this to mean that her prayer was offered with a bitter spirit, and from here we may derive the *koved rosh* requirement. This paradigm is rejected since it is possible that Hannah, who was extremely distraught at not having been blessed with children, should not be taken as a role model. Her exceedingly bitter circumstances suggest that she should hardly be the yardstick for all.

Another possible biblical exemplar is entertained by the Talmud. King David the psalmist sang: *As for me, through Your abundant kindness, I will come to Your house, I will prostrate myself towards Your holy sanctuary, in awe of You* (Psalms 5:8). The implication is that prayer necessitates awe. This source too is challenged. Perhaps King David was different, for his approach to prayer went beyond that which is demanded of a regular person (*B. Berakhot* 3b–4a). How then can we draw a conclusion from his conduct? Moreover, the king himself indicated that he was referring only to himself – *as for me* – and not setting a standard for all.

A third biblical source is offered, once again from Psalms, only here King David was not describing his own practice; rather he was addressing others: *Bow before God in holy splendour* (Psalms 29:2). The Talmud suggests that the word for splendour (*hadrat*) should be read with the Hebrew letter *ḥet* instead of the almost silent letter *heh*. That leaves us with *ḥerdat*, meaning trepidation, instead of *hadrat*. King David was instructing people to prostrate themselves before God in awe, and thus we have a source for *koved rosh* meaning veneration in prayer. The sages, however, were still unsatisfied with this source. Perhaps King David really meant that people should bow with splendour, namely that they should adorn themselves with appropriate clothing before prayer. Indeed, we have accounts of sages who would don their finest attire before beginning to pray.

A final suggestion is made: *Serve God with awe, and rejoice with trepidation* (Psalms 2:11). Though the verse refers to the Temple service, our prayer services stand in place of the lost Temple service and must likewise be conducted with awe. Thus the rule that prayer requires *koved rosh* can be attributed to a biblical source.

Let us return to the unique turn of phrase *koved rosh*. Hasidic masters creatively offer a further dimension to the rabbinic directive. Our sages are not merely defining appropriate posture or even requiring a reverent attitude; the requirement of *koved rosh* demands far more.

Rosh, meaning head, in esoteric parlance can be understood as referring to the Holy Presence, the head of everything. The Hasidic ideal of nullifying the self in favour of grasping the entirety of the Divine is voiced in this passage. Prayer is no longer aimed at beseeching the Almighty to grant our earthly requests, requests that are merely based on the supposition of our own existence and the assessment of our base, material needs.

True prayer, say the Hasidic masters, entails overcoming this outlook. Our prayers should not be filled with requests connected to our livelihood; rather they should focus on the pain of God, Who is troubled by the unredeemed state of the world. The pain of the Jewish people should be felt as the anguish of the Almighty, not as our own temporal aching. Prayer should be undertaken with the weight of God on our shoulders. This is indeed a challenging level of prayer.

To be sure, we have here a creative reading that goes beyond the intent of the rabbinic instruction. Moreover, this approach changes the entire landscape of prayer – its central path, its byways, its challenges and its ultimate goals. Yet one master suggests that prayer on this level guarantees a positive response to our requests, for we ask not for ourselves but for the sake of the Almighty.

BERAKHOT 30B–31A

Tempering enjoyment

"MAZAL TOV!" CRIES the crowd as the glass is broken at the end of a wedding ceremony. The response is so ingrained that no matter where we are, a glass that shatters – or for that matter any dish – is immediately followed by a chorus of shouts of *mazal tov*.

In truth, joyous exclamations are a strange reaction to the custom of breaking a glass under the wedding canopy, for this practice is really an acknowledgment of our unredeemed state. The joy of this blissful day for the newlyweds, and indeed this festive occasion for the Jewish people, is momentarily toned down as we place the fallen Jerusalem above our highest joy (Psalms 137:5–6). Why do we seek to dull our happiness at its height? Why must we mingle our enjoyment with sadness?

On the biblical verse, *Serve God with awe, and rejoice with trepidation* (Psalms 2:11), the Talmud explains the unusual pairing of *rejoice with trepidation*: "Where there is rejoicing, there should also be trepidation" (*B. Berakhot* 30b–31a).

Continuing with this line of thought, the Talmud relates that Abbaye was sitting before Rabba, his teacher, when Rabba noticed that he was excessively cheerful. "It is written *rejoice with trepidation*," reminded the teacher.

Abbaye sought to alleviate his concern, saying: "I am wearing *tefillin*." This implied that there was no need to worry since he was keenly aware of the heavenly yoke.

In a similar episode, Rabbi Yirmiya was sitting before his teacher, Rabbi Zeira. Here too, the teacher perceived that the pupil was excessively cheerful. "It is written *in all sorrow there is benefit* (Proverbs 14:23)," the teacher told him, quoting a verse that seems to advocate being sad.

The response was similar: "I am wearing *tefillin*." Thus the two students – Abbaye and Rabbi Yirmiya – each understood that the problem with excess cheer is that it indicates that the heavenly yoke has been discarded. Awareness of their *tefillin,* they assured their teachers, had a sobering effect and tempered their joy.

Some commentators suggest a different explanation of the students' response. They were explaining the reason for their high spirits. It was the opportunity to wear *tefillin* that led to their exuberance. Thus the teachers need not be concerned that their good mood was misplaced (*Rabbeinu Yona Gerondi*).

Either way, our sages appear to frown upon unrestrained joy. To buttress this contention, the talmudic passage relates three wedding tales. The sage Mar bar Ravina made a wedding feast for his son. The host saw that his rabbinic guests were excessively cheerful, so he brought a precious glass cup worth 400 *zuz* and smashed it before them. Though it is generally forbidden to destroy useful objects, where the damage is purposeful the prohibition does not apply. Here Mar bar Ravina sought to check the levity of his guests, and indeed succeeded, as they were saddened by the loss of this valuable item.

In a similar episode, Rav Ashi made a wedding feast for his son. When he perceived that his colleagues were excessively jovial, he brought a cup of white crystal and broke it in their presence. Once again the broken vessel had the desired effect as the guests became more subdued. One commentator suggests that these accounts and the desire to dampen the festive atmosphere are the source for our custom to break a glass under the wedding canopy (*Tosafot*).

A third tale is told, this one from the wedding feast of Mar bar Ravina himself. The sages called Rav Hamnuna Zuti and requested: "Let the master sing for us." Perceiving the frivolous atmosphere, Rav Hamnuna Zuti began: "Woe to us that we are destined to die! Woe to us that we are destined to die!" He favoured a dirge over a wedding ditty (*Ein Yaakov*). By recalling death, Rav Hamnuna Zuti succeeded not only in reducing the levity, but in changing the entire atmosphere of the party.

With dampened spirits, the sages asked: "How can we respond after what you have said?"

Rav Hamnuna Zuti was not finished. He then cited a more frightening end than mere death: "Where is the Torah and where are the commandments that can protect us?" Dying with no spiritual achievements is even more depressing, he was suggesting.

The Talmud, it appears, advocates tempering joyous occasions. Even at a wedding we are encouraged to keep our merriment in check, to break a glass to sadden the joyous occasion and to talk about death at this celebration of life.

Why are we so gloomy? Our unredeemed state is an inseparable part of our existence; do we really need to further diminish happy occasions by recalling our woeful circumstances? Shouldn't we enjoy these flashes of joy, momentarily allowing ourselves to forget our doleful condition?

While these dicta may seem to advocate a denial of pure pleasure, the concluding rule in this talmudic series puts a different spin on the joys of this world. Rabbi Yoḥanan recounts a tradition in the name of Rabbi Shimon bar Yoḥai: "It is forbidden to fill our mouths with laughter in this world." The source for this rule is the biblical promise that *Then will our mouth be filled with laughter and our tongue with joyous song* – that is, at a time when *they will say among the nations: "God has done great things with these people"* (Psalms 126:2). Rabbi Yoḥanan's student-colleague, Reish Lakish, took this lesson to heart, and tradition relates that once he heard this teaching he never again filled his mouth with laughter.

The goal of curtailing enjoyment is not to limit our interaction with the delights of this world. The constraints suggested in this passage are designed to ensure that we continue to hope and strive for a better age. The ultimate goal may be to enjoy life, yet absolute pleasure is not possible in an unredeemed state. Certainly we have moments of temporary delight, such as the creation of a new family at a wedding. Yet even at these occasions, we are encouraged to curb our joy and spare a thought for the greater goal of a redeemed world where enjoyment will belong to all.

BERAKHOT 31A

Saying goodbye

SAYING GOODBYE IS never an easy task. What parting words do we hope will linger in the air after we have departed for a new destination? What blessing should we bestow until we meet again?

Our sages tell us that people should not part ways amid chatter, on a note of laughter, with light-headedness or idle words. Saying goodbye is a key moment and parting words should relate to halakha (*B. Berakhot* 31a). A spiritual leave-taking is far preferable to the alternatives.

To buttress this contention, the Talmud cites the practice of the prophets. Though they were Divinely moved to warn the people of impending punishments, they conclude their messages with words of hope and comfort. For example, the first thirteen chapters of Hosea contain prophecies of doom, and the theme of the book appears to be a harsh critique of Israel. Yet the concluding chapter abandons this theme, and promises that God and Israel will eventually be reconciled. Parting words need to be carefully considered, as they leave a lasting impression. The final note struck before taking leave of people should be a spiritually uplifting one, not stark prophecies and certainly not inane babble.

The Talmud continues by citing a similar tradition, which adds an explanation of the significance of parting with words of halakha: "For this way he will remember him." Who is remembering whom?

One option is to suggest that God recalls the parting friends. Earlier in our tractate, our sages discuss God's presence in various holy undertakings (*B. Berakhot* 6a). Quoting the biblical verse *Then those who feared God spoke to one another, and God listened* (Malachi 3:16), our sages tell us that when two people study Torah together, the Divine Presence is with them. Furthermore, the Almighty is at hand not only when two people study Torah, but even when an individual sits alone and studies Torah. This is indicated by God's assurance: *Wherever I permit My name to be mentioned, there I will come to you and bless you* (Exodus 20:21). The Talmud asks the obvious question. Since God is present when an individual learns Torah, surely the Divine Presence rests on two people who study! The Talmud suggests a difference between the Divine Presence at a lone study session and God's company when two people learn. When an individual studies Torah, the Almighty is present; when two people learn Torah, not only is God present but the words of their study session are recorded in a heavenly book of remembrance. Thus the Torah study of parting friends is recorded before the Almighty, and it is God Who remembers the parties and their Torah interaction long after they have parted ways.

While this approach elegantly invites God into the interaction between two friends, the straightforward reading of our passage does not seem to endorse it. A more likely interpretation has the friends remembering one another after they have said goodbye.

Why should offering parting words of halakha improve the chances of friends remembering each other?

Perhaps we can understand this in light of another rabbinic directive. Our sages tell us that citing Torah sources brings redemption to the world (*M. Avot* 6:6). They add that not citing sources brings a curse on the world. In one place, they go even further, suggesting that people who refrain from mentioning sources effectively kill, as they act as if the person from whom they received the teaching does not exist. Moreover, the Talmud states that when people attribute a Torah statement to its original source, they should imagine the statement's author standing before them as they share the teaching (*Y. Kiddushin* 61a). Based on this encouragement to cite sources and the understanding that the original author is present when we do so, we can understand why taking leave with Torah thoughts will help people to remember one another.

In an inspiring autobiographical passage, Zalman Shazar (1889–1974) tells of his last Shabbat with his grandfather in the Byelorussian town of Mir. This took place before the young idealist made his journey to Palestine. Shazar grew up in an ardently Ḥabad Hasidic family. At a young age he was drawn to Zionism, and his student days were filled with Zionist activism. After the establishment of the State of Israel, Shazar served as the first Minister of Education and Culture in 1949, and his tenure in that position is commemorated today on the NIS 200 banknote. In 1963, he became the third President of Israel.

In 1924, Shazar – or Shneur Zalman Rubashov as he was then known – began the journey to Palestine. En route to the Promised Land, he spent a nostalgic Shabbat with his grandfather. As the time to part arrived, grandfather and grandson made their way out of the town. They walked together and the old man spoke of the unique value of a melody that is connected to the soul of the singer. As Ḥabad Hasidim, explained the grandfather, the souls of the Rubashov family were tied to the melody of the "Alter Rebbe" or "Old Rav," Rabbi Shneur Zalman of Lyady (1745–1812). When the two were about to part, the old man followed the talmudic directive, posing a complicated legal problem and offering a solution.

The warm memory of that parting from his grandfather stayed with Shazar for the rest of his life. However, it was not because of the halakha they discussed as the wagon driver urged his passenger to board; the details of that lesson later remained sketchy in the mind of Shazar.

Instead, Shazar took with him the parting melody that his grandfather had lauded. "During difficult periods of my life, whenever I suddenly wished to remember the melody of the Old Rav and the wonderful tune came to mind, I felt new strength welling up within me, evidence that I am heading in the right direction. All despair conquered, I continued on my way with hope and inner peace."

BERAKHOT 31A

Windows for prayer

WHEN BUILDING A new synagogue or choosing one to join, there are many things we consider. Is the space conducive to prayer? Can I get a seat that I will be happy with? Is the community inviting? One aspect that we may neglect to consider is whether the synagogue is built according to halakhic guidelines. When relating to the laws regarding the proper place, time and manner for prayer, the Talmud tells us: "A person should always pray in a house where there are windows" (*B. Berakhot* 31a, 34b). The Talmud offers Daniel's manner of prayer as a source for this requirement: *He had windows open in his upper storey, towards Jerusalem, and he kneeled upon his knees three times a day and prayed and gave thanks to his God as he did previously* (Daniel 6:11). What is the purpose of these windows? Commentators offer different insights. The reason for the windows may bear on the appropriate location for them, as we shall see.

One commentator suggests that windows can assist concentration, as supplicants look heavenward during prayer (*Rashi*). According to this approach the windows should be placed such that those praying can look out towards the sky during the service. Moreover, the windows should not open up to an area whose sights will disrupt focus in prayer. Perhaps the windows should even be placed high, so that supplicants' eyes will be raised heavenward during prayer.

Another commentator also suggests that the windows are aimed at improving focus during prayer, albeit by a different means. Windows allow light to filter into the synagogue and this has a calming effect on those present, helping them to concentrate on their prayers (*Rabbeinu Yona Gerondi*). The windows, according to this approach, should be placed so that they will allow maximal light to pour into the space dedicated to prayer.

A third approach returns to the biblical source. As we saw, Daniel opened windows towards Jerusalem. Thus, our synagogue windows should face Jerusalem. These openings are thus an extension of the mandated direction of prayer, a way of further channelling our prayers through the Holy City (*Maimonides*).

Elsewhere in the Talmud we are instructed to pray with our eyes lowered towards the ground and our heart raised heavenward (*B. Yevamot* 105b). How can we fulfil both these mandates – looking out towards Jerusalem and looking down towards the ground?

One halakhist suggests that the rule initially requires lowered eyes during prayer. If we lose concentration, however, we are advised to look fleetingly through the windows heavenward and in the direction of Jerusalem, in order to refocus our thoughts (*Magen Avraham*). Others suggest that the windows should be looked at before the onset of prayer, after which our eyes should be directed downward (*Peri Megadim*). Both opinions agree that the windows serve as a stimulus to bring us back to the task of heartfelt, sincere prayer.

In bygone times, windows were not nearly as common as they are today. Building technology did not allow for gaping holes in walls, and the cost of glass was prohibitive. It is against this background that we can understand the question posed to Maimonides by a troubled observer, who noted that there were many houses of prayer that had no windows at all. Why did widespread practice ignore the talmudic rule?

In his responsum, Maimonides introduces a heretofore unheard-of distinction. Windows are necessary only for those who pray at home; however, this requirement does not apply to synagogues. Buttressing this distinction, Maimonides points out that Daniel prayed at home. Notwithstanding this point, later halakhists note that the accepted practice is to have windows in the synagogue and not to reserve them for prayers at home (*Peri Megadim*).

A further issue under discussion involves whether the windows should be open or closed. Some authorities advocate closed windows, and recommend that supplicants distance themselves from open windows (*Rabbi Akiva Eiger*). Other authorities are in favour of open windows. One halakhist singles out the holiest day of the year, Yom Kippur, as the only time when windows need to be open during prayer (*Peri Megadim*). There are those who note that the Hasidic master Rabbi Ḥayim Elazar Shapira of Munkács (1872–1937) would enter the synagogue on Yom Kippur eve and ask those present to open all the windows.

Esoteric tradition goes further, describing the ideal number of windows. The *Zohar* dictates that a synagogue should have no fewer than twelve windows, corresponding to the twelve heavenly channels for prayer, one for each of the twelve tribes of Israel. This may be the source of the popular practice of having the tribes' insignia cast in the windows of the synagogue. One Hasidic master who was steeped in the kabbalistic tradition, Rabbi Yitzḥak Isaac Yehuda Yeḥiel Safrin of Komarno (1806–1874), even formulated minimum dimensions for each window: four handbreadths by four handbreadths. In some cases twelve windows is a tall order, so one authority suggests that each window pane – rather than each hole in the wall – be counted as a separate window (*Eshel Avraham Buczacz*).

Normative Jewish law adopts the position that the windows should face Jerusalem and recommends the kabbalistic twelve windows (*Shulḥan Arukh, Oraḥ Ḥayim* 90:4). However, not all of them need to face the Holy City (*Mishna Berura*).

While the kabbalistic significance of these windows may be beyond the ken of many, we can nevertheless find relevance in the window requirement. Let us return to Maimonides' responsum to the troubled observer. Maimonides concludes by recalling that no wall or beam can separate between us and our Creator in heaven. To sum up, a window is primarily a means to assist supplicants in visualising themselves standing in Jerusalem before the Almighty. As we look out the window, beyond our physical confines, we seek to journey to holy spaces on the wings of our prayers.

BERAKHOT 31B

Quest for balance

HANNAH, WIFE OF Elkanah, was barren. Each year when the family made the journey to Shiloh to offer up sacrifices in the Tabernacle, Hannah experienced great anguish as she saw Peninnah, her co-wife, travelling with her brood. Though Elkanah tried to soothe Hannah's pain by giving her larger portions of food and by declaring his commitment to her, his efforts were unsuccessful. Hannah refused to be comforted.

Seeking a solution to her plight, Hannah turned to God, bitterly crying and beseeching the Almighty for a child: *O Lord of hosts, if You will indeed look upon the affliction of Your maidservant, and remember me and not forget Your maidservant, and You will grant Your maidservant seed of men* (zera anashim), *then I will give him to the Lord all the days of his life and no razor shall come upon his head* (1 Samuel 1:11).

The sages are intrigued by the turn of phrase *zera anashim*, "seed of men," and offer a number of explanations for Hannah's choice of words (*B. Berakhot* 31b). The first explanation focuses on the term *anashim* (men). Hannah was asking for a man among men, namely a person unique among his peers.

A second approach separates the two terms *zera* and *anashim*. Hannah was prophetically asking for a child (*zera*) who would anoint great men (*anashim*). Eventually, Hannah's son Samuel would anoint Saul and David, the first two kings of Israel (1 Samuel 10:1, 16:13).

A third suggestion focuses on the juxtaposition of the two nouns. Hannah was requesting a child (*zera*) who was the equal of two men (*anashim*, the plural of *ish*). Citing the verse *Moses and Aaron among His priests, and Samuel among those who invoke His name* (Psalms 99:6), the Talmud further clarifies Hannah's prayer. She was pleading for a son of the calibre of two men, Moses and Aaron.

The fourth explanation offered by the Talmud takes an entirely different approach. Hannah was not asking for an outstanding child in any way; rather she was requesting a child (*zera*) who would be inconspicuous among other people (*anashim*). The Talmud elaborates on this last approach, sharing with us the specifics of Hannah's prayer: "Let him be neither tall nor short, neither thin nor stocky, neither pale nor ruddy, neither wise nor foolish."

While we can understand that a mother might not want her child to stand out because of his peculiar physical appearance, asking for a child who is not wise seems strange. Parents want everything for their children. Which mother does not want her child to be wise? Moreover, thrice daily we include a passage in our prayers in which we specifically request knowledge, wisdom and understanding. Our sages tell us that King Solomon, wisest of leaders, fasted for a full forty days in order to be granted wisdom (*Midrash Mishlei* 1:1). Why then did Hannah shy away from this coveted trait? Perhaps driven by this concern, one commentator tempers her request. Hannah did not want her son to be excessively wise. If he were out of the ordinary, he would draw excess attention and arouse the evil eye (*Rashi*).

Still, this is a strangely cautious attitude and surprising, coming from a woman who so desperately wanted a child.

Further on in the talmudic passage we are told that when the young Samuel came to the Tabernacle at Shiloh, he caused some turmoil. Samuel saw that people who brought sacrifices sought a priest to slaughter the animal. The young lad protested: "Why do you seek a priest? The slaughter can be performed by any person!" Samuel was quickly brought before Eli the *Kohen Gadol*, who asked the youngster for his source. Samuel deftly quoted and interpreted the relevant biblical passage, and Eli was forced to admit that the boy was right. "You have spoken well," pronounced the *Kohen Gadol*. "Nevertheless, you have rendered a decision in the presence of your teacher" – referring to himself – "and are hence liable to the death penalty!"

While the underage Samuel would not normally have been held liable for his actions, perhaps Eli sought to nip this problem in the bud. Better to do away with a potential rabble-rouser before he manages to agitate the masses and cause mayhem. Indeed, this is the logic behind the Bible's harsh treatment of a rebellious son (*M. Sanhedrin* 8:5).

In light of this tale, Hannah's concern before she was even pregnant about having an overly wise child appears to have been well-founded. Young Samuel's sharp intellect almost got him killed. Hannah's response to Eli's ruling was: *For this child I prayed* (1 Samuel 1:27). She was recalling her prayer for his limited wisdom and assuring the *Kohen Gadol* that the future held no dangers.

Perhaps we can read the passage slightly differently, not focusing on Hannah's prescience, but suggesting that she was asking for the golden quality of balance. The importance of equilibrium is illustrated by a tale recounted by Rabbi Shmuel Bornsztain (1855–1926). He told it upon the return from the funeral of his father, Rabbi Avraham Bornsztain (1839–1910), Hasidic master in Sochaczew, Poland. Rabbi Avraham was a respected legal authority and author of two important halakhic works – *Eglei Tal* on the laws of Shabbat and *Responsa Avnei Nezer*.

After his wedding, the young Rabbi Avraham resided in the house of his famed father-in-law, Rabbi Menaḥem Mendel Morgensztern (1787–1859), Hasidic master in the Polish town of Kock (pronounced Kotzk). The young man was often sick, and the doctors could offer no medical explanation for the youth's ill health. The Kotzker

Rebbe explained to his young son-in-law that his infirm constitution was a result of an imbalance: Rabbi Avraham's mental capacity far outweighed his physical capabilities. The cure was obvious. The studious Rabbi Avraham needed to eat more in order to strengthen his physical disposition and correct the disparity.

Returning to Hannah's prayer, we can understand her request. This mother-to-be was beseeching God for a child with a balanced makeup. Thus Hannah juxtaposed her requests regarding physical features with her hopes for the child's mental prowess.

Of course we have high hopes for our children. However, our tradition may be suggesting that more important than standout intellect or noticeable physique is a balanced approach to life. Such balance between our physical capabilities and mental faculties surely reflects equilibrium in our soul.

BERAKHOT 31B

Potency of Shabbat

We all seek remedies for our iniquities, spiritual medicine to wipe our slates clean and allow us to start afresh. Our sages advise us of the strongest elixir for our sins: fasting on Shabbat. We are told that the heavenly court tears up an evil judgment of seventy years for anyone who fasts on Shabbat (*B. Berakhot* 31b). Thus sins committed over the course of a lifetime – seventy years in this world – are erased as if they never were, thanks to a Shabbat spent abstaining from food and drink.

Why might someone choose to fast on Shabbat? The commentators offer two explanations. The popular and oldest-recorded approach suggests that our sages are referring to a fast undertaken after an ominous dream (*Hai Gaon*). Elsewhere in the Talmud we are told that fasting effectively incinerates a sinister dream, much as fire consumes the flammable fibres of flax (*B. Shabbat* 11a). Our sages there add that a fast is particularly effective on the day following the dream, even if this day is the holy Shabbat.

Later authorities limit the fasting following a bad dream to specific cases, such as if someone was visited by the same dream thrice. Alternatively only certain dreams are ill omens, such as dreaming of a Torah scroll being burned, picturing the final moments of Yom Kippur, seeing the beams of your house crashing down or your teeth falling out.

Other authorities counter that in our time we do not really understand dreams and therefore cannot ascertain whether a dream is an evil omen or a favourable sign. As a result, nowadays fasting on Shabbat is generally not a recommended course (*Shulḥan Arukh, Oraḥ Ḥayim* 288:5).

Let us return to our talmudic passage. An entirely different approach notes that the sages make no mention of a dream. Hence, the discussion must be talking about another type of fast on Shabbat – a fast undertaken in repentance for a particular sin. The person fasting desires to return to the Almighty. His regret for the sins he committed is so deep that he fasts on the day when the community celebrates Shabbat (*Shitta Mekubetzet*). Alas, relying on the silence of our sages in this passage is not so clear cut, for another talmudic account (*B. Ta'anit* 12b) does make a connection between fasting on account of a bad dream and the requirement to atone for such a fast if it is undertaken on Shabbat.

How does the panacea of a Shabbat fast work? Why is fasting on Shabbat more potent than penance undertaken on any other day of the week? Shabbat is a time when we all joyfully celebrate. One way this cheery atmosphere manifests itself is in the culinary dimension. An extra meal is served, and delicacies procured during the week are saved for Shabbat. In this communal festive atmosphere, depriving oneself by fasting is more challenging than usual. Undertaking this fast despite the difficulty is clear acknowledgment of complete regret, which results in the revoking of evil decrees (*Rashi*).

This magical elixir, however, is fraught with problems. After stating the power that fasting has on Shabbat, the sages immediately issue a dire warning. Despite the merit of such abstention, the heavenly court exacts punishment from the one fasting for neglecting *Oneg Shabbat*, the requirement of enjoying this holy day.

Confounded by this paradox, the Talmud asks: how can the sin of disregarding *Oneg Shabbat* be rectified? The suggested remedy is fascinating. The person who fasted on Shabbat must observe an additional fast to atone for the Shabbat fast.

If the Shabbat fast constitutes an infraction of *Oneg Shabbat*, a violation so serious that it requires another fast to atone for it, why is it allowed in the first place? One commentator explains that for the individual who fasts, abstaining from eating on Shabbat actually constitutes *Oneg Shabbat*. The fast acts as a calming tonic for the troubled soul, quelling fears due to his ominous dream or his sinful state. Nevertheless, the fasting person has not celebrated Shabbat in the proper *Oneg Shabbat* spirit, and therefore must make amends with an additional fast (*Rashba*).

Another commentator offers an insightful suggestion. If God sent an ill-omened nightmare on Friday night, forcing the dreamer to fast and thereby violate *Oneg Shabbat*, it is probably because the dreamer had not previously been scrupulous about *Oneg Shabbat*. The nightmare, the resultant Shabbat fast and the subsequent penitential fast should awaken dreamers to the fact that they have not been rigorous in their *Oneg Shabbat* observance (*Iyun Yaakov*).

When should this additional fast be observed? The commentators suggest that it should be held on the Sunday immediately following the Shabbat spent without eating (*Rashi*). It is the same urgent need for atonement that led to fasting on Shabbat which guides the timing of the second fast. Moreover, the proximity of the two fasts ensures that the penance is immediate, and publicly demonstrates that the supplementary fast is aimed at atoning for the breach of *Oneg Shabbat*. Fasting on the following Sunday, however, is not obligatory. If such a course would be too physically taxing, the additional fast can be delayed (*Rashba*).

With the exception of Yom Kippur, a public fast that falls on Shabbat is not observed on Shabbat. Instead, it is either brought forward to the preceding Thursday, as in the case of the Fast of Esther, or delayed until the following Sunday, as in the case of *Tisha B'Av* (the Ninth of Av), *Shiva Asar B'Tammuz* (the Seventeenth of Tammuz), the

Fast of Gedalya and *Asara B'Tevet* (the Tenth of Tevet) (*Shulḥan Arukh, Oraḥ Ḥayim* 550:3).

Shabbat is not something to be trifled with. Its holiness is enshrined in our tradition. When personal circumstances necessitate deviation from the Shabbat atmosphere, we must realise that it comes at a price. Thus our sages require a compensating fast to atone for the fast on Shabbat. On the one hand, a Shabbat fast can atone for one's sins; on the other hand, such action breaches the sanctity of Shabbat and therefore is considered problematic. This duality demonstrates the unique potency of the holy Shabbat.

BERAKHOT 31B–32A

Filing claims against the Almighty

THE TALMUD RELATES that three heroes of Jewish history filed claims against the Almighty (*B. Berakhot* 31b–32a).

The first is Hannah. In her fervent prayers to God for a child, she flung harsh words heavenward. This is derived from the biblical passage which describes her supplication using an unusual preposition to introduce the prayer: *And she prayed against God* (I Samuel 1:10). We would have expected her to pray to (*el*), not against (*al*), the Almighty. Given that Hannah's prayer came from a place of anguish, should she be accused of speaking too harshly to the Almighty? The commentators explain that even though her prayers were undoubtedly heartfelt, they should have been formulated respectfully rather than flung at the Almighty (*Rashba*).

The second person accused of improper prayer is Elijah the prophet. In his day, many of the Jewish people had turned to Baal worship. A confrontation was organised on Mount Carmel between the followers of Baal and the prophets of the Almighty in which each group would attempt to offer a bull sacrifice without any fire. The custodian of the true belief would be the party whose offering was consumed by heavenly flames. With the eyes of Israel focused on this trial, the Baal faction went first. Despite its cries, no fire descended from heaven. It was then Elijah's turn, and he turned heavenward with a simple prayer whose opening words have become a staple of our liturgy: *Answer me, God, answer me, and let the people know that You are the God Almighty and it is You Who has turned their hearts backward* (1 Kings 18:37). With these last words, Elijah appeared to be accusing the Almighty of being the cause of the people's improper behaviour. He was implying that God should have directed the people's hearts (*Rashi*), or at least not prevented them from repenting (*Maimonides*).

The third personality who flung words against the Almighty was Moses, though it is unclear to which incident the Talmud is referring.

When the Jews in the desert complained about God, a heavenly fire descended, singeing the edge of the camp. At that point, *The people came crying to Moses, and Moses prayed to God and the fire died down* (Numbers 11:2). True, the appropriate preposition is used here – Moses prayed to (*el*), not against (*al*), the Almighty. Nevertheless, one school of exegesis expounds the verse by interchanging the silent *alef* with the guttural *ayin*, since many people (including the majority of Modern Hebrew speakers today) do not differentiate between these two letters. Thus the verse could be read as Moses praying against (*al*), instead of to (*el*), the Almighty. According to one commentator this unflattering reading of the biblical text was precipitated by the curious fact that the content of Moses' prayer is not revealed (*Tzlaḥ*).

Another opinion in the Talmud cites a different episode in which Moses filed a claim against God. The final book of the Pentateuch opens with a description of the location in which Moses gave his farewell talks to the Jewish people (Deuteronomy 1:1). The last place mentioned is Di Zahab, which the sages interpret as a reference to the Golden Calf. At this episode Moses turned accusingly to God with the claim that the Almighty brought about the making of the Golden Calf. Thus Moses said: "Master of the universe, this happened because of the silver and gold (*zahav*) that You lavished upon Israel, when they went out of Egypt, until they said 'Enough!'" The word for "enough" is *dai*, which is written with the same letters as the word Di (as in Di Zahab). Based on his assertion, Moses maintained that God ought to show clemency and not destroy the Jewish people for their sin.

What is the upshot of these paradigms? In two of the cases – Elijah and Moses – the sages present biblical support to indicate that God later concurred with their accusations. Regarding Hannah, the sages are silent, and no such vindication is offered. Nevertheless, we may assume that her claims were also accepted, as she was granted a child – the famed prophet Samuel. Moreover, Hannah was not punished for her brazen prayer. Can we conclude that flinging words against the Almighty is a possible approach to prayer? Is this mode of prayer endorsed for us?

Let us reread the talmudic passage. God's consent is presented as *ex post facto* authorisation rather than *ex ante* approval. Our sages are hardly suggesting that this is recommended behaviour.

On the other hand, certain Hasidic masters were famed for calling God to account, none more so than the beloved Rabbi Levi Yitzḥak of Berdyczów (1740–1810). He was often called the "Defender of Israel" for his willingness and audacity to plead for Israel. According to one tradition, Rabbi Levi Yitzḥak would converse frankly with the Almighty on Rosh HaShana after *kiddush*, saying: "Master of the universe, all the wealth granted to the Jewish people is spent for You. A Jew who has plenty spends more on Torah study, makes a finer Shabbat and contributes generously to charity. Why then do You not repay the kindness and deliver Your people?"

In another episode, Rabbi Levi Yitzḥak hesitated before sounding the *shofar* and turned heavenward: "Do You think I will sound the *shofar* before You this year? Let the evil forces to whom You have given power against us sound it! Yet I, who eternally love You, will bend my will and sound it. So too You should bend Your will and forgive Israel."

Which course is endorsed for prayer? A bold, candid and somewhat impudent dialogue with God, or a reverent and respectful offering of supplications before the Almighty?

Perhaps we have two different paradigmatic relationships with God. Those who relate to the Almighty with the appropriate veneration and awe would never entertain brazenly flinging words heavenward. Yet there are those who feel so close to God – like Hannah, Elijah, Moses, Rabbi Levi Yitzḥak of Berdyczów and others – that they irreverently file claims against the Almighty. They are like children arguing with a parent. The child may be disrespectful and the parent may rightly rebuke the child, but the relationship is based on love and the overwhelming feeling is one of mutual caring. For this reason, the parent still heeds the claims of the child.

BERAKHOT 32A

Grabbing God by the lapels

As MOSES COMMUNED with God on Sinai, the Jewish people rejoiced in the idolatrous service of the Golden Calf. Perceiving this, God told Moses: *Go down, for your people whom you brought up from Egypt have become corrupt* (Exodus 32:7).

The Talmud states that God's instruction was more than merely a directive to descend the mountain (*B. Berakhot* 32a). This is apparent from the continuation of the passage. Rather than Moses immediately leaving the Holy Presence, a conversation between Moses and the Almighty ensues.

The Talmud explains that God told Moses that his exalted station was due to his being the leader of the Jewish people. Once the people had sinned, Moses could no longer lay claim to this high position. At the news of his demotion from his lofty post, Moses' strength immediately waned and he was unable to advocate for the sinful Jewish people. Moses' inability to speak is indicated in the biblical passage by the use of two verbs for God's speaking. At the initial opening of God's speech to Moses it says *vayedaber*, and He spoke (verse 7), and then a subsequent, seemingly superfluous opening is indicated with the word *vayomer*, and He said (verse 9). An enfeebled Moses was evidently unable to say anything in response to God's initial speech.

The Almighty then instructed Moses: *And now leave Me alone so that My wrath may flare against them and I will annihilate them*

(Exodus 32:10). Moses immediately comprehended that he had the ability to entreat the Almighty, protest the impending punishment and intervene on behalf of the Jewish people. In light of this revelation, Moses marshalled his strength so that he could pray and plead for mercy.

The Talmud makes use of a parable to explain the course of events. A king was angered by his son the prince and he began to hit him. The king's friend sat there witnessing the beating, but was afraid to speak out in defence of the prince. The king turned to the prince and said: "If not for this friend of mine who is sitting before me, I would kill you." At that point, the friend realised that the matter was dependent on him, and he immediately rose to the defence of the prince and saved him.

One talmudic sage describes Moses' response with greater vividness. Before offering his explanation, the sage warns: "If the explanation were not written in Scripture, it would be impossible to say it." Thus he is acknowledging the audacity and perhaps danger of what he is about to present. The sage continues: By God saying *Leave Me alone*, we understand that Moses grabbed the Almighty like a person seizing a friend by the jacket lapels, and said: "Master of the universe, I will not let You go until You forgive and pardon them."

One of the great Hasidic masters before the Holocaust, Rabbi Ḥayim Elazar Shapira (1872–1937), finds this graphic portrayal of Moses grabbing God by the lapels intriguing. The Munkatcher Rebbe was both Hasidic master and the rabbi in Munkács, which was formerly in Hungary, then in Czechoslovakia and today in Ukraine. This colourful personality, whose quick tongue offended many, was known for his legal acumen as well as his knowledge and understanding of the esoteric realms of the tradition.

The Munkatcher Rebbe asks: why is such physical imagery employed? Corporeal descriptions clearly have no place when referring to the Almighty. It would have been more appropriate to depict Moses coming before the heavenly court with persuasive arguments and heartfelt urgings on behalf of his client, the Jewish people.

After raising his eyebrows at the talmudic passage, the Munkatcher Rebbe offers an insightful explanation for the dramatic description. He begins by assessing the case at hand and reaching the conclusion that God was truly justified in wanting to destroy the Jewish people, for the crime was great and the intended retribution appropriate. The only matter preventing the execution of the judgment was the likely response of the nations of the world, in particular Egypt, which would have interpreted the episode as an apparent weakness in God's ability to lead the recently redeemed Chosen People into the Promised Land. It would appear as though the Almighty's power was not so all-mighty. The likelihood of such heresies left God in an untenable position; the Almighty had no choice but to forgive the Jewish people, not because they deserved forgiveness, but for the sake of God's own reputation.

The counsel for the defence, Moses, fully understood the situation. The Jewish people were indeed guilty. External considerations, however, meant that punishment could not be seriously entertained. It was these peripheral factors, these layers of clothing that covered up the true state of events, that Moses evoked when arguing on behalf of the Jewish people. Figuratively, Moses grabbed the lapels of God's garments, persuasively indicating that external factors dictated forgiveness for the Jewish people.

The Munkatcher Rebbe ends his explanation, as he so often finishes his expositions, with encouraging words that allude to a better era when all will recognise God's dominion. In this conclusion he expertly cites the biblical promise of a day when the Teacher shall no longer hide Himself (Isaiah 30:20). The root which the prophet employs to mean "hide" is the unusual root *k-n-f*, which can also refer to the corner of a garment (Numbers 15:38). This is a reference to the very lapel that Moses grabbed.

The Munkatcher Rebbe's interpretation indicates the significance of a desecration of God's name. It is so important to avoid this, that the fear of such a result overrides the regular dictates of justice. In this context we can recall another biblical passage in which God pledges salvation to the Jewish people and a return to the Promised Land (Ezekiel 36). The promise is made, not for the sake of the undeserving Jewish people, but for the forsaken Land of Israel whose desolation is a source of desecration of God's name. Once again the profanation of the Divine name is a consideration that takes precedence over regular rules of justice.

Thus it appears that the need to avoid the desecration of the Divine name is so acute that the possibility of it occurring is a factor in deciding whether a deserved punishment will be meted out. Indeed, before undertaking any action one must assure that it will not lead to a profanation of God's name.

BERAKHOT 32B

The power of tears

WHAT IS THE most effective route to reach the Almighty? At first glance the answer is prayer. Indeed, the Talmud records various statements of the sage Rabbi Elazar with regard to the potency of prayer, each supported by a biblical verse (*B. Berakhot* 32b). Thus, Rabbi Elazar tells us that prayer is greater – meaning more effective – than good deeds. To support this contention, he points to the biblical episode in which Moses beseeched the Almighty to allow him to enter the Promised Land. This request was denied; yet due to his heartfelt prayer, Moses was granted the opportunity to see the land from afar. Even Moses, whose actions were unsurpassed, was answered only when he turned to prayer. Rabbi Elazar goes further: not only is prayer more effective than good deeds, but prayer – the service of the heart – was more valuable in Temple times than the sacrificial service.

At the same time, Rabbi Elazar seems to deem the tremendous potency of prayer obsolete. He asserts: "From the day that the Temple was destroyed, the heavenly gates of prayer were locked" (*B. Berakhot* 32b; *B. Bava Metzia* 59a). Thus our prayers are no longer accepted as they once were. The source offered for this conclusion is Jeremiah's lament following the destruction of the First Temple: *Though I will cry out and plead, He has shut out my prayer* (Lamentations 3:8). Commentators, perhaps shaken by this radical conclusion, suggest that the Almighty continues to answer prayers, yet they are not as readily received or as quickly answered (*Meiri*).

Rabbi Elazar appears to add a postscript of hope: "Though the gates of prayer have been locked, nevertheless the gates of tears have not been locked." This exception is derived from the verse *Hear my prayer, O God, give ear to my outcry; to my tears be not silent* (Psalms 39:13). We beseech the Almighty to hear our crying prayers and not to be indifferent to our tears. The verse implies that while our prayers are not heard by God at all – hence the plea that God listen to them – our tears are indeed registered by God, though God may sadly choose to ignore them. Hence we do not need to ask for the tears to be heard; rather we ask God to respond to them. We see that our tears do make their way before God, even when our prayers are locked out (*Rashi*). Thus the most valuable path to the Almighty is through heartfelt tears.

How did the razing of the Temple affect the acceptance of our prayers? Rabbi Elazar explains that along with the Temple's destruction an iron wall was introduced that separates Israel from the Almighty. This unyielding separator effectively closes the prayer channels to God.

Given this iron curtain between us and our Creator, how can tears still make their way heavenward? The famed scholar Rabbi Akiva was inspired at a late age to begin learning Torah after he saw water dripping on a stone and slowly eroding a hole through the rock. "If soft water can pierce hard rock, surely the Torah can penetrate my callous heart," he reasoned (*Avot DeRabbi Natan* A 6). So too, even though an iron curtain stands between us and the Almighty, a persistent stream of tears can pierce this barrier and make its way before God.

Why can tears find the elusive path to the Almighty, while prayers cannot? A leading ethics teacher of the last generation offers an explanation for the relationship between tears and prayers.

Rabbi Eliyahu Eliezer Dessler (1892–1953) – who was known as Rabbi Elya Lazer – was born in Latvia and educated in the spirit of the *Musar* movement, the Jewish ethics movement popularised in nineteenth-century Eastern Europe. When his father lost his successful timber business after the Russian Revolution, the family relocated to England. In the late 1940s, Rabbi Dessler moved to Palestine and was appointed the spiritual counsellor in Bnei Brak's Ponevezh Yeshiva, a position in which he served until his death.

Rabbi Dessler suggests that the closed gates of prayer are not to be found in heaven; in fact, the Talmud is referring to our hearts, which have been cordoned off from spirituality. Our insides are so sealed that we cannot break out and approach the Almighty. Even though we know intellectually that we should escape our self-imposed entrapment, we cannot emotionally overcome the blockage. Only through prayer that is so intense, so earnest that we are brought to tears, can we break through the blockade and draw near to God. Thus Rabbi Dessler sees prayer and tears as the same act, albeit with different levels of heartfelt intensity. It is the depth of sincerity indicated by the tears that penetrates the heavenly fortifications.

In another talmudic passage, a different sage boldly states that even an iron barrier cannot separate Israel from God (*B. Pesaḥim* 85b; *B. Sota* 38b). We might suggest that the two understandings of the separating wall are not contradictory. An iron barricade does stand between us and the Almighty, a barrier that our prayers cannot penetrate. Yet it cannot succeed in preventing our communion with the Almighty, for our tears are able to pierce this metal obstruction.

The Hasidic master Rabbi Menaḥem Mendel Morgensztern of Kotzk (1787–1859) related that upon the death of his colleague Rabbi Yitzḥak Kalish of Warka (1779–1848), he expected his friend to visit him in a dream and share with him the nature of his journey through the supernal worlds after death. When the Warka Rebbe did not come, the Kotzker embarked upon a spiritual voyage to find his friend. He travelled from supernal palace to palace, but his friend was nowhere to be found. Finally he discovered the Warka Rebbe leaning on his stick by a sea that was making an awful sound.

"What are you doing here, my friend?" asked the Kotzker Rebbe.

"Don't you recognise this?" replied the Warka Rebbe. "It is the ocean of tears of pain and anguish, of longing and of hope." It was then that the Kotzker recognised the sound of bitter crying. The Warka Rebbe continued: "I promised that I would stand by this ocean until God dries up all the tears of the world."

Such is the value of our tears. Why then does society often look askance at people who cry?

BERAKHOT 32B

Types of encouragement

OUR SAGES TELL us that there are four undertakings which require constant encouragement: the study of Torah, the practice of good deeds, the prayer encounter and the pursuit of a livelihood (*B. Berakhot* 32b).

To buttress this contention, the Talmud brings scriptural support for the need to strengthen each of these undertakings. For Torah study and doing good deeds, the Talmud cites a verse from Joshua's first prophecy after the death of Moses: *Only be strong* (ḥazak) *and be very courageous* (ematz), *to observe* (lishmor) *to act* (la'asot) *according to all the Torah which Moses My servant has commanded you; do not depart from it to the right or to the left, so that you will prosper wherever you may go* (Joshua 1:7). The sages explain that the heartening *ḥazak*, be strong, refers to learning Torah, while the encouraging *ematz*, be courageous, refers to doing good deeds. The additional two verbs in the verse – *lishmor*, to observe, and *la'asot*, to act – may also correspond to these two actions. Indeed, elsewhere in the Talmud, the Hebrew root *sh-m-r*, meaning to guard or observe, is understood as referring to Torah study; and the root *a-s-h*, to do, refers to good deeds (*B. Kiddushin* 37a).

The Talmud continues with a biblical source for the need to strengthen the third undertaking, prayer: *Hope to God, be strong* (ḥazak) *and He will give your heart courage* (veya'ametz), *and hope to God* (Psalms 27:14). When looking to the Almighty in prayer, we need to be strong and of brave heart. The biblical source employs two terms of encouragement, though our sages derive from this verse only one field that needs strengthening – prayer.

The fourth pursuit that calls for encouragement is that of earning a living, which is often challenging. Our sages offer the following verse as a source: *Be strong and let us strengthen ourselves* (venitḥazak) *on behalf of our people and on behalf of the cities of our Lord, and God will do that which seems good in His eyes* (II Samuel 10:12). The verse is taken from General Joab's tactical discussion with his brother and fellow general, Abishai, during the battle against Ammon and Aram. Joab was offering encouraging words before the two generals parted, each taking with him part of the army. In context, the encouragement refers specifically to soldiering, but our sages apply it to all worldly occupations (*Rashi*).

Looking back at this talmudic passage, we see that two Hebrew terms are used to define the need for reinforcing various areas: *ḥazak* and *ematz*. Why are two different verbs employed? What are the nuances of each term? A possible answer may be derived from the explanation that one biblical commentator offers for God's first words of encouragement to Joshua.

Rabbi Meir Leibish ben Yeḥiel Michel Weiser (1809–1879), better known by the acronym Malbim, was born in Volhynia, which was then part of the Russian empire. He served as rabbi in a number of European cities, eventually taking the post of Chief Rabbi of Bucharest, Romania. Malbim was a staunch defender of Orthodoxy, and his disagreements with those advocating Reform led to his imprisonment. Through the intervention of Sir Moses Montefiore he was released, on condition that he left the country. Malbim travelled to various cities where he served in the rabbinate; at each post he clashed with those seeking to change normative practices. A hallmark of his biblical commentary is his attempt to explain the subtle differences in meaning between seeming synonyms.

In reference to God's words to Joshua, "*ḥazak ve'ematz*," Malbim suggests that the term *ḥazak* refers to an initial effort, the encouragement to embark upon a new quest, the strength for that first push that goes against the flow. The term *ematz*, on the other hand, encourages the continued effort to perform once the glamour of the first encounter has dulled; it is the courage to struggle against the tedium of repetition in the pursuit of lofty goals.

Using Malbim's definitions as a springboard, perhaps we can better understand the talmudic passage. The inaugural Torah study session is the most challenging. Finding the time and the mental space to embark upon the intellectual and emotional journey of encountering our tradition requires focus. Once this initial step is taken, the continuation of the pursuit is less demanding, for the excitement of this stimulating journey fuels its continuation. Thus for Torah study, the term *ḥazak* is employed to encourage us to begin the voyage.

Similarly, a new job entails particular hurdles: becoming acquainted with new colleagues, the work environment, accepted procedures and other norms of the workplace. Once a worker adjusts to a new position, the memory of initial difficulties fades. Yet at the initial stages of acclimation, *ḥazak*-type words of encouragement are invaluable. In the biblical passage, both Joab and Abishai were faced with a new reality. Accordingly, Joab offered the blessing of *ḥazak* and added that he too needed to strengthen himself to deal with the new situation – *venitḥazak*.

The performance of good deeds is starkly different. The first-time act is the most exciting; with time, even altruistic pursuits can become tedious. The struggle is to persevere with what was once a novelty. Thus for the practice of worthy acts the term *ematz* is used, to encourage the continuation of a journey begun in earnest.

Prayer – perhaps the pursuit that requires the most strengthening – is difficult to embark upon and difficult to continue. Sincere, focused prayer is a constant struggle from which there is no respite; many of us are familiar with the challenge of regular heartfelt prayer. Thus both *ḥazak* and *ematz* are offered for this trying venture: *ḥazak* to begin, and *ematz* to continue.

There are many times in our lives when we need encouragement from our peers. At times we find ourselves offering words of support, assisting others in their time of need. Encouragement is not all of one type; sometimes an initial push of *ḥazak* is needed, while at other times an *ematz* of persistence is called for.

BERAKHOT 32B

Fine-tuning our prayers

With the advent of the Hasidic movement in the late eighteenth century, the contours of the regnant prayer model were challenged and many new paths to heartfelt communion with God were explored. One of the popular innovations was delaying the beginning of the service to provide the opportunity for mental, emotional and spiritual preparation for the prayer journey.

Undeniably, preparations for prayer were not the invention of the eighteenth-century Hasidim. Our sages tell us that the pious people of old – who were referred to as "*ḥasidim*" long before the eighteenth century – would tarry for one hour and only then pray, so that they might direct their hearts to the Almighty. One sage adduces scriptural support for the practice of preparatory meditation (Psalms 84:5): *Fortunate are those who bide in Your house* – that is, in order to ready themselves for prayer, and only afterwards *they will yet praise You* (*M. Berakhot* 5:1; *B. Berakhot* 32b).

Following this model, some eighteenth-century Hasidim would spend much of their day involved with prayer. Many traditionalist opponents of the fledgling movement viewed this preoccupation with prayer with distaste, asserting that such lengthy prayer preparation went beyond the rabbinic paradigm (*Rabbi Yaakov Emden*).

Hasidim, for their part, felt that preparation was no indulgence; indeed, it was a necessity for successfully and effectively venturing into the Divine world of prayer. To highlight the importance of attaining the proper mindset before embarking upon prayer, Hasidic masters composed prayers that were to be recited before the onset of the service.

The idea of a prayer to precede prayer is already found in the Talmud. Though the *Amida* originally began with the blessing recalling the unique relationship between our forefathers and the Almighty, a biblical verse (Psalms 51:17) was added beforehand: *God, open my lips, and let my mouth declare Your praise* (*B. Berakhot* 4b, 9b). This verse is not considered essential, and one who inadvertently omits it is not required to repeat the *Amida* (*Mishna Berura*). Nevertheless, our sages tell us that this verse, which requests Divine guidance, does not constitute an unnecessary interruption and is a valid extension of the prayer.

Drawing on this talmudic passage, the much-loved Hasidic master, Rabbi Levi Yitzḥak of Berdyczów (1740–1809), explains that the additional line was a later addition, born of the need to focus before commencing the *Amida*. According to Rabbi Levi Yitzḥak, the former greats did not have the same regular need for this preparatory formula. To be sure, even the heroes of old had occasion to turn to God before beginning their prayers. This is how Rabbi Levi Yitzḥak understands Moses' statement: *And I pleaded with God at that time, saying…* (Deuteronomy 3:23). Having exhausted all known prayer avenues, Moses turned to God beseeching guidance as to how to pray effectively. Moses was saying: *And I pleaded with God at that time*, and having been unsuccessful, I asked God what I should be *saying*, that is, how I should pray.

A disciple of Rabbi Levi Yitzḥak, Rabbi Yosef of Nemirov, related a wonderful parable in his correspondence with an anti-Hasidic activist. There was a king who delighted in music. He chose musicians who would visit the palace daily to play for his enjoyment. The musicians were handsomely rewarded for their efforts, and those who arrived before the appointed time were awarded a bonus. For the musicians this was a labour of love, for they were driven by adoration for the king, paying little attention to the payment.

As nature would have it, some of the musicians were more talented and diligent than others. These more committed musicians would arrive well before their peers with instruments that were in splendid condition. Yet all the musicians made sure to arrive by the appointed time, playing out of love for their master and enchanting the king with a magnificent daily musical routine.

Time passed and the children took the place of their parents. The children, alas, lacked the talent and the pure motives of their predecessors. They were single-mindedly interested in the remuneration for their services, paying little attention to the quality of the music. Some of the new musicians followed the example they had seen in their youth, arriving early at the palace. Sadly, their instruments were not tuned properly nor had they adequately practiced. All that concerned them was the monetary bonus for early arrival. The others followed in the footsteps of their predecessors by arriving at the appointed time, but regrettably with no preparation. Their musical achievements were sorely lacking as well. Their late arrival meant they hurriedly went through the routine, always with an eye to their wages.

When the king heard the cacophony these so-called musicians produced, he walked out. Unfortunately, the musicians were so oblivious that they did not perceive the displeasure of the king, and continued the daily ritual in his absence.

Among these slackers were a few worthy people, who realised that their instruments were not in good working order and that they lacked the necessary talent to please the king. They decided to devote time and energy to fixing their instruments and improving their skills. This investment meant they would be late arriving at the palace. When they entered, they would hear the racket of their colleagues and not be able to concentrate on the task at hand. Thus they would find a quiet corner where they could play in earnest.

Having fulfilled their daily quota and earned their coveted reward, the oblivious musicians would leave the palace while their devoted peers lingered, trying their utmost to improve their playing. The king beheld their sincere efforts and was pleased. True, they lacked the talent of their predecessors and their instruments were not as finely tuned, yet they were troubled by these issues and were going to great lengths to attempt to rectify them.

Preparing for prayer is like tuning a musical instrument – a necessity before any quality performance. It is the difference between a harmonious symphony and a discordant cacophony. Preparation for the prayer journey can be as simple as reciting a biblical verse beseeching God for Divine assistance, or it can constitute hours of meditation. It is this groundwork that enhances the melodious harmony of our prayers.

BERAKHOT 32B–33A

Slithering prayers

WHEN DO OUTSIDE distractions legitimise an interruption of prayer? The Mishna offers a terse but clear guideline. Even if the king inquires as to your welfare, you should not interrupt the *Amida* to respond; and even if a snake is coiled around your heel, you should not interrupt to rid yourself of the reptile (*M. Berakhot* 5:1).

Our sages temper the tone of the Mishna by qualifying the rule (*B. Berakhot* 32b–33a). First the Talmud limits the rule by stating that only kings of Israel may be ignored, presumably because they should know better than to disturb supplicants during their prayers. A gentile king, however, is not assumed to have the same priorities, hence supplicants may interrupt their prayers to respond rather than endanger their lives.

Our sages also qualify the rule about dangerous animals. Only when a snake is wrapped around your leg must you continue to pray; if a scorpion is present, an interruption is warranted. This is because a scorpion is more dangerous, as it is likely to sting repeatedly even unprovoked. Following this principle, another talmudic source states that if the snake is agitated and appears set to strike, one is permitted to interrupt the prayers and remove the hissing serpent (*Y. Berakhot* 9a). One commentator permits shaking off any snake or walking away even in the middle of the *Amida*, in cases when calling for help would be considered an unsanctioned interruption of prayer (*Rabbeinu Yona Gerondi*).

Even with these qualifications, the law is still difficult to grasp. On the one hand, it is nigh impossible to expect regular people to ignore a snake wrapped around their leg and continue in heartfelt prayer. On the other hand, the Mishna clearly dictates such a course of inaction. For this reason, as we have seen, authorities seek to limit the scope of the Mishna: one is forbidden to interrupt only if the snake is not dangerous; scorpions and potentially harmful snakes should not be ignored.

Normative Jewish law has accepted these qualifications (*Shulḥan Arukh, Oraḥ Ḥayim* 104).

An extreme expression of the discomfort with this mishnaic teaching can be found in the writings of the Hasidic master and halakhic authority, Rabbi Ḥayim Elazar Shapira of Munkács (1871–1937). In his commentary to the *Shulḥan Arukh* he was uncharacteristically troubled by this law. The Munkatcher Rebbe was a champion of tradition; his works are filled with suggested sources and justifications for common practices that at first blush appears to deviate from halakha. He also dedicated his life to upholding normative law, often using harsh words in his critiques of those who wished to change it. It is therefore surprising to find the Munkatcher Rebbe questioning a talmudic law and saying that it "shatters the roof," meaning that it is extremely difficult to comprehend.

The Munkatcher Rebbe's primary difficulty here is that we seem to be dealing with a life-threatening scenario. In such cases, we do not start doing complicated calculations as to the statistical likelihood of becoming the victim of a lethal snake bite. In life-threatening situations, we do not rely on probability. Thus, even if we were to conclude that most snakes do not bite, and that even among those that bite the majority are not venomous, we would still expect the law to take into account the minority of lethal snakes and allow the person praying to act accordingly. In this vein, elsewhere the Talmud dictates that even if it is doubtful whether a situation is life-threatening, the laws of Shabbat are suspended because life must be preserved (*B. Yoma* 84b). If the laws of Shabbat recede when there is even the possibility of a life-or-death situation, surely if there is a snake wrapped around your leg an interruption of prayer is justified!

The Munkatcher Rebbe also comments on the mindset of the supplicant in this situation. Could such a person truly concentrate on a single word with a snake curled around his leg?

With regard to the licence to walk away but not to call for help, the Munkatcher Rebbe goes further, asking: "How will this save the person? What will he do if the snake does not fall from his leg? Will he try to remove it with his hands? Won't that just provoke the snake? Then it will most certainly bite him!" The Munkatcher Rebbe feels that sometimes there is no choice. The supplicant must interrupt his prayers to call an expert who knows how to charm the snake or pry it from his leg with tongs.

The Munkatcher Rebbe entertains the possibility that the talmudic passage speaks of a pet snake that poses no real danger and is almost a member of the household. This explanation is roundly rejected, for no other commentator or codifier suggests that the rabbinic dictum refers only to a tame snake.

One commentator quoted by the Munkatcher Rebbe tries to explain the rabbinic rule. Once the snake is curled around a person's leg, it poses no danger for it is expressing its love and affection by cuddling up to the person. This approach is difficult to swallow; it certainly does not apply to a boa constrictor, and even a venomous snake can hardly be said to be hugging. Indeed, elsewhere in the Talmud detailed instructions are offered as to how to rid oneself of a snake coiled around one's leg; this cold-blooded creature is not expressing its warmth and friendliness (*B. Shabbat* 110a).

The Munkatcher Rebbe's conclusion is clear: except on a mystical level, this law is incomprehensible. He boldly rules that the law does not apply, and that if a snake glides up while you are in the midst of prayer, you should suspend your supplications and assure your safety.

By the employment of methods of interpretation internal to the halakhic system coupled with an analysis of reality, the law of praying with snakes coiled around our legs may have slithered away.

BERAKHOT 33A

Close encounters with an *arod*

As MENTIONED, THE Mishna rules that even if a snake is coiled around your leg as you stand in prayer, you must continue your supplications without interruption. The Talmud qualifies: the rule applies only to a non-lethal snake; a venomous snake or a scorpion warrants stopping prayer (*M. Berakhot* 5:1; *B. Berakhot* 33a; *Y. Berakhot* 9a).

In this connection, our sages recount a marvellous story about

Rabbi Ḥanina ben Dosa. Often stories of our sages are retold in different sources with slight variations. The story of Rabbi Ḥanina ben Dosa appears in a variety of rabbinic sources, with each redaction casting the tale a bit differently.

The earliest recorded version implicitly describes the greatness of Rabbi Ḥanina ben Dosa (*T. Berakhot* 3:20; *Tanḥuma, Va'era* 4). An animal called an "*arod*" approached and bit Rabbi Ḥanina ben Dosa as he stood in meditative prayer. Rabbi Ḥanina ben Dosa did not allow this serpent-like creature to disrupt his prayers and continued as if nothing had happened. His students searched for the *arod* and found it lying dead near its hole. They promptly proclaimed: "Woe to a person who is bitten by an *arod*, and woe to the *arod* that bites Ben Dosa!" Thus in the context of interrupting prayers, Rabbi Ḥanina ben Dosa is presented as the paradigm of concentration in prayer. The account suggests a connection between single-minded, undiverted focus and Rabbi Ḥanina ben Dosa's miraculous ability to withstand and even reverse the *arod* bite.

A parallel version of this tale adds detail and colour, explicitly making the connection suggested in the earlier account (*Y. Berakhot* 9a). In this version of the story, the students turned to Rabbi Ḥanina ben Dosa and incredulously wondered: "Master, did you not feel the bite?" He responded by assuring the students that due to his intense concentration in prayer he felt nothing; so focused was he that even a lethal bite did not disrupt his supplications. In this source the animal is called a "*ḥabarbur*," but the commentators agree that the *ḥabarbur* and the *arod* are the same creature. After recounting the events, the passage relates to this unknown creature and describes its curious properties.

Clearly the *arod* is serpent-like, for it is always mentioned in the context of snakes. In this case, its encounter with Rabbi Ḥanina ben Dosa is reported after we are told that a prayer interruption is not justified even if a snake is coiled around one's leg. One commentator suggests that the *arod* is related to the toad, but concludes that we do not have the requisite expertise to identify it (*Meiri*). Later commentators suggest that it is a cross between a snake and a toad, and acknowledge that it is extremely dangerous.

Whatever its origins, the *arod* or *ḥabarbur* has an extraordinary feature. Though its bite is lethal, the bite itself does not end the ordeal.

Rather, the bite begins a race – a race to a body of water. The winner lives, while the loser – whether the biter or the bitten – dies.

The account makes no mention of Rabbi Ḥanina ben Dosa racing to a body of water; indeed the point of the story is that he did not move from his place of prayer. How then was he saved? The talmudic passage concludes by saying that the Almighty created a spring beneath his feet and thus he reached water before his animal adversary.

The passage concludes with the verse: *He will fulfil the desire of those who fear Him, and He will hear their cry and will save them* (Psalms 145:19). This version, therefore, focuses not only on Rabbi Ḥanina ben Dosa's greatness but on the Divine protection afforded to those who do the Almighty's will.

We now come to the third version of the story recorded in the Babylonian Talmud (*B. Berakhot* 33a). The reference point of the story is the same – the rule that a snake coiled around one's leg does not justify a prayer disruption – yet this account changes the focus from the description of Rabbi Ḥanina ben Dosa's focused prayer and its efficacy.

In a certain place there was an *arod* that was wreaking havoc. Seeking a solution, the people came to Rabbi Ḥanina ben Dosa. Rabbi Ḥanina ben Dosa said to them: "Show me the hole where the *arod* lives." When he came to the *arod*'s lair, Rabbi Ḥanina ben Dosa calmly put his heel on the mouth of the hole. The *arod* darted out and bit the proffered foot, whereupon the *arod* dropped dead. Rabbi Ḥanina ben Dosa picked up the dead animal, slung it over his shoulder and brought it to the *beit midrash*. As he entered the *beit midrash*, perhaps holding the *arod* in plain view for all to see, he declared: "Look my children, it is not the *arod* that causes death but sin that causes death."

In this account Rabbi Ḥanina ben Dosa is not a passive supplicant devoted solely to heartfelt prayer; he actively goes out to combat the *arod* crisis. Even once this dangerous creature has been neutralised, Rabbi Ḥanina ben Dosa takes the opportunity to teach an important lesson. He brings the carcass to the *beit midrash* to show the people that they should be more careful to follow God's commandments and to avoid sin, rather than run from the *arod* who is merely one of the Almighty's messengers. The power of death does not lie with the *arod*, but with the *arod*'s Creator.

This version of Rabbi Ḥanina ben Dosa's encounter with the *arod* does not mention his piety in prayer; it is presented as an educational lesson about the dangers of this world. It also points to the course of action expected from worthy leaders, and the guidance they should provide, boldly confronting the challenges of the day and using every encounter as a teaching moment.

BERAKHOT 33A

Compassion for fools

EVERY SATURDAY NIGHT, we accompany the departing Shabbat with the recitation of the *havdala* prayer. The theme of this prayer is the demarcation between the holy and the mundane, and its recitation separates between the sanctity of Shabbat and the work week. This prayer is first said as part of the silent *Amida* and a different form is recited over a cup of wine following the evening prayer.

When in the *Amida* should *havdala* be inserted? The Mishna offers three opinions. All three agree that the prayer should be recited as part of the evening *Amida*; the disagreement surrounds the form and placement of *havdala* (*M. Berakhot* 5:2; *B. Berakhot* 33a).

According to the first approach, *havdala* should be added to the fourth blessing – *Ata Ḥonen* – which deals with the intellect. The sages offer two explanations for the placement. The first suggests that this fourth blessing is the first weekday benediction, as the first three sections of the *Amida* are included in the Shabbat liturgy as well. We therefore distinguish between Shabbat and the work week in this first weekday blessing. The second explanation suggests that differentiating between the holy and the mundane, between the sacred Shabbat and the routine weekdays, is an exercise in wisdom. The most suitable place for *havdala*, therefore, is in the fourth blessing, where we acknowledge the wisdom, understanding and knowledge that are Divinely bestowed upon us.

The second approach of the Mishna suggests that *havdala* deserves to have its own additional blessing. Thus it should slot in as a new fourth section of the *Amida*, preceding all the weekday blessings.

The third approach holds that *havdala* should be recited towards the end of the *Amida* as part of the benedictions of thanksgiving. After all, we are thanking the Almighty for the gift of Shabbat and for the ability to distinguish between the holy and the mundane.

While disagreements are a staple of the Talmud, here our sages are intrigued by the *havdala* dispute. The Men of the Great Assembly are credited with laying the foundations of our liturgy, including the introduction of the *havdala* requirement. The Talmud asks: how can there be a disagreement as to where *havdala* should be said? The answer should be simple – wherever the Men of the Great Assembly instituted it. Furthermore, how could a dispute arise regarding a weekly prayer ritual that was no doubt practiced for many years?

The Talmud responds by recounting an interesting historical chapter leading up to the dispute. *Havdala* was first instituted as part of the prayer service. At that time, the Jewish people were not affluent, and the Men of the Great Assembly did not wish to burden them financially by requiring anything more than a paragraph of prayer. Once the people's fortunes improved, *havdala* was removed from the evening prayer and allocated its own space after the service. It was to be said over a cup of wine. Thus Shabbat was ushered in with *kiddush* over wine and ushered out with *havdala* over wine. Later, the people became impoverished again, and the sages sought to revert to the original requirement of *havdala* in prayer.

While consciousness of the financial needs of the people is praiseworthy, and seeking to adapt the law accordingly is certainly laudable, this continuous state of *havdala* flux may have engendered uncertainty. A new arrangement was therefore introduced: *havdala* was to be said by all as part of the evening prayer, and those who had the means to do so would also recite it over a cup of wine. It was at this stage – after the period when *havdala* had been said over wine only and not as part of the prayer service – that the disagreement arose as to where the prayer should be recited.

Let us return to the placement of *havdala* in the *Amida*. Halakha adopts the first approach. *Havdala* is said as part of the fourth blessing, which deals with the mind. In this context, the Talmud launches into an exposition of the supreme value of the intellect. Knowledge is great as demonstrated by the fact that the first weekday blessing in the *Amida* petitions God for mental acuity: "You favour humans with knowledge and teach mortals understanding. Please grace us with knowledge, understanding and insight. Blessed are You, O God, gracious giver of knowledge."

One commentator adds that only with understanding can we hope to recognise to Whom we are addressing our subsequent requests for repentance, forgiveness and satisfaction of our needs (*Rashba*).

According to one sage in the Talmud, we equate possessing knowledge to reconstructing the Temple. A later commentator expands on this theme. A different talmudic passage states that if the Temple has not been rebuilt in your time, it is as if it has been destroyed in your time (*Y. Yoma* 38c). Thus acquiring knowledge, which is akin to rebuilding the Temple, is a way to demonstrate that our central place of worship was not laid to waste in our time (*Kedusha UVerakha*).

Elsewhere (*Vayikra Rabba* 1:6) our sages ask a rhetorical question: if people possess gold and silver, precious stones and pearls, and all the most exquisite valuables of this world, yet they lack knowledge, what have they really acquired? One sage reports that it is unanimously accepted that the only true pauper is one who is impoverished in knowledge (*B. Nedarim* 41a).

In the Land of Israel, a popular aphorism encapsulated the centrality of knowledge: "Those who have it within them have everything within them; those who do not have it within them have nothing within them. If they possess it, what do they lack? If they do not possess it, what do they possess?" The apparent repetition in this proverb may indicate that there are two types of knowledgeable people. Those who are born with a sharp intellect are fortunate to have this gift. Yet even those who are not born with this gift can still be knowledgeable, through application and commitment to acquiring wisdom (*Anaf Yosef*).

Yet among these talmudic statements lauding the value of the mind, we find a startling – and troubling – proclamation. "It is forbidden to have mercy on someone who does not have knowledge." Scriptural support is offered for this unexpected declaration: *For it is not a people of understanding; therefore its Maker shall not have mercy on it* (Isaiah 27:11).

While we can understand the value and pivotal role of intellectual pursuits, it is nevertheless troubling to hear that mercy is withheld from the mentally incompetent. Moreover, this statement even appears absurd. Could it be that there is an intellectual threshold that defines who deserves our compassion? Different explanations for this passage have been offered, as we shall see.

Let us return to the biblical passage cited. The prophet describes how the Almighty will not compassionately alleviate the troubles of the Jewish people as long as they fail to understand that their suffering is due to their iniquity. God hopes that the nation's continued torment will ultimately lead to repentance (*Radak*). In this light the lack of compassion for the ignorant could be seen as a tactic to goad the development of the intellect. Of course, one could question the effectiveness of this method.

According to another approach, lack of knowledge is itself accompanied by a lack of compassion. People who have no knowledge will have no mercy on others, and therefore the sages declare that we need not have mercy on them (*Rabbi Naḥman of Bratslav*). This approach may not sit easy with many of us. Are the sages teaching that compassion should be *quid pro quo*, that only one who can be considerate is deserving of sympathy?

One Hasidic master departs from the straightforward reading of the text to offer an innovative reading with a powerful message. Rabbi Yitzḥak Kalish (1779–1848) of Warka in Poland was known for his compassionate style of leadership. He was a humble leader and his love for others served as a worthy example.

The Warka Rebbe was once asked how he could so liberally show kindness and concern, particularly for people who lacked knowledge. The master replied: "As humans, we naturally feel empathy towards others. This innate response, however, is generally reserved for those with knowledge who have fallen on difficult times. With regard to someone whose intellect is lacking, the Talmud urges us to ignore our instincts and feel compassion towards such people."

"But doesn't the passage say it is *assur*, forbidden to have mercy on the ignorant?" inquired the disciples.

Punning on the double meaning of the Hebrew word *assur,* the Warka Rebbe replied: "The Talmud teaches that we are *assur,* bound to be compassionate to such unfortunate people."

BERAKHOT 33A

Revenge

THE TALMUD QUOTES a sage who tells us that knowledge (*de'ah*) is "great," meaning of primary importance. For this reason knowledge is the subject of the first of the weekday petitions in the *Amida* (*B. Berakhot* 33a). A further proof of the significance of knowledge is that it appears between two Divine names in a biblical verse: *For the God of thoughts (de'ot) is the Almighty* (1 Samuel 2:3).

Following this method of identifying premier values, another sage suggests a second critically important item. The Temple is "great," for it appears between two Divine names in the Song at the Sea: *The foundation of the dwelling place You have made, O God; the Temple, O God, that Your hands have established* (Exodus 15:17). Moreover, the two values – knowledge and the Temple – are understood to be intrinsically connected. "When one has knowledge (*de'ah*), it is as if the Temple was rebuilt in his days," for both values appear in the Bible between two Divine names.

One sage is driven to question the reliability of identifying major values using this method. He objects that "According to this, you would have to say that revenge is also great, for it too is found between two Divine names – *Almighty of vengeance, O God, Almighty of vengeance, appear* (Psalms 94:1)." The Talmud concedes that vengeance is indeed great in appropriate circumstances, but not all vengeance is justifiable. The biblical verse, as we have just seen, mentions vengeance twice: at times revenge is called for, and such vengeance is surrounded by two Divine names; at other times vengeance is evil and should be eradicated.

Despite acknowledging the possibility of justifiable vengeance, halakha appears to eschew revenge. The Torah instructs: *You shall not avenge, nor bear any grudge against the children of your people, and you should love your neighbour as yourself; I am God* (Leviticus 19:18). No opening is given in this biblical verse for the option of vengeance.

What type of vengeance could be considered justifiable? The Talmud finds an example in the Divine realm: God's vengeance against the nations of the world, who rejected Torah, is justifiable revenge.

Though revenge is generally shunned, we are not enjoined merely to stand by silently if we are disparaged. In his thirteenth-century enumeration of the 613 commandments, the unknown Barcelonan author of *Sefer HaḤinukh* rejects the notion that the command against revenge proscribes any type of response to abuse. He writes: "If someone comes and wickedly pains his fellow with evil words, the intention is not that the vilified person should not respond, for it is impossible for a person to be like an unmoving rock. Moreover, if he is silent it is as if he is conceding the truth of the defamatory attack. In truth, the Torah does not command that one be like a rock, maintaining silence when abused just as he is silent when blessed."

The author continues by comparing a verbal response in the face of a defamatory attack to legitimate self-defence in the face of a physical assault. The prohibition against revenge does not include a prohibition against self-defence, so a person is permitted to respond to attacks. At the same time, though, such a response does not include revenge.

We have seen that barring Divine vengeance and legitimate self-defence, classic revenge is shunned. What is so bad about vengeance? One biblical commentator – Rabbi Naftali Zvi Yehuda Berlin (1816–1893), known by the acronym Netziv – offers practical societal reasons for avoiding revenge. He explains that the act of revenge often begins a vicious cycle, in which each vengeful act is reciprocated by another vengeful act.

This approach echoes an early passage in Maimonides' halakhic *magnum opus, Mishneh Torah*. In the laws against revenge and bearing a grudge, he concludes with the lofty words: "And this," that is, not taking revenge or bearing a grudge, "Is the correct way to behave. It enables the world to be settled and allows people to have dealings with one another."

In the eyes of Maimonides the injunction against revenge and bearing a grudge is so important that he treats it towards the beginning of his work where he deals with matters of character refinement, rather than relegating its treatment to a subset of the laws of damages.

Netziv, however, also advocates a utilitarian approach, as embodied in another biblical verse: *If your enemy be hungry, give him bread to eat; and if he be thirsty, give him water to drink. For you will heap coals of fire on his head* – and thus prevent him from reacting badly towards you in the future – *and God will reward you* (Proverbs 25:21–22).

In succinct but lucid terms the Talmud illustrates the folly of revenge using vivid imagery (*Y. Nedarim* 41c). You are cutting meat, and by mistake your right hand cuts your left hand. Would your left hand pick up the knife and chop off your right hand?!

As a people we are one body. Taking revenge against another person is as silly as one hand taking revenge against the other; in the end the body has just incurred more injuries. If we internalise the notion that taking revenge harms only ourselves, we will quickly shy away from this path. The prohibition against revenge reflects our reciprocal relationship with one another.

Revenge is a dangerous tool. While it may be permitted in clearly delineated circumstances, it should generally be avoided. To be sure, we are not commanded to take the path of non-resistance in the face of physical or verbal assaults from an aggressor. Yet our response should be tempered, because spiteful revenge reflects a lack of brotherhood and is harmful to those who seek it. Perhaps this is what the Talmud means when it says that vengeance is "great" – not great in the celebratory sense, but great in the sense that it is a powerful and dangerous tool. Revenge is an act that is aimed at harming another and appears not to affect the avenger. However, this is an illusion; in truth it is the avenger who is harmed most.

BERAKHOT 33B

Lessons learned

EDUCATORS ARE ALWAYS looking for innovative methods with which to teach their students. How can we effectively convey a message to pupils so that the teaching moment becomes a learning experience rather than a short-lived transfer of information? The Talmud provides us with a number of examples where our sages sought to instruct students and convey lessons which would leave indelible impressions.

The Mishna proscribes certain additions to the text of the *Amida*, and the Talmud explains what is problematic with these insertions (*M. Berakhot* 5:3; *B. Berakhot* 33b).

A supplicant may not repeat the word *modim*, as if to say "We give thanks to You, we give thanks to You," for it would appear as if two deities were being addressed. One may not repeat the word *shema*, saying "Hear, hear," for the same reason.

Likewise, the phrase "Your name shall be remembered for goodness" may not be added, for this implies that we thank the Almighty for the good things we experience but do not acknowledge God's hand in the bad things that befall us (*M. Berakhot* 9:8).

Similarly it is forbidden for the prayer leader to say: "Your mercy, God, extends to the bird's nest." This refers to the requirement to chase a mother bird away before taking her eggs or chicks (Deuteronomy 22:6–7). The Talmud offers two possible problems with this formulation. First, the addition intimates that God's mercy extends to birds only. Alternatively, this phrase implies that God's directives are to be followed because they express mercy, whereas in truth the rules must be respected as decrees of the unknowable Divine will (*Rashi*).

In all these instances the ruling is the same: we silence the supplicant who has added such phrases.

The Talmud recounts a related incident in which Rabba and his student Abbaye heard a certain prayer leader say: "You, God, have shown mercy on the bird's nest; so too may You have compassion and mercy on us."

Hearing this Rabba exclaimed: "How well this sharp Torah scholar knows how to appease his God!"

Abbaye was shocked. He retorted: "Didn't we learn in the Mishna that such a supplicant must be silenced? Why did you praise him?"

The Talmud explains that Rabba – who was certainly aware of this ruling – had intended to test Abbaye, and wanted to see whether his pupil would challenge him.

The commentators question Rabba's approach. This was no time to test Abbaye; the supplicant should have been silenced in accordance with the law! They offer various solutions. Perhaps we can suggest that for the sake of the opportunity to teach Abbaye, Rabba was willing to set aside the rule momentarily. Undoubtedly, such a dramatic experience would leave a stronger impression on the mind of a young pupil than a rote recitation of a legal dictum.

Another talmudic tale further illustrates the value of the practical educational experience, perhaps even at the expense of the law (*B. Kiddushin* 32a). Rav Huna once tore silks in the presence of his son. Ripping the expensive cloth to shreds, Rav Huna said to himself: "Let me see if my son gets angry at me or whether he is able to honour his father and control his fury."

The Talmud dissects the scenario, questioning Rav Huna's conduct. Had his son failed to live up to the challenge and cursed his father's wanton destruction, Rav Huna would effectively have caused his son to sin. Rav Huna would thus have violated the biblical prohibition *Before a blind person you shall not place a stumbling block* (Leviticus 19:14). The answer is that Rav Huna must have waived the honour due to him, circumventing any possibility of his son sinning. Nevertheless, the Talmud continues, it would seem that Rav Huna himself violated a prohibition, the one against destroying useful property (Deuteronomy 20:19). The Talmud goes on to explain that Rav Huna must have torn the garments along the seams so as not to ruin them, for they could easily be sewn back together. The Talmud objects to this suggestion, though, saying that perhaps this was the reason that the son was not infuriated – because his father had rent the silk at the seam. If so the test was useless. The passage concludes by saying that Rav Huna must have staged this test while his son was already upset regarding another issue. Due to his preoccupation with this other matter, the son would not have noticed that the tear was along the seam. The test, therefore, was real.

While the Talmud presents a complicated scenario to explain why there was no transgression in this act, we may add that Rav Huna appears to have been willing to walk a fine line for the sake of creating a challenging situation for his son.

Of course we may wonder whether there is a limit to the techniques used to teach a lesson. Can any law be temporarily set aside for the sake of a teaching moment? Such a conclusion would be most surprising, and is hardly the thrust of these talmudic accounts.

In fact, another talmudic passage belies the premise that educational experiences should be arranged at all costs (*B. Bava Metzia* 75a). After a lengthy discussion of the parameters and severity of the prohibition of taking interest on loans, the Talmud makes a surprising statement. It is permitted for people to charge interest to their children and other household members, in order to let them taste the bitterness of paying interest. Interest is generally proscribed, yet here it is allowed for educational purposes. The hope is that the child will feel the distress and the hopelessness of someone caught in the net of interest payments and will refrain in the future from engaging in such practices. Nevertheless, this proposed educational exercise is quickly rejected by the Talmud. Such an experiment is too dangerous, for the child may realise how easy and tempting it is to earn money by charging interest. Instead of discouraging the youngster from taking interest, this may have the opposite effect.

While there may be room for bending the rules for the sake of educational experiences, there is no licence for disregarding the law. Teaching moments are extremely valuable, but need to be handled with care, lest the lessons learned be different from the ones we are trying to teach.

BERAKHOT 33B–34A

Heavy metal in prayer

As we have seen, the Mishna proscribes three particular additions to the text of the *Amida*: "Your mercy, God, extends to the bird's nest," "Your name shall be remembered for goodness," and "We give thanks to You, we give thanks to You." The Talmud goes on to explain what is problematic with each of these insertions. It also adds a fourth proscribed statement: "Hear, hear" (*M. Berakhot* 5:3; *B. Berakhot* 33b–34a).

In all of these instances we silence the supplicant who adds the phrase. One talmudic sage questions the harsh condemnation in the two cases of word repetition. Perhaps the person is not concentrating when he first recites the word, and therefore repeats it in an earnest attempt to focus. The repetition in such a case does not reflect a misguided belief in two deities – the reason we silence the supplicant – but rather is an expression of a sincere desire to have proper concentration during prayer. Surely such an approach should be lauded, not censured!

The Talmud explains that if this is the reason for the repetition, the prayer leader does deserve a reprimand, for when we talk to the Almighty we must dedicate our undivided attention to the task. Thus the entire situation is shameful. In the rhetorical words of the Talmud: "May one act towards heaven with the familiarity with which one acts towards a *ḥavruta*, a study partner!?" Thus the Talmud does not take lightly the possibility of repeating a few innocent words. Rather, it proclaims: "Supplicants who do not focus at the outset should be struck with a blacksmith's hammer until they do."

One commentator tempers the talmudic dictum, noting that educators need not walk around with metal clubs hitting people over the head without warning if they lose concentration while praying. Rather, it means that we first instruct supplicants to focus in prayer, and if necessary strike them should they persist in repeating words (*Rashi*).

Moving further away from any violent interpretations, we turn to the world of Hasidism. One of the foremost students of the famed Besht (c. 1700–1760) and the author of the first published work of Hasidic thought, Rabbi Yaakov Yosef of Polonnoye (1710–1782), writes that his master uses this talmudic passage to explain one of the foundational tenets of early Hasidic thought.

The Besht begins by noting that the talmudic passage barely deals with our earlier question. Why is repeating words because one is striving for greater focus considered so heinous a crime? Perhaps the reiteration is in fact an attempt to concentrate; why should we assume that it reflects a philosophical position about the Almighty's oneness?

The Besht explains that the supplicant's concentration is likely disturbed by some "foreign thought" which enters his mind when he first attempts to pray. Rather than rejecting this distracting thought out of hand, he should acknowledge it as being of Divine origin. Thus it is possible to elevate it to a spiritual plane. The mistake of the supplicant who repeats the words is that he does not acknowledge that the invasive thought has been sent by God and thus can be rectified or reclaimed for sacred purposes.

The talmudic image of a blacksmith's hammer is a metaphor for the foreign thought that hammers at a person, pleading to be elevated to a spiritual plane. At that moment, the supplicant's task is to grasp this thought, find the kernel of truth within it and transform it into something positive. Elsewhere in his writings, Rabbi Yaakov Yosef cites an example given by the Besht: a lustful thought should be channelled in the direction of loving-kindness.

Trying to recite the prayer a second time indicates that one is discarding the thought. This is a denial of the Divine spark in that invading thought, which is comparable to trying to limit the presence of the Almighty.

The Besht acknowledges that some foreign thoughts should be set aside, and he provides a formula for distinguishing between different types of mental intrusions. If, as soon as the distracting thought shows up, the supplicant has an idea as to how this thought can be spiritually elevated, then rather than discarding the thought, it should be sublimated. If, however, no such idea presents itself immediately, the thought has indeed come to disrupt and disturb. In this case only, the person should discard the intruding thought.

This is not merely a theoretical model; Rabbi Yaakov Yosef concludes his exposition with a historical report. Once someone pointedly asked the Besht whether he was allowed to repeat words from *Shema* or the *Amida* if they were recited without concentration. The Besht responded by applying his theoretical position to this practical case.

It should be noted that the early Hasidic idea of elevating foreign thoughts irked the opponents of Hasidism, and the doctrine was largely abandoned by the masses of Hasidim in later generations. The elevation of foreign thoughts was left to only the most spiritually adept. The doctrine nevertheless reflects an ever-present ideal: to identify God's Presence in every item, every space and every scenario. This is truly a lofty goal.

It may be easy to say that everything is from the Almighty, but the challenge lies in internalising this ideal. We need to move from a cosmetic Judaism, concerned most with superficial catchphrases, to a Judaism of substance and depth.

BERAKHOT 34A

Refusing to lead

HOW EAGER SHOULD we be to lead the prayer services? Should we jump at the chance to guide fellow supplicants? Or should we balk at the responsibility, leaving the privilege of directing the service to others?

Our sages declare that one who is invited to serve as *sheliaḥ tzibur*, the prayer leader, must at first decline this honour (*B. Berakhot* 34a). The mandated refusal reminds the leader that he is unworthy of the distinction of being the community's representative (*Rashi*). This may reflect the goal of humility in general, not just in the realm of leading the prayers. You should always hesitate rather than immediately accept a position of honour (*Rabbi Yehonatan HaKohen of Lunel*).

The Talmud continues with a metaphor. If the person asked to lead does not initially decline, his attitude is deemed tasteless. It is likened to food cooked without salt: just as such a dish gives sustenance but lacks flavour, so too this prayer leader fulfils the task adequately but in a bland way that lacks zest. On the other hand, the service would never start if everyone adamantly refused to lead. Therefore our sages add that if someone declines excessively, he is compared to a dish that has been oversalted.

Seeking a happy medium, the Talmud asks: how should the potential leader behave? A guideline is provided. The first time a person is asked to lead the service, he should simply refuse. The second time, he should appear to be wavering. Finally, when he is asked a third time, he should step forward to where the leader stands during the service and guide the congregation in prayer.

In conclusion, the Talmud quotes an earlier source that succinctly tells us that three things are bad in excess but are fine in moderation: yeast, salt and refusal.

Jewish law limits this talmudic passage in two ways (*Shulḥan Arukh, Oraḥ Ḥayim* 53). First, the instruction applies only to a leader who is not the established *sheliaḥ tzibur*. A person who officially serves the community in this capacity need not go through the motions of being asked thrice before the onset of each service. Furthermore, if the potential *sheliaḥ tzibur* is approached by a great person, he should acquiesce without delay.

The Hasidic master Rabbi Yehuda Zvi Eichenstein of Rozdol (d. 1827) was known for his asceticism and his understanding of the hidden realms of Torah. Addressing his disciples, he told of his personal journey, which gave expression to the stages described in our talmudic passage. "When I was a young man, I had a beautiful voice and I knew how to make all the prayers sound Divine. I was often asked to lead the service, as many people desired to listen to my melodious prayer. As for me, I was at war with my evil inclination. Each time I rose to lead the service I battled against feelings of self-importance and vanity. I would tell myself: 'I am obligated to lead the service and am doing so without arrogance and conceit.' Eventually, I decided that I would never lead the service, so that no hint of haughtiness would enter my heart. Moreover, I decided to switch places in the synagogue. No longer would I sit by the eastern wall, which enjoys pride of place in any synagogue. For in that place people would gather around me to hear the harmonious sound of my personal prayer. Instead I decided to stand in the corner where no one could hear my voice.

"As I stood humbly in the corner, offering my heartfelt prayers, I felt that I had reached the lofty goal of worthy prayer with unadulterated humility.

"Suddenly I realised that the evil inclination had misled me into feeling proud at my prayer achievement! I said to the evil inclination: 'I thought that at least here in the corner you would leave me be and not disturb my thoughts. Since I see that here too you intend to pursue me, I will continue to serve as leader of the service as was the custom of my forefathers. Thus at least I can serve my Creator with the vocal gift Divinely bestowed upon me.'"

In tackling the personal challenges of sincere prayer, Rabbi Yehuda Zvi of Rozdol journeyed through the three stages described in the Talmud. At first he flatly declined to serve as *sheliaḥ tzibur*, thinking that a blanket refusal – the Talmud's first stage – would help him avoid the challenges of arrogant thoughts during prayer. This move, however, did not have the desired result.

As Rabbi Yehuda Zvi stood in the corner, he found himself in a quandary. Should he lead the congregation and risk feeling proud of his musical capabilities, or should he stand off to the side? If he stood to the side he would still be subject to the evil inclination. It would relentlessly continue attempting to lead him to pride – not on account of his melodious prayer, but on account of the earnest prayer that he was offering away from the eyes and ears of others. This was the second stage described in the Talmud – the stage of wavering.

Finally, Rabbi Yehuda Zvi decided to lead the prayers with his pleasing voice and thus serve the community and the Almighty. This was the Talmud's third stage – the stage of acceptance.

Hesitating before serving as the *sheliaḥ tzibur* is not only an exercise in self-restraint, nor is it merely an expression of humility. It also allows the person approached to evaluate whether undertaking the proffered leadership role will be a constructive experience for himself and his community. True, the service requires a prayer leader, but it is only someone who will serve the community's needs and who will grow through the experience who should accept this responsibility. This may serve as a paradigm for leaders in all walks of life. True, leaders may be necessary; but before people accept the mantle of leadership, they must first evaluate it and do their best to ensure that accepting the job will be beneficial both for them and for their community.

BERAKHOT 34A

How much time should it take to pray?

RABBI MENAḤEM ZIEMBA (1883–1943 in the Warsaw Ghetto), one of the outstanding rabbinic leaders of Polish Jewry, would often finish his silent *Amida* well ahead of many of the congregants. When asked how it was that a rabbinic personality such as himself could complete his supplications with such speed, he replied: "I say the words; I don't know what everyone else is doing!"

What are the limits of lengthy and abbreviated prayers? When does the service become too drawn out and, conversely, when is it considered too brief? Our sages recount two tales that provide guidance regarding the appropriate length of time for prayers (*B. Berakhot* 34a).

A student of Rabbi Eliezer once led the services in front of his teacher. As he lengthened the service excessively, perhaps by adding extra supplications (*Meiri*), the other students present commented to their teacher: "Our master, what a prolonger this person is."

Rabbi Eliezer calmed his disciples with reference to a biblical episode. "Does he prolong his prayers more than our master Moses did? As Moses said: *And I threw myself down before God for forty days and forty nights* (Deuteronomy 9:25)." Following the sin of the Golden Calf, Moses prayed to the Almighty to avert the annihilation of the Jewish people. His supplications lasted for forty days and forty nights, and thus provide an example of protracted prayer. Rabbi Eliezer appears to be chiding his students, explaining that their prayer leader need not be condemned, for he had not exceeded the bounds of extended prayer.

Immediately following this account, the Talmud offers a similar tale, but one reflecting the opposite extreme. A certain student once led the prayer services in the presence of his teacher, Rabbi Eliezer. This time the student markedly abbreviated the service. The other students griped to their teacher: "What an abbreviator this person is."

Again Rabbi Eliezer provided a biblical source in defence of the leader of the service. "Does he abbreviate his prayers more than our teacher Moses did?" The Torah records Moses' concise and crisp prayer for the healing of his sister Miriam: *Please God, please heal her* (Numbers 12:13). Succinct prayers also have their place.

The commentators seek to differentiate between the two statements of Rabbi Eliezer. Returning to the biblical verses quoted, they distinguish between times when lengthy prayers are called for, and circumstances when concise supplications are appropriate.

One commentator notes that Moses' terse prayer was offered when he sought a cure for Miriam's malady, while his protracted supplications were for the salvation of the entire Jewish people (*Maharsha*). From this we can extrapolate that when praying for the broader community, it is appropriate to pray at length; when praying for the needs of an individual, the supplication should be kept short and to the point.

Following the paradigm of Moses' prayer for Miriam, our sages teach us that when one seeks Divine mercy for a friend, the individual's name need not be mentioned. As one commentator explains, the Holy One will see into the heart and know the intent of the supplicant (*Maharsha*). Later authorities limit this ruling to when the prayer is offered in the presence of the person for whom the supplicant is praying; if the subject of the prayer is elsewhere, however, the supplicant should explicitly mention the name (*Maharil*).

Another commentator, using the same method of examining the biblical verses quoted, suggests a different distinction (*Anaf Yosef*). Moses' clipped prayer was for Miriam's physical well-being; his extensive supplications were for the spiritual survival of the Jewish people. Accordingly, when one's prayers are for physical well-being, a concise prayer is suitable; when the prayers concern sacred matters such as spiritual survival, the supplicant may maximise the length of the prayers.

Perhaps we can suggest another approach that focuses not on the biblical verses quoted but on the juxtaposition of the two tales and Rabbi Eliezer's seemingly contradictory teachings. As an enterprise of the soul, prayer should not be artificially bound by the dictates of time. It would be incongruous to suggest that a sincere, heartfelt prayer must fit into a predetermined time frame. The sum of Rabbi Eliezer's two statements is that there is no set length of time for prayer.

The juxtaposition of Rabbi Eliezer's two responses is not the only way we can derive this lesson. According to an earlier rabbinic source, the contrast between Moses' two prayers teaches us that there is a time for concise prayer and a time for extended prayer (*Mekhilta*). Pointedly, the sources are silent as to when these times are. This leaves a gap that – as we have seen – the commentators attempt to fill. Perhaps the silence leaves room for a flexible approach to the length of prayers in general.

Moses also provides us with a third paradigm of prayer to complement the lengthy forty-day-and-night prayer and the terse, one-line supplication. After hitting the rock rather than speaking to it in order to extract water for the Jewish people, Moses was barred from entering the Land of Israel (Numbers 20:7–13). In his parting speech to the Jewish people, Moses revealed that he beseeched the Almighty to allow him to enter the Promised Land. Our sages tell us that the word used to describe Moses' supplication – *va'etḥanan*, and I besought (Deuteronomy 3:23) – contains a hint about his prayer approach. The *gematria* – numerical value of the Hebrew letters – of the word *va'etḥanan* is 515. This indicates that when Moses beseeched the Almighty to grant him access to the Land of Israel, he offered 515 supplications (*Yalkut Shimoni*).

Alongside the concise prayer and the extended prayer, we now have the repeated supplication offered over a longer period of time. Moses' three types of prayer and Rabbi Eliezer's responses to two types of prayer suggest that our prayers need not conform to a set time schedule. In certain circumstances we may be moved to lengthy supplications. At other times a heartfelt prayer may be short and soulful. And there may be cases when we repeat a prayer over and over again. The varied options for prayer can thus reflect our varied moods and experiences.

BERAKHOT 34B

Whom you marry

OUR SOCIETY ACKNOWLEDGES that in recognition of achievements or contributions, certain people deserve to be accorded respect and even material benefits. In Jewish tradition, one class that undeniably falls into this category is the scholarly. Throughout rabbinic literature we find statements expressing the value of supporting the wise, providing them with material benefits and giving them preferential treatment.

The Talmud urges us to host the wise in our home and use our possessions for the benefit of *talmidei ḥakhamim*, Torah scholars. Doing so is lauded and compared to other great religious activities, such as offering sacrifices in the Temple or bringing *bikkurim*, the first fruits, to the Temple (*B. Berakhot* 10b, 63b; *Vayikra Rabba* 34:13). Helping the wise is so significant that, according to one source, a simpleton who assists Torah scholars in this world will be taught Torah in the World to Come (*Yalkut Reuveni*). Moreover, attaching oneself to a scholar is akin to cleaving to the Holy Presence (*B. Ketubot* 111b).

Those who toil in Torah are given preference when charity is distributed (*Kohelet Rabba* 11:1). According to one commentator, money set aside for charity may be given to those who study Torah, even if they do not fit all the criteria to be considered needy (*Penei Moshe*).

But the greatest gift one can grant the wise is to give one's daughter's hand in marriage to a scholar. The Talmud tells us that the prophets prophesied only for those who marry off their daughters to the wise, use their possessions for the benefit of scholars and do business on their behalf (*B. Berakhot* 34b).

How important is it to marry off a daughter to a scholar? Laban, justifying his switching Jacob's wives, states: *This is not done in our place to give the younger one before the eldest one* (Genesis 29:26). This statement is generally accepted – we do try to marry off older children before younger children. However, Rabbi Yekutiel Yehuda Halberstam (1904–1994), the Klausenburger Rebbe, rules that a younger daughter can marry a scholar even though her older brother is still single, for such a union brings blessing into the house and will benefit the older, unmarried sibling. Thus the importance of marrying someone wise is so great that it takes precedence over the principle that we marry off the older before the younger.

Talmudic advice is directed not only at the parents of a young girl seeking to find her a match. Elsewhere in the Talmud, instructions are provided for a groom looking for a bride (*B. Pesaḥim* 49b). A person should sell all his possessions if necessary to marry the daughter of a Torah scholar. If he cannot find the daughter of a scholar, he should marry the daughter of one of the leaders of the generation who excel in good deeds. If no such bride is available, he should marry the daughter of a synagogue leader. Where this is not a possibility, the daughter of an honest custodian charged with the collection and distribution of charity is the next preference. If such a bride cannot be found, then he should seek a daughter of a schoolteacher. The Talmud also discourages marrying the daughter of the unlearned.

Thus parents are advised to find Torah scholars for their daughters, while young men are encouraged to look for scholars' daughters. In the context of this two-pronged advice, we recall a tale from nineteenth-century Hasidic Poland.

At the age of fourteen, Rabbi Avraham Bornsztain of Sochaczew (1839–1910) married the daughter of the famed Kotzker Rebbe, Rabbi Menaḥem Mendel Morgensztern (1787–1859). He was once asked whether he was satisfied being the son-in-law of this illustrious personality. Before answering the question, Rabbi Avraham described the first attempt at finding him a suitable match. It was suggested that he marry the daughter of Rabbi Ḥayim Halberstam (1793–1876) of Nowy Sącz, Poland. Known as the Tzanzer Rebbe, he was a serious talmudist, a famous halakhic respondent and an influential Hasidic master.

A meeting between the father of the bride and the prospective son-in-law was arranged. The goal of the appointment was for the Tzanzer Rebbe to ascertain whether the young scholar was an appropriate match for his daughter. Since the Talmud says that a father should ensure that his daughter marry a scholar, the Tzanzer Rebbe opened the meeting by testing the young Rabbi Avraham on some of the finer points of Jewish law. After much Talmud page turning, questions and answers, arguments and counter-arguments, the Tzanzer Rebbe was satisfied. The young Rabbi Avraham was truly a noteworthy scholar and would be a worthy son-in-law.

The Tzanzer Rebbe closed the tome of Talmud and with a smile congratulated the young Rabbi Avraham. For his part, the precocious youthful scholar did not feel that the interview had finished. He reopened the volume of Talmud in his hands, saying: "Our sages teach us that a person should sell all his possessions to marry the daughter of a scholar. Now it is my turn to test you." Incensed at the cheek of this young whippersnapper, the Tzanzer Rebbe promptly threw him out, ending any chance of a match.

Let us take a step back from the specific recommendations outlined above. The thrust of the words of our sages above is clear. Scholars should be afforded material benefits. Those who are involved in the intellectual pursuits of Torah should not only reap abstract, intangible rewards, they should also merit assistance in this-worldly matters. Thus we urge people with material wealth to assist Torah scholars. One authority writes that the entire community is accountable for supporting them. This responsibility goes beyond regular charity obligations and should be considered a salary as compensation for the time they invest in study on behalf of the community (*Rabbi Ḥayim ben Betzalel*).

A sceptic could always dismiss these statements as self-serving attempts by Torah scholars to encourage the masses to provide financial support for them. Yet it is also possible to read the sources as a reflection of the Jewish people's value system and priorities. While the sources talk of "marrying off daughters," which may be distant from our contemporary reality, these timeless texts still carry a lasting message. As a society we wish to encourage intellectual pursuits, and we do so by supporting people who have dedicated themselves to the quest for Torah knowledge, understanding and wisdom.

BERAKHOT 34B

Where penitents stand

THE TALMUD TELLS us that biblical prophecies of reward refer to the next-worldly just desserts of *ba'alei teshuva*, penitents. As for the completely righteous who never sinned, the Talmud simply quotes a biblical verse: *No eye except Yours, O Lord, has seen* (Isaiah 64:3). The reward for the wholly virtuous is indescribable in human terms, even prophetic ones, for only the Almighty can imagine what good is in store for them. The Talmud immediately presents a dissenting view that suggests a different hierarchy: "Where penitents stand, the completely righteous cannot stand." This means that the level of remorseful sinners is so lofty that even the wholly righteous will not be privileged to stand in the same heavenly section with them (*B. Berakhot* 34b; *Rashi*).

What is the logic behind this surprising hierarchy? While the first position seems intuitive, how should we understand the alternative suggestion that repentant sinners are greater than those who never sinned?

Elsewhere our sages tell us that the iniquities of a sinner who repents are considered as merits in the eyes of the Almighty (*B. Yoma* 86b). In this way a repentant sinner can apparently leapfrog over a righteous person in spiritual standing. Alternatively, wrongdoers who have tasted the allure of sin are faced with a greater challenge in resisting temptation, while the perfectly righteous who have never become accustomed to sin are not tangled in its web. Thus penitents need to exert greater effort in overcoming their evil tendencies and are rewarded accordingly (*Maimonides*).

To buttress this unexpected hierarchy, the Talmud cites a biblical verse: *Peace, peace to the distant and to the near* (Isaiah 57:19). First the Almighty extends greetings to someone distant – meaning the repentant sinner – and only then to someone righteous who has always been near God.

The Talmud proceeds to defend the original position. It suggests that *Peace, peace to the distant* refers to people who are distant from sin, meaning the righteous; *and to the near* refers to people who were near sin but who have now distanced themselves from it, meaning penitents. Thus precedence is given to those who have never sinned.

Despite this endorsement of the original suggestion that the righteous take precedence over penitents, it appears that our passage accepts the alternative hierarchy: where penitents stand, even the wholly righteous do not stand.

In reading this passage, a number of Hasidic masters focus on the physical posture – standing – used to describe the relative positions of the righteous and the penitent. Thus Rabbi Ḥayim Elazar Shapira of Munkács (1871–1937) explains that a remorseful sinner has already withstood a challenge, for a true penitent is one who has the opportunity to sin again and resists the temptation. Penitents, therefore, know that they will be able to stand up to the attraction and enticement of sin. The righteous, however, who have never been similarly challenged, do not know if they would be able to confront and defy the lure of sin. In this manner, where penitents stand firm, the righteous are not guaranteed that they could stand up to temptation.

Another approach focusing on the standing posture is offered by Rabbi Yisrael Friedman of Czortków (1854–1934). Righteous people must be constantly on the move, trying to reach higher levels of spiritual accomplishment. Such paragons of virtue continuously seek to develop and hence never contemplate standing in place. Repentant sinners, who also seek to grow, need not move in order to attain higher levels of spirituality; they can stay where they are, for they have much to repair. In the very place they stand, penitents can come close to the Divine by fixing all that they have damaged.

Repentance is unique in that it can be achieved with a flash of sincere remorse. The Talmud tells us of a man who betroths a woman and says that the betrothal is conditional on his being totally righteous. In such a case, the Talmud rules that the betrothal is valid, for perhaps at that instant, while standing right there, the potential groom resolutely decided to repent (*B. Kiddushin* 49b). Rabbi Yisrael of Czortków explains that while remorseful sinners can stand still and achieve levels of spirituality, the totally righteous cannot afford to rest in one place and must progress towards the highest possible level of spiritual attainment.

Perhaps Rabbi Yisrael of Czortków is drawing on the more esoteric explanation of his uncle, Rabbi Avraham Yaakov Friedman of Sadigora (1820–1883). This approach follows the Hasidic-kabbalistic doctrine that in every situation we are charged with elevating the sparks of godliness entrapped in physical reality. Contrite sinners have already walked the paths of filth, and the mud in which they have rolled has stuck to their souls. Their repentance is fully effective if they once again find themselves in those same places and, instead of rolling around in the muck, they stand tall and elevate the hidden sparks of holiness. The righteous, however, have no reason to stand in those muddy places, for their duty is not to elevate the sparks from such dirt. Thus where repentant sinners stand in order to elevate Divine sparks, the righteous do not stand.

Let us return to the talmudic passage. The sinner has a potential that goes beyond that of the righteous person. The question remains: will the sinner realise this latent power? Once the beloved Hasidic master Rabbi Levi Yitzḥak of Berdyczów (1740–1810) grabbed a known sinner by the lapels and, to the surprise of onlookers, brusquely said: "I am jealous of you!" Even the sinner was shocked by the rabbi's declaration. Seeing the astonishment on the face of the sinner, Rabbi Levi Yitzḥak loosened his grip and explained: "Once you repent, all your crimes will be considered virtues and then your merits will be innumerable."

BERAKHOT 34B

Unique contributions

OUR SAGES TELL us that Rabbi Ḥanina ben Dosa was well aware of the efficacy of his prayers (*M. Berakhot* 5:5). When he prayed for the sick, he would immediately know whether his supplications had been accepted. "This one will live and this one will die," he would announce at the conclusion of his prayers. Fascinated by his declaration, those around him asked: "How do you know?"

Rabbi Ḥanina ben Dosa shared the key to his perceptive powers: "If my prayer is fluent, then I know it has been well received and the ailing person will recover. But if not, then I know that my prayer has been rejected by the heavenly court and torn up."

The Talmud illustrates the power of Rabbi Ḥanina ben Dosa's prayer with two tales. The first one provides the background for the aforementioned exchange (*B. Berakhot* 34b).

When Rabban Gamliel's son fell ill, he sent two scholars to request that Rabbi Ḥanina ben Dosa pray on his son's behalf. As soon as Rabbi Ḥanina ben Dosa saw the two emissaries approach, he went up to the attic and begged Divine mercy for the sick child. Once he finished his prayers, he descended and curtly told the messengers to return to their master, for the child's fever had abated.

Sceptically, the two scholars asked: "Do you claim to be a prophet?"

"I am neither a prophet nor the son of a prophet," Rabbi Ḥanina ben Dosa replied. "Rather, I know from experience that if my prayer is fluent, then it has been favourably received. If not, then I know that my prayer has been rejected."

The two visitors made a note of the exact time and returned to Rabban Gamliel. Upon their arrival they reported the entire episode to their teacher. Rabban Gamliel exclaimed: "You have neither deducted from nor added to the exact time of his recovery! It happened just so – at that very moment the fever left him and he asked us for some water to drink."

Building on the first story, the second tale compares Rabbi Ḥanina ben Dosa's force in prayer to the powers of the famed Rabban Yoḥanan ben Zakkai. While Rabbi Ḥanina ben Dosa was learning Torah from Rabban Yoḥanan ben Zakkai, the latter's son fell ill. The master turned to his disciple with an impassioned plea: "Ḥanina, my son, request Divine mercy for him that he may live." Rabbi Ḥanina ben Dosa promptly laid his head between his knees and offered a heartfelt prayer. As a result, the boy's life was saved.

Seeing the power of this prayer, Rabban Yoḥanan ben Zakkai exclaimed: "Had Ben Zakkai stuck his head between his knees for an entire day, the heavenly court would pay no heed to him!"

Hearing this admission, his wife turned to him and queried: "Is Ḥanina greater than you?" Rabban Yoḥanan ben Zakkai placated his wife with a cryptic reply: "No, but he is like a servant before the king, while I am like a minister before the king."

What is the meaning of this analogy? According to one approach, a servant benefits from regular, unimpeded access to the king and is therefore on intimate terms with the ruler. Despite his lowly station, the servant can approach the king at will. The minister, however, appears before the king for important business only. Since the minister's relationship is more structured and formal, he cannot make requests of the king as he pleases (*Rashi*).

Another approach suggests that if people view themselves as servants of the Almighty, they are rewarded *quid pro quo*, such that God subjugates the Divine will before their requests. In comparison, if people hold lofty positions of authority, wield power and do not acquiesce to every request they receive, they are treated in kind by the Almighty. For this reason, the modest, servant-like Rabbi Ḥanina ben Dosa was worthier than Rabban Yoḥanan ben Zakkai, and so his prayers were answered immediately (*Ben Ish Ḥai*).

A third approach proposes that a minister understands that the king's decrees are for the betterment of his subjects. Thus the minister accepts the king's will with no argument or objection. The servant, however, is not aware of the complex considerations behind the decrees and does not comprehend the decision-making process, and therefore he prays fervently and unremittingly until his requests are granted (*Rabbi Tzadok HaKohen of Lublin*).

Perhaps a further lesson can be drawn from Rabban Yoḥanan ben Zakkai's explanation. Rabban Yoḥanan ben Zakkai was at the apex of the learning pyramid. Thanks to his foresight, Torah Judaism survived the Roman destruction of Jerusalem and the razing of the Second Temple. He successfully reconstituted the world of Torah study in Yavne, and his legacy continues to impact upon our lives today. It is no wonder that he is lauded as a hero, for we value Torah study greatly, perhaps more than anything else.

Nevertheless, study is not the only field of Jewish achievement. Rabban Yoḥanan ben Zakkai's admission that Rabbi Ḥanina ben Dosa was more effective than he in the realm of prayer may be pointing to the different roles played by different people. Every person can make his or her own unique contribution. We need not make value judgments in recognising that a palace needs ministers as well as workers; each plays a distinct, necessary and irreplaceable role.

Rabban Yoḥanan ben Zakkai remained the teacher of Rabbi Ḥanina ben Dosa, yet the disciple was able to achieve something that the master could only dream of doing. With humility, Rabban Yoḥanan ben Zakkai recognised that his strengths lay in the realm of scholarship and communal leadership; to attain other objectives he needed to turn elsewhere.

The viability of a community may be measured by its relationship to every individual's unique role. Those entrusted with leadership positions are challenged to acknowledge their own limitations, and to recognise the inimitable contribution of each and every one of their constituents.

SOURCES CITED

Abudraham: Rabbi David Abudraham, Seville, Spain, fl. 1340

Afikei Yam: Rabbi Yitzḥak Isaac Ḥaver (Wildman), Lithuania, 1789–1852

Ahavat Yisrael: Rabbi Yisrael Hager of Vizhnitz, 1860–1936

Anaf Yosef: Rabbi Ḥanoch Zundel, Białystok, d. 1867

Arukh: Rabbi Natan ben Yeḥiel of Rome, c. 1035–1106

Arukh HaShulḥan: Rabbi Yeḥiel Mikhel HaLevi Epstein, Lithuania, 1829–1908

Avot DeRabbi Natan: aggadic compilation from the period of the Geonim, c. 700–900

B.: *Talmud Bavli* (Babylonian Talmud), c. 200–500

Baḥ: Rabbi Yoel Sirkis, Poland, 1561–1640

Bahag: Halakhot Gedolot, Babylonia, c. 840

Bartenura: Rabbi Ovadya of Bertinoro (commonly pronounced Bartenura in Hebrew), Italy and Jerusalem, died c. 1500

Be'er Sheva: Rabbi Yissakhar Ber Eilenberg, Italy, 1550–1623

Bemidbar Rabba: aggadic Midrash on Numbers, compiled no earlier than the twelfth century

Ben Ish Ḥai: Rabbi Yosef Ḥayim, *Benayahu* and *Ben Yehoyada*, Baghdad, 1834–1909

Bereshit Rabba: aggadic Midrash on Genesis, compiled in the fifth or sixth century

Benei Yisaskhar: Rabbi Zvi Elimelekh Shapira of Dynów, 1783–1841

Derekh Eretz Rabba, Derekh Eretz Zuta: midrashic compilation, divided into two sections – *Rabba* and *Zuta*, possibly compiled in the ninth century

Devarim Rabba: aggadic Midrash on Deuteronomy, compiled no earlier than the twelfth century

Ein Yaakov: Rabbi Yaakov ibn Ḥabib, Spain, Portugal, Salonika, c. 1450–1516

Eliyahu Rabba, Eliyahu Zuta: also known as *Seder Eliyahu* and *Tanna DeVei Eliyahu*, Midrash attributed to Elijah the prophet, divided into two sections – *Rabba* and *Zuta*, compiled at the end of the tenth century

Eshel Avraham Buczacz: Rabbi Avraham David Warman of Buczacz, Galicia, 1771–1840

Geonim: Babylonian heads of talmudic academies, 589–1038

Gra: Rabbi Eliyahu of Vilna, 1720–1797

Hai Gaon: Pumbedita, Babylonia, 939–1038

Hagahot Maimoniyot: Rabbi Meir ben Yekutiel HaKohen, Rothenburg, Germany, killed in Rintfleisch massacres of 1298

Ḥida: Rabbi Ḥayim Yosef David Azulai, Jerusalem, scores of other places and finally Livorno, Italy, 1724–1806

Ḥizkuni: Rabbi Ḥizkiya ben Manoaḥ, France, fl. thirteenth century

Ibn Ezra: Rabbi Avraham ibn Ezra, Spain and many other places, 1089–1164

Iyun Yaakov: Rabbi Yaakov Reischer (Bechofen), Prague, Rzeszów, Anspach, Worms and Metz, 1661–1733

Kalonymus ben Kalonymus: Provence, 1286–after 1328

Kedusha UVerakha: Rabbi Naftali Katz, Poland, Germany, Prague, 1645–1719

Ketav Sofer: Rabbi Avraham Shmuel Binyamin Sofer, Pressburg, Hungary, 1815–1871

Kohelet Rabba: aggadic Midrash on Ecclesiastes, compiled before the thirteenth century

M.: *Mishna*, c. 220

Magen Avraham: Rabbi Avraham Abele Gombiner, Kalish, Poland, c. 1633–c. 1683

Maharal: Rabbi Yehuda Löwe, Prague, 1512?–1609

Maharil: Rabbi Yaakov HaLevi Moelin, Germany, c. 1360–1427

Maharsha: Rabbi Shmuel Edels, Poland, 1555–1631

Maharshal: Rabbi Shlomo Luria, Poland, 1510–1573

Maimonides: Rabbi Moshe ben Maimon, Córdoba, Spain, and Fostat, Egypt, 1138–1204

Maor VaShamesh: Rabbi Kalonymus Kalman HaLevi Epstein, Kraków, 1751–1823

Mekhilta: *Mekhilta DeRabbi Yishmael,* halakhic Midrash on the book of Exodus, compiled third century

Meiri: Rabbi Menaḥem HaMeiri, *Beit HaBeḥira,* Provence, 1249–1315

Menorat HaMaor: Rabbi Yitzḥak Abuhav, Spain, fl. end of the fourteenth century

Meshekh Ḥokhma: Rabbi Meir Simḥa HaKohen of Dvinsk, 1843–1926

Midrash Mishlei: aggadic Midrash on Proverbs, compiled in the eighth century

Midrash Shmuel: aggadic Midrash on Samuel, compiled before the eleventh century

Midrash Tehillim: aggadic Midrash on Psalms, compiled before the eleventh century

Mishna Berura: Rabbi Yisrael Meir HaKohen of Radin, 1839–1933

Mordekhai: Rabbi Mordekhai ben Hillel HaKohen, Germany, born c. 1250, killed in Rintfleisch massacres of 1298

Paḥad Yitzḥak: Rabbi Yitzḥak Lampronti, Italy, 1679–1756

Pardes Yosef HeḤadash: Rabbi David Avraham Mandelboim

Perisha: Rabbi Yehoshua HaKohen Falk, Poland, 1555–1614

Pirkei DeRabbi Eliezer: aggadic Midrash, compiled in the eighth century

Penei Menaḥem: Rabbi Pinḥas Menaḥem Alter, Poland and Jerusalem, 1926–1996

Penei Moshe: Rabbi Moshe Margolies, Lithuania, c. 1710–1780

Peri Megadim: Rabbi Yosef ben Meir Teomim, Galicia and Germany, 1727–1792

Ra'avad: Rabbi Avraham ben David, Posquières, Provence, c. 1125–1198

Rabbeinu Baḥya: Rabbi Baḥya ben Asher ibn Ḥalawa, Saragossa, Spain, d. 1340

Rabbeinu Ḥananel: Rabbeinu Ḥananel ben Ḥushiel, Kairouan, Tunisia, 990–1053

Rabbeinu Yona Gerondi: Spain, c. 1200–1263

Rabbi Akiva Eiger: Eisenstadt and Poznań, 1761–1837

Rabbi Avraham Yaakov Friedman of Sadigora: Hasidic master from the Ruzhin dynasty, 1820–1883
Rabbi Avraham son of the Gra: Vilna, d. 1808
Rabbi Ḥayim ben Betzalel: Friedberg, 1520–1588
Rabbi Elazar Azikri: Safed, 1533–1600
Rabbi Menaḥem Mendel of Rymanów: Hasidic master, 1745–1815
Rabbi Naḥman of Bratslav: Hasidic master, 1772–1810
Rabbi Samson Raphael Hirsch: Germany, 1808–1888
Rabbi Shlomo Sirilio: Spain, Constantinople, Adrianople, Salonika, Safed and Jerusalem, died c. 1553–1555
Rabbi Yaakov Emden: Altona, Germany, 1697–1776
Rabbi Yehonatan HaKohen of Lunel: Provence, c. 1135–after 1210
Rabbi Yehuda Arye of Modena: Italy, 1571–1648
Rabbi Tzadok HaKohen of Lublin: Hasidic master, 1823–1900
Radak: Rabbi David Kimḥi, Narbonne, Provence, 1160–1235
Rema MiFano: Rabbi Menaḥem Azarya da Fano, Italy, 1548–1620
Ramban: Rabbi Moshe ben Naḥman (Naḥmanides), Spain and Land of Israel, 1194–c. 1270
Ramḥal: Rabbi Moshe Ḥayim Luzzatto, Padua, Amsterdam and Acre, 1707–1746
Ran: Rabbi Nissim ben Reuven Gerondi, Spain, 1320–1376
Rashba: Rabbi Shlomo ben Aderet, Barcelona, 1235–1310
Rashbam: Rabbi Shmuel ben Meir, France, c. 1084–c. 1158
Rashbatz: Rabbi Shimon ben Tzemaḥ Duran, Majorca and Algiers, 1361–1444
Rashi: Rabbi Shlomo Yitzḥaki, France, 1040–1105
Reshit Ḥokhma: Rabbi Eliyahu di Vidas, Safed, 1518–1592
Ri: Rabbi Yitzḥak of Dampierre, died c. 1185
Riaf: Rabbi Yoshiya Pinto, Damascus, 1565–1648
Rif: Rabbi Yitzḥak al-Fasi, Fes, Morocco, 1013–1103
Ritva: Rabbi Yom Tov ben Avraham Asevilli, Seville, Spain, 1250–1330
Rosh: Rabbi Asher ben Yeḥiel, France, Germany, and later Toledo, Spain, c. 1250–1327
Sa'adia Gaon: born in Egypt, 882/892, died in Baghdad 942
Sefer HaḤinukh: anonymous author from Barcelona, thirteenth century
Sefer HaManhig: Rabbi Avraham HaYarḥi, Lunel, Provence, c. 1155–1215

Semaḥot: minor tractate, also called *Evel Rabbati*, no earlier than the middle of the eighth century

Semak: Rabbi Yitzḥak of Corbeil, France, fl. second half of the thirteenth century

Shadal: Shmuel David Luzzatto, Italy, 1800–1865

Sha'arei Teshuva: Rabbi Ḥayim Mordekhai Margoliot, Dubno, d. 1818

Shemot Rabba: aggadic Midrash on Exodus that is not uniform in composition, compiled at the latest in the twelfth century

Shitta Mekubetzet: Rabbi Betzalel Ashkenazi, Egypt and Jerusalem, c. 1520–c. 1592

Shulḥan Arukh: Rabbi Yosef Karo, Spain, Portugal, Turkey and Safed, 1488–1575

Shulḥan Arukh HaRav: Rabbi Shneur Zalman of Lyady, 1745–1812

Sifrei: halakhic Midrash on Numbers and Deuteronomy, compiled around the middle of the third century

T.: *Tosefta*, addition to the Mishna, c. 220

Tanḥuma: aggadic Midrash on the Pentateuch, compiled by the eighth century

Tashbetz Katan: Rabbi Shimshon ben Tzadok, Germany, d. 1312

Taz: Rabbi David HaLevi Segal, Poland, c. 1586–1667

Tiferet Yisrael: Rabbi Yisrael Lipschuetz, Germany, 1782–1861

Torah Temima: Rabbi Barukh HaLevi Epstein, Lithuania, 1860–1941

Tosafot: talmudic scholars from western and central Europe, twelfth–fourteenth centuries

Tur: Rabbi Yaakov ben Asher, also known as *Ba'al HaTurim*, Cologne, Germany, and Toledo, Spain, c. 1269–c. 1343

Tzemaḥ Tzedek: Rabbi Menaḥem Mendel Schneersohn of Lubavitch, 1789–1866

Tzlaḥ: Rabbi Yeḥezkel Landau, Poland and Prague, 1713–1793

Vayikra Rabba: aggadic Midrash on Leviticus, compiled in the fifth, sixth or seventh century

Y.: *Talmud Yerushalmi,* also known as Jerusalem Talmud, Palestinian Talmud or Talmud of the Land of Israel, c. 200–400

Yad Ramah: Rabbi Meir ben Todros HaLevi Abulafia, Burgos, Spain, c. 1170–1244

Yalkut Reuveni: Rabbi Avraham Reuven HaKohen Sofer, Prague, d. 1673

Yalkut Shimoni: aggadic Midrash on the Bible, largely compiled from other works, probably in the thirteenth century

Zohar: foundational work of Jewish mystical thought, first appeared in Spain in the thirteenth century

ABOUT THE AUTHOR

LEVI COOPER, ORIGINALLY from Australia, teaches at the Pardes Institute of Jewish Studies in Jerusalem and serves as the rabbi of *HaTzur VeHaTzohar* Congregation in Zur Hadassa, Israel. His PhD, awarded by Bar-Ilan University's Faculty of Law, explored the interaction between Hasidism and Jewish Law. Rabbi Cooper is a member of the Israel Bar Association and the Tzohar rabbis organisation, and serves as a historian with Heritage Seminars. He publishes "The Tisch," a column on Hasidism in *The Jerusalem Post,* and is a contributing editor for *Jewish Educational Leadership,* the Lookstein Center for Jewish Education journal.

The fonts used in this book are from the Arno family

Maggid Books
The best of contemporary Jewish thought from
Koren Publishers Jerusalem Ltd.